Imaginary Crimes

Also by Tom Ferguson

*Trusting Ourselves: A Crash Course
in the Psychology of Women*
(with Karen Johnson, M.D.)

Helping Smokers Get Ready to Quit

*The No-Nag, No-Guilt,
Do-It-Your-Own-Way Guide
to Quitting Smoking*

The People's Book of Medical Tests

*Medical Self-Care:
Access to Health Tools*

Imaginary Crimes

Why We Punish Ourselves and How to Stop

Lewis Engel, Ph.D.
Tom Ferguson, M.D.

Houghton Mifflin Company
Boston 1990

For information about permission to reproduce selections from
this book, write to Permissions, Houghton Mifflin Company,
2 Park Street, Boston, Massachusetts 02108.

Library of Congress Cataloging-in-Publication Data

Engel, Lewis.
Imaginary crimes : why we punish ourselves and how to stop /
Lewis Engel, Tom Ferguson.
p.   cm.
Includes bibliographical references.
ISBN 0-395-46556-7
1. Guilt.   2. Psychology, Pathological.   3. Psychotherapy.
I. Ferguson, Tom, 1943–.   II. Title.
RC569.5.G84E54   1990   89-77067
616.89—dc20   CIP

Printed in the United States of America

FFG 10 9 8 7 6 5 4 3 2 1

To Harold Sampson, who introduced me to Control Mastery Theory and supported this project unstintingly. His deep understanding and enormous respect for his clients have been a profound inspiration to me.

— L.E.

To health-active, health-responsible laypeople everywhere, who *do* want to take more control of their own lives — in their own way and in their own time.

— T.F.

Contents

Acknowledgments

Much of the material in this book grew out of the work of Joseph Weiss, Harold Sampson, and their associates in the Mount Zion Psychotherapy Research Group.

Weiss's painstaking thirty-year study of psychotherapy process notes and transcripts provided the basis for Control Mastery Theory, the powerful new set of psychological principles that inspired this book. All the essential insights, terminology, and much of the approach to research were the products of Weiss's inspiration and enormous hard work. We are grateful for his enthusiastic support for our efforts to bring portions of Control Mastery Theory to the attention of a wider audience.

The ongoing collaboration between Joe Weiss and Hal Sampson, which began in 1964, has been a particularly fruitful one. From the very beginning of their work together, they focused on developing a strategy for bringing the tools of the scientific method to bear on the process of psychotherapy. In 1972 they established the Mount Zion Psychotherapy Research Group, which now includes over fifty members — psychologists; psychiatrists; psychoanalysts; marriage, family, and child counselors; clinical social workers; and graduate students. In 1986, with the help of the Mount Zion Group, Weiss and Sampson published *The Psychoanalytic Process: Theory, Clinical Observation, and Empirical Research*, the first book-length introduction to the ideas and research techniques of Control Mastery Theory.

Hal Sampson has been an important friend and mentor and has spent hundreds of hours discussing Control Mastery Theory with Lewis Engel. In addition, he has given unselfishly of his time and energy in reviewing several early drafts of the manuscript.

John Curtis and George Silberschatz, codirectors of the Brief Therapy Research Project, along with Weiss and Sampson, have been responsible for much of the groundbreaking Control Mastery research and have done a great deal to involve others in this work.

We would also like to acknowledge the important contributions of other past and present members of the Mount Zion Psychotherapy Research Group: Edward Ballis, Sandra Bemesdorfer, Anne Black, Marcia Black, Kay Blacker, John Bogardus, Diana Bowling, Jessica Broitman, Abbot Bronstein, David Brown, Suzanne Brummer, Martel Bryant, Jack Bugas, Marshall Bush, Lynn Campbell, Joseph Caston, Sandra Cohen, Joshua Coleman, Lowell Cooper, Janet Cumming, Barbara Dallas, Kathy DePaola, Jack Dolhinow, Carol Drucker, Heather Folsom, Steven Foreman, Polly Fretter, Michael Friedman, Suzanne Gassner, Jess Ghannam, John Gibbins, William C. Glover, Ruth Goldman, Rachelle Goodfriend, Irwin Gootnick, Seppe Graupe, Phyllis Greene, Harriete Grooh, Forrest Hamer, Sheryl Hausman, Arthur Hoffman, Leonard Horowitz, Sue Hulley, J. Rod Hundley, Marla Isaacs, Susan Jenny, Cynthia Kale, Thomas Kelly, Michael Kirsch, Andrew Knier, Anya Lane, Lisa Levine, Georgine Marrot, Elizabeth Mayer, Terry McCall, Mary Margaret McClure, Ellen Mowery, Roxanne Norville, Lynn O'Connor, Jacob Ofman, Harvey Peskin, Judy Pickles, Don Propstra, Paul Ransohoff, Owen Renik, Saul Rosenberg, Arlene Rothschild, Eleanor Sampson, Frances Sampson, Jan Schreiber, Cynthia Shilkret, Robert Shilkret, Ellen Siegelman, Alan Skolnikoff, Norman Sohn, Ronald Spinka, April Stan, Thomas Stein, Stanley Steinberg, Diane Suffridge, Phyllis Toch, Estelle Weiss, Michael Windholz, Abby Wolfson, John Wotkyns, Neil Young, and Ellen Zuckerman.

We were fortunate indeed to have the help of a number of friends and colleagues who devoted much time and energy to reviewing the manuscript:

Eugene Alexander, marriage, family, and child counselor, and member of Family Therapy Institute of San Francisco; Edward Bourg, provost, California School of Professional Psychology, Berkeley-Alameda campus; Esther Bourg, psychiatric social worker, Berkeley; Stephanie Brown, psychologist, lecturer, and author in the field of alcoholism, Palo Alto; Marshall Bush, psychologist and member of the San Francisco Psychoanalytic Institute; Beverley Cone, marriage, family, and child counselor, Belmont, California; John Curtis, psychologist and codirector of the Brief Therapy Research Project, San Francisco; Meredith Dreiss, consulting archaeologist, Austin, Texas; Judith Elman, National Wellness Institute, University of Wisconsin, Stevens Point; Barbara Engel, consultant and trainer in the area of women's issues and former director of Women's Services, Chicago YWCA; Brandy Engel, marriage, family, and child counselor, San Francisco; Frieda Engel, psychiatric social worker, former associate professor of social work, University of Illinois, Chicago, former Core Faculty, Antioch University, San Francisco; Paula Engel, coordinator of the Outreach Program, Round Valley School District, Covelo, California; Joseph Engel, organizational consultant, Organizational Consultants, Inc., San Francisco; Heather Folsom, medical director of East Bay Activity Center, private practice of child and adult psychiatry, playwright, Berkeley, California; Steve Foreman, psychiatrist, director of Child Psychiatry, Pacific Medical Center, Clinical Faculty, University of California Medical Center, San Francisco; Michael Friedman, psychiatrist, Berkeley, California; Joe and Terry Graedon, authors of *The People's Pharmacy* books and the syndicated column of the same name, Durham, North Carolina;

Rose Levinson, social worker and organizational consultant, Berkeley, California; George Silberschatz, psychologist and co-director of Brief Therapy Research Project, San Francisco; Evelyn Whitlock, a physician specializing in preventive medicine, Portland, Oregon; and Stuart Yudofsky, chairman, Department of Psychiatry, University of Chicago School of Medicine.

We owe a special debt of gratitude to Lonnie Barbach, psychologist, author, and friend, who reviewed several early drafts and generously shared her insights, experiences, and advice from the very beginning of this project. We would also like to thank John Sterling, Nan Talese, Carole Pisarczyk, and Tony Lopopolo for their enthusiasm and support for the book.

We are grateful to our able and enthusiastic literary agents, Charlotte Sheedy and Vicki Bijur of the Charlotte Sheedy Literary Agency, who guided us through the initial stages of planning the book and finding a publisher.

We owe a special debt of thanks to Ruth Hapgood, our editor at Houghton Mifflin and her assistant editor, Tara Hartnett. Ruth served as our advocate, collaborator, and chief support person from the very beginning of this project, providing enthusiasm, constructive criticism, and a quiet New England confidence. Her unstinting efforts made this a much better book. Jayne Yaffe, our manuscript editor, polished and tightened what we had written, adding ease and grace to the final product. Publicity director Marly Rusoff, publicist Sandy Goroff-Mailly, and their colleagues worked long hours to get the word out.

A special thanks to Rachel Sanborn, who helped to prepare the manuscript. Her continuing patience and nearly superhuman good cheer through our seemingly endless revisions made the process of writing and rewriting this book a real pleasure.

Our spouses, Brandy Engel and Meredith Dreiss, have supported this project in a thousand ways — by reading and commenting on the manuscript, by taking on an extra portion of household and parenting tasks, by keeping our spirits high, and, when necessary, by reminding us that there were other things in life than "the book." Neither of us could have taken on a work of this magnitude were it not for the solid bond we each feel for our life partner.

Our children, Nicholas Engel and Adrienne Dreiss, provided us with valuable reminders of the struggles that children go through to make sense of this complex and sometimes difficult world we live in. Our involvement with them has helped us appreciate the enormously difficult task of parenting and has reminded us that there is often a huge difference between the way something is intended by a parent and perceived by a child.

Finally, we would like to express our deep appreciation to our own parents, Frieda and Joseph Engel and Helen and Wallace Ferguson. In the course of this project we both came to understand the magnitude of the gift we have received from them.

Introduction

Many of our most serious psychological problems are due to a special kind of guilt: the hidden guilt we feel toward our parents — and sometimes toward our brothers and sisters.

Some of us are partially aware of these feelings and their grip on us. But for many of us, this guilt is completely unconscious. Somewhere back in childhood we came to believe that we wounded our parents (and perhaps our brothers and sisters). These wounds constitute *imaginary crimes* against our loved ones, which cause us to be driven by a powerful hidden guilt. Our guilt is baffling precisely because it is unconscious. We are aware only of the problems it produces:

- Some of us sabotage our own success.
- Some of us are unable to achieve a satisfactory intimate relationship.
- Some of us find it impossible to relax and enjoy life.

These problems are often our way of punishing ourselves for our imaginary crimes.

Six types of imaginary crimes appear to be most common: *outdoing, burdening, love theft, abandonment, disloyalty,* and *basic badness:*

- **Outdoing.** This crime can occur if we surpass a family member in any way. If we perceive ourselves as happier, more successful, more popular, or more capable of enjoying life than our parents, brothers, or sisters, we may judge ourselves guilty of the imaginary crime of outdoing.

• **Burdening.** If one or both of our parents seemed burdened or weighed down, or if either parent was unsuccessful or unfulfilled, we may feel that their unhappiness was our fault. We may unconsciously believe that the burden of taking care of us was the cause of their misery and dissatisfaction.

• **Love Theft.** If we believe that we received the love and attention another family member needed in order to thrive, we may judge ourselves guilty of the imaginary crime of love theft. As a consequence, we may feel unconsciously responsible for all the trouble and difficulties that our neglected sibling or parent later experienced.

• **Abandonment.** This is the crime of wanting to separate from our parents, to make our own choices, to move away from the family home, and to establish a separate and independent life. If we feel that by growing up and leaving home we deprived our parents of their principal focus, or if we feel that our parents are deeply unhappy without us, we may feel guilty of the imaginary crime of abandonment.

• **Disloyalty.** This is the crime of being critical of our parents, of breaking family rules, of disappointing parental expectations, or of making independent life choices. If we have critical thoughts about our parents, if we rejected the profession, religion, or lifestyle they had planned for us, if we adopted different political or philosophical ideas, or if we married a person of a different faith, race, or social class, we may feel guilty of the imaginary crime of disloyalty.

• **Basic Badness.** Negative messages, abuse, or neglect may have caused us, as children, to conclude that there was something fundamentally wrong with us. Even today, we may believe that no matter how kind and caring we appear on the surface, on the inside we are still loathsome, repulsive, and unlovable.

*

Whatever our imaginary crime — or combination of crimes — we first mistakenly judged ourselves as guilty in the innocence of childhood. And we have been punishing ourselves ever since.

This self-punishment can take many forms: We may find ourselves engaging in self-defeating behavior. We may be plagued by feelings of anxiety or depression. We may sabotage our own efforts to form intimate, rewarding relationships. Or we may find ourselves destroying the relationships we already have. Our hidden guilt drives us to deny ourselves the very things we want most in the world — success, intimacy, pleasure, and peace of mind.

The ideas in this book are based on Control Mastery Theory, an exciting new theory of psychotherapy developed by the San Francisco psychoanalyst Joseph Weiss. Although based on classical psychoanalytic thinking, Control Mastery provides a powerful, different, and hopeful new picture of the human psyche. This book focuses primarily on only one aspect of the broad theory that Weiss developed: the enormous role that unconscious guilt plays in many of our psychological problems. For further information on Control Mastery Theory, see Appendix I, "A Note to Mental Health Professionals" and Appendix II, "Recommended Reading."

We realize that the name Control Mastery Theory may have a slightly authoritarian ring. Let us hasten to assure you that the theory itself is anything but authoritarian. Control Mastery offers a tremendously optimistic view of human nature, a view similar to those proposed by Carl Rogers and Abraham Maslow.

The word *control* is not used to imply that we must control ourselves or others. Rather, it suggests that we can control certain important aspects of our mental life when we feel it is safe to do so. The word *mastery* reflects Control Mastery's assumption that we all have an inborn drive to master our psychological problems.

One of Control Mastery Theory's key themes is the importance of safety. When people feel safe, they can grow and develop toward their maximum potential. When they are overwhelmed by fear, guilt, or shame, they cannot. Thus the task of the Control Mastery therapist is to create a climate of safety so that clients can "remember" and master the traumatic experiences that led to their psychological problems.

The principles presented in this book will be especially useful for those who are troubled by the feeling that they are continually getting in their own way, sabotaging their own most cherished goals. Control Mastery traces the origins of our self-defeating behaviors back to their roots — in our childhood interactions with other family members.

Control Mastery Theory holds that many psychological problems are the result of a false or exaggerated sense of responsibility for the misfortunes that befell our loved ones. The chapters that follow present dozens of case histories of people who have worked in therapy to absolve themselves of their imaginary crimes. For upon close inspection, it almost always turns out that we are innocent of the crimes with which we have unconsciously charged ourselves. Once we identify these crimes, we can begin to discover how irrational or exaggerated our unconscious guilt really is and we can begin to free ourselves. As our unconscious guilt feelings lose their grip on us, we will find ourselves becoming less and less self-defeating and self-punishing.

Although Control Mastery Theory offers fresh and potent insights to help us deal with our psychological dilemmas, we do not mean to suggest that reading this book will bring about the quick and miraculous resolution of long-standing psychological difficulties. Real psychological growth requires considerable time and effort. What this book *can* do is help us direct and focus our effort in a positive, constructive way — by providing a powerful new perspective on our own problems and on those of our friends and family members.

As we are continuing to study the ways these ideas can help solve psychological problems, we would be particularly interested in receiving feedback from readers who have attempted to apply these approaches. We'd like to hear your opinion of this book: What was most helpful? What bothered you the most? How might we improve the next edition? What should be added? What should be cut? We invite you to respond to the "Reader Feedback" questions on p. 247.

Three brief technical notes:

• Our case histories are based on the actual experiences of real people, but they have been thoroughly disguised to protect the confidentiality of those involved. Some case studies have been combined or simplified to illustrate an important point.

• In an effort to present our ideas in nonsexist language, we have used the male and female pronouns interchangeably when speaking of people in general — instead of using the male pronoun to refer to both.

• Although this book is a truly collaborative effort between the authors, the concepts and case examples come from Lewis Engel's years of experience as a psychotherapist. We have thus sometimes used the first-person singular to refer to Lewis Engel.

Control Mastery Theory has already aroused much enthusiasm among many psychotherapy researchers and psychotherapists. We believe that in the years to come, it will have a major impact on the way therapists practice — and on the way we all think about our psychological problems. Unfortunately, the results of new psychotherapy research frequently take a long time to spread; this fascinating new theory is still not widely known, even among psychotherapists.

We wrote this book because we wanted to help speed this process. Control Mastery Theory is a secret too good to keep. We are convinced that Joseph Weiss's theories can be enormously helpful to most people right now, and that we should not have to wait the years it might take for the news to seep out of scientific psychology circles into the mainstream of American life.

We hope that *Imaginary Crimes* will serve as a useful introduction to this exciting and powerful new set of psychological concepts.

Lewis Engel, Ph.D.
Tom Ferguson, M.D.

Imaginary Crimes

1

Hidden Guilt

A Key to Our Psychological Problems

―――――

Our patients do not believe us when we attribute to them an unconscious sense of guilt. In order to make ourselves at all intelligible, we must tell them of an unconscious need for punishment.

— SIGMUND FREUD

Many of our most troubling psychological problems are caused by guilt. I had long realized that guilt played a powerful, usually destructive, role in the lives of many of my clients. Nevertheless, as I learned more and more about Control Mastery Theory, I began to see that I had gravely underestimated its importance.[1]

My clients have told me of thousands of incidents that made them feel guilty. If they had acted in ways that were cruel or dishonest, I advised them that their guilt was justified and tried to help them make what amends they could. But many clients were plagued with intense guilt over the most trivial or even nonexistent offenses — minor misdeeds, unkind thoughts, sex-

ual fantasies, and other situations in which the supposed misdeed produced little or no harm. In these cases, I tried to help
my clients understand that their guilt was greatly exaggerated
or even completely unwarranted.

Yet the guilty feelings my clients reported — justified or not
— were only the guilt feelings of which they were conscious.
Conscious guilt is troublesome enough. Unconscious guilt can
be much more insidious. We are not aware of it and so cannot
fight against it. And while conscious guilt can stem from either
real or imagined injuries to others, unconscious guilt almost
always stems from imagined or greatly exaggerated misdeeds.
As we shall see, hidden guilt is part of the price we pay for our
imaginary crimes.[2]

You Can't Feel It

As you read these pages and think about your own problems,
don't assume that you will be able to feel your hidden guilt. You
may find that you can perceive this guilt only indirectly — you
may notice that you may behave in ways that make you feel
frustrated, unhappy, lonely, or unsuccessful. Or you may be
vaguely aware of certain patterns of self-sabotage or self-defeating behavior. You may find that you are plagued by feelings of
anxiety or depression for no apparent reason, as if you have a
need to punish yourself. And you do. You are punishing yourself to assuage your hidden guilt.

Let's now look at three people who came to understand how
their hidden guilt was driving them to sabotage their own happiness.

Lydia was a tall, quiet twenty-nine-year-old law school graduate, a native Texan with an aw-shucks, down-home manner, a

perpetual stoop, and a painfully low opinion of herself. She was a terrible procrastinator who struggled with deadlines all the way through college and barely made it through law school. After graduating, she felt completely burned out. She came into therapy after repeatedly failing the bar exam. She had been unable to bring herself to do the necessary studying.

Lydia's mother was a nervous, perfectionistic homemaker who'd given up a career as a clothing designer when Lydia was born. Lydia soon became the be-all and end-all of her life. The only time Lydia's mother seemed content was when she was advising or criticizing her daughter. Each time Lydia wanted to play with her friends or showed any other signs of independence, her mother became depressed. Lydia's father was an egotistical, socially inept biology teacher. He loved to flaunt his scientific knowledge but showed little interest in Lydia's opinions or accomplishments.

In therapy, Lydia came to understand that she had already experienced some hidden guilt over leaving home to attend law school. She felt that by passing the bar and becoming financially independent of her parents she would be abandoning her clingy mother and threatening her competitive, know-it-all father. She unconsciously believed that her success would even further sadden her unhappy mother and hurt her insecure father. Lydia had judged herself guilty of the imaginary crimes of abandonment and outdoing. The anxiety and lethargy that had kept her from studying for her bar exam had been caused by her hidden guilt.

David was a handsome, soft-spoken thirty-three-year-old ski store clerk. He wore rugby shirts and jeans and exhibited an athlete's natural grace. But in contrast to his youthful, bright appearance, David always seemed abstracted, as if troubled by some deep sorrow.

He earned top grades in high school, but after graduation David became a ski bum, drifting through a series of low-level jobs as a skiing instructor and sporting goods salesman. At the same time, he had experienced a succession of shallow, unsatisfying relationships with women. Though athletic and very attractive, he thought of himself as stupid, unattractive, and unmotivated. He seemed unable to let himself be successful — at work, with women, or in his own eyes. He had even found himself thinking of suicide. These thoughts scared him so badly that he decided to enter therapy.

David had been his mother's favorite. His older brother, Rob, had been a physically and socially awkward computer nerd. In contrast, David was bright and popular. During his sophomore year of high school, he was named to the state all-star baseball team. While David was away receiving the award, Rob made his first serious suicide attempt. After that, Rob was admitted to a series of mental hospitals. He eventually took a job as a low-level programmer and never fulfilled his early promise.

In therapy, David began to see that he suffered from hidden guilt over having received so much attention and approval when his brother had had so little. He had unconsciously concluded that Rob's rapid deterioration was the result of his own social, academic, and athletic successes. David had judged himself guilty of the imaginary crime of love theft. To ease his guilt, he had punished himself by being unrealistically self-critical and by making himself unsuccessful.

Maria was an attractive forty-seven-year-old chef. She was a talkative, outgoing Italian-American with an easy laugh and a warm, spunky personality. Although her career was going well, Maria constantly found herself involved with a succession of unsuccessful men who treated her badly and ran around with other women. Maria came into therapy complaining that men were impossible and that her love life was a disaster.

After Maria's mother and father had divorced, Maria's mother had taken up with a never-ending series of alcoholics, ne'er-do-wells, philanderers, and con men. In therapy, Maria realized that she was unconsciously choosing inappropriate partners — just as her mother had done. Maria unconsciously believed that by choosing a worthwhile partner and developing a happy relationship, she would be betraying her mother. She had judged herself guilty of the imaginary crime of outdoing. Maria's hidden guilt about having what her mother never had caused most of her problems with men.

As these examples indicate, our hidden guilt is usually based on the unconscious idea that we have hurt or are in danger of hurting our parents or siblings. Such mistaken ideas often include the irrational belief that by succeeding or being happy we will somehow become responsible for the unhappiness of other family members.

A Profound Misunderstanding

Lydia, David, and Maria each misunderstood the reason for their continuing problems. They thought their difficulties stemmed from personal defects such as laziness, unintelligence, or unattractiveness, or from wanting something they felt was unrealistic — such as a loving and trustworthy partner, a stimulating career or an enjoyable and satisfying life. They all suffered from the irrational belief that by pursuing their own legitimate goals they would hurt someone else. Because of this misunderstanding, their many attempts to escape from their dysfunctional patterns had been unsuccessful.

• Lydia was sure that her problems stemmed from her "laziness and lack of discipline." She castigated herself constantly and tried to drive herself to work harder. But once she began to understand that she was unconsciously avoiding success — to keep from "abandoning" her parents — she was able to pass the bar exam and find work as an attorney.

• David saw himself as unintelligent, unattractive, and unmotivated. He convinced himself that he was so inept that he would never amount to much. But once David realized that he unconsciously believed he was responsible for his brother's misfortunes, and that by becoming happy and successful he might cause his brother even more anguish, he was able to see his lack of motivation in a very different way. Once he understood the origins of his unconscious guilt, his self-esteem began to improve. He accepted a long-standing offer to manage the ski shop where he worked and eventually arranged to buy it.

• Maria went back and forth between two equally discouraging views — one, that there were simply no good men available, and two, that she was simply too uninteresting and unlovable to attract a good man. Once she came to understand the guilt that was keeping her from achieving a happy love relationship, she realized that neither of these gloomy views was correct. She found herself increasingly attracted to less flashy, more reliable men. She eventually became engaged to a man who loved her and treated her with courtesy and respect.

Most of us, like Lydia, David, and Maria, remain stuck in our psychological problems because we misunderstand how these problems arose in the first place. Control Mastery Theory provides a powerful and straightforward explanation: psychological problems are due to constricting unconscious beliefs.[3]

We develop these beliefs as the result of our childhood experiences. As children, we use logic and our powers of observation to draw conclusions about how the world works. But children sometimes misunderstand what they see and hear. Thus we frequently grow up feeling responsible for problems we did not really cause.

• As a child, Lydia noticed that whenever she felt happy and confident, her mother became tense and unhappy. However, when she was troubled and insecure, her mother became interested and cheerful. Lydia unconsciously concluded that her happiness made her mother sad, while by acting troubled and unsure, she could make her mother happy.

• As a child, David noticed that the more awards and popularity that came to him, the worse his brother seemed to do. He unconsciously concluded that his success came at his brother's expense.

• When her mother told her, "Men are all bastards. You can't live with 'em and you can't live without 'em," Maria believed her. Maria saw her mother hurt and disappointed by man after man. Yet her mother continued her desperate pursuit of undesirable males, choosing one inappropriate partner after another. Maria unconsciously concluded that she too would always long for but never achieve a satisfying intimate relationship.

It is important to remember that even though these beliefs are, for the most part, unconscious, they continue to control our behavior. If Lydia, David, and Maria had been asked if they believed in these depressing ideas, they would probably have denied it. We are not usually aware of our grim, unconscious beliefs or of the imaginary crimes that give rise to them.

Why We Falsely
Blame Ourselves

As children, we became unconsciously convinced that we were responsible for the suffering, disappointments, and inadequacies of our parents or siblings. It is this unconscious idea — that we are to blame for our parents' and siblings' misfortunes, inadequacies, and sufferings — that we call an imaginary crime.

Even if a parent or sibling was chronically unhappy, endlessly critical, unable to love, or given to inexplicable fits of rage, we were not responsible. If a parent or sibling was taken from us by death, divorce, separation, or incarceration, nothing we could have done would have changed matters. If a parent or sibling was made unavailable, unpredictable, or unreliable by physical illness, alcoholism, drug addiction, schizophrenia, depression, or manic-depressive illness, we were not to blame. Yet we do unconsciously blame ourselves for all these painful events. And we punish ourselves for these imaginary crimes, crimes that we never committed, crimes that never really occurred.

The Imaginary Crime of Writing This Book

I experienced a relatively minor but instructive example of unconscious guilt while writing this book. I had played with the idea of writing a book about Control Mastery Theory for about a year and had actually made a start on it before Tom and I decided to make it a joint effort. Although I sincerely wanted to write such a book, I had grave doubts about my ability to complete it or to get it published on my own. It was only after Tom, an experienced and successful author, agreed to collaborate with me, that I felt certain the book really would get written and published. The night we agreed to do the book together, I went to sleep elated and optimistic.

I awoke the next morning nearly paralyzed with anxiety. I lay there trembling, overwhelmed by a profound sense of dread. I worried that Tom and I would not be able to agree, that our twenty-year friendship might break up over the project. I worried that Hal Sampson, from whom I first learned about Control Mastery, and Joe Weiss, who originated the theory, would feel I was trying to steal their thunder and would repudiate me. I worried that jealous colleagues would shun me. I worried that there would be widespread contempt and disdain for our feeble, pop-psych effort.

I replayed the tapes of my own internal dialogues over and over again:

"Hal and Joe don't really want me to write this book."

"That's ridiculous! They've supported us every step of the way."

"They're going to try to keep me from writing it."

"Not true. They want to get their ideas out to the widest possible audience."

"They'll be envious of the attention and success we'll receive for writing our book."

"Wrong. Hal and Joe are both highly successful and widely respected. Neither has ever acted the least bit competitive or envious."

"Not so far — but what if they pull the rug out from under me at the last minute?"

This silent dialogue went on endlessly, painfully, and pointlessly. Instead of leading me to any useful conclusions or plan of action, it only made me more and more anxious and depressed.

I obsessed about the potential calamities for several days. Then it suddenly struck me that my worries were a textbook example of what Control Mastery Theory calls *punishment thoughts* — obsessive negative thoughts we use to punish ourselves for our imaginary crimes. (For more on punishment thoughts, see Chapter 7.) I stopped ruminating on these distressing but unlikely outcomes and began to ask myself the questions

Control Mastery Theory would suggest: Why would it be a crime for me to write a successful book? Why am I seeking to punish myself?

After much soul-searching, I realized that what lay beneath all my fears was guilt over the imaginary crime of outdoing my father. Although he has been very supportive of me in recent years, as a child it seemed to me that he was never satisfied with my efforts. From a very early age, I always wanted to do things my own way, and it often seemed to me that my father disapproved unless I did things his way. I derived the erroneous but deep impression that if I didn't do things his way, I would never receive his full approval. In addition, some years ago my father had considered writing a book about his own work, but the project never proceeded beyond the talking stage. Thus I felt that writing a successful book of my own would mean succeeding where he had failed. Finally, while growing up, it was my impression that my father wasn't happy with his work and didn't feel particularly successful. In contrast, I love my work and feel quite successful. Writing a useful book would make me feel even more so. I felt by writing and publishing a book, I would be outdoing my father.

As I became aware of these deep feelings, my sweaty anxiety receded and I became profoundly sad — sad for my father, for all the years he spent struggling with a job situation he didn't really like. Sad for the difficult parts of our relationship. And I also felt sad for myself. I grieved for the persistent low-level anxiety that has plagued me all my adult life. I felt a sense of loss for the many ways it had robbed me of happiness and satisfaction.

This incident led to an important self-understanding: I realized that I have a powerful unconscious belief that by being successful I might cause so much envy that others might feel inclined to attack and repudiate me. Because of this belief, I unconsciously feared that Hal and Joe would attack me for writing a successful book — in spite of their obvious enthusiasm for the project. The real cause of my fear was not anything they had said or done, but my imaginary crime against my father.

Although I am still occasionally troubled by these worries, it is now much easier for me to recognize them for what they are. As a result, they are less intense and less persistent. And, as the book you are reading demonstrates, they did not keep me from reaching my goal.

Are We Exclusively Motivated by Self-Interest?

As I began to understand the principles of Control Mastery Theory, I noticed that many of my clients' problems seemed, at bottom, to be covering up guilt and sadness toward their parents. Those clients who became aware of the guilt and sadness seemed, over time, to gain more and more mastery over their symptoms.

I wondered why I hadn't previously noticed the importance of this guilt. I wondered why my clients, an extremely bright and psychologically sophisticated group, rarely considered that their difficulties might be due to guilt regarding their parents and siblings. I realized that to think along these lines one would have to assume that we all have a very powerful urge to protect and care for our loved ones — particularly our parents and siblings. Such ideas rarely occur to us because we all usually assume that we are motivated almost exclusively by self-interest. Because we take our selfish nature so much for granted, we do not usually consider the possibility that some of our most persistent problems may be due to our irrational worries and concerns about others.

It is the purpose of this book to open up this hidden territory — our powerful altruistic impulses — for exploration. For it is only by understanding the intensity of our need to care for others that we can begin to understand our hidden guilt — and the varieties of self-sabotage and self-punishment that can result from it.

False Assumptions

Because I assumed that I was motivated exclusively by self-interest, I had never seriously considered the idea that I had suffered from anxiety and self-sabotage for most of my adult life out of a kind of empathy and misplaced loyalty to my father. I gave myself other explanations: I was basically lazy. I was filled with rage. I had a tremendous fear of failure. I was basically incompetent. And so on.

Now there is some truth in each of these notions: I do have a tendency to put off hard work. I do sometimes harbor resentments. I don't like to fail. And although I do a number of things very well, there are other things I do poorly. But none of these explanations went to the heart of the matter. None of them made me any less anxious. In fact, they made me feel worse. None of them freed me to begin to work effectively toward my goal of writing a useful and successful book.

It was only when I began to realize that I was avoiding success much more than avoiding failure, avoiding the work I wanted to do rather than putting off work I didn't want to do, and avoiding feeling guilt and sadness for my father rather than wallowing in self-pity, that my work on the book began to go smoothly.

Even Babies Are Altruistic

Freud and many of his contemporaries, acting on incomplete data, concluded that human beings are exclusively egoistic.[4] Until very recently, this view was widely held among social scientists, psychiatrists, and psychologists, but new evidence contradicts Freud's notion.[5]

Current research now strongly supports the idea that there is a powerful instinctive drive in many animals — and in particular, in human beings — to aid others in distress.[6] For the species that exhibit this tendency, including *Homo sapiens,* this drive is particularly intense toward offspring, parents, and siblings. These studies do not contradict the idea that human beings are strongly motivated by self-concern, but they do add another powerful instinctual motive — our inborn concern for others.

A team of University of Michigan psychologists found that day-old babies became distressed when they heard another baby crying, but showed little or no distress when exposed to a similarly loud tone.[7] Their response was clearly instinctive.

The distress with which one-day-old infants respond to the sound of other infants crying is a kind of rudimentary empathy. The fact that another infant is distressed causes them to be distressed. Yet one-day-olds have no way to put their empathic feelings into action. There is nothing they can do to help. However, almost as soon as they are able to engage in helping behavior, children begin to do so.

When researchers at the National Institute of Mental Health studied infants between nine months and two years of age, they found a surprisingly high level of helping behavior. Here is one observer's description of one-and-a-half-year-old Julie's response when confronted with a crying baby:

> The baby began to shriek and pound his fists on the floor. He was very upset by my efforts to comfort him, so I finally put him in a highchair and gave him some cookies.

As soon as he began to cry, Julie looked very worried, startled, and anxious. Her body stiffened. She leaned toward him and cocked her head. She kept reaching toward him but didn't actually touch him.

When he began to throw his cookies and cry, Julie tried to return them to him. She looked very worried: her eyebrows were up and her lips were pursed. When I put him back on the floor, she hovered over him, whimpering and looking up at me questioningly.

I put him in the playpen. He continued to cry. Julie continued to look very anxious and on several occasions began crying herself. She patted his hair and stroked his shoulder. He pulled away from her. She made concerned, cooing sounds.

A bit later she came back to me, took my hand, and led me back to the playpen, glancing up at me with a concerned, worried look. She took my hand and tried to put it on the baby's head.[8]

Current research strongly indicates that, from a very early age, children feel an instinctive empathic distress when they see a fellow human in pain. And as this anecdote clearly indicates, even as early as the second year of life, this instinctive urge leads the child to help others.[9]

Psychologists had formerly believed that altruism is a learned behavior that does not develop until the fifth year of life. But ethnologists have long been aware that many animals who live in groups show a strong inborn urge to help their comrades. This altruistic impulse is believed to increase the chances for survival of all group members.[10] Human beings now appear to be one of the species with this powerful inborn altruistic impulse.

How Altruism
Gets Us into Trouble

The ability to empathize with others is the source of those aspects of humanity we most admire: caring, nurturing, sacrifice, and all the complex varieties of love. The lifelong sacrifice of Mother Theresa, Gandhi, Albert Schweitzer, Martin Luther King, and other humanitarians is even more impressive. Such people represent a noble flowering of the altruistic spirit.

Our powerful urge to care for others is responsible for some of our most inspiring behavior. A colleague of ours was badly burned when he ran into a blazing bedroom to save his baby daughter. Concern for her welfare completely outweighed his concern for his own safety. Control Mastery Theory suggests that our psychological problems come about in much the same way: Our decision to make ourselves unhappy because one or both of our parents were unhappy is just as altruistic as our friend's decision to run through flames to save his daughter.

Control Mastery Theory proposes that most psychological problems are the result of our altruistic impulses run amok. Our altruism is such an important and powerful part of our nature that, when misdirected, it can inspire intense impulses to punish ourselves and to sabotage our lives.

If your mother was chronically unhappy during your childhood, you probably felt a compelling urge to cheer her up. If you were unable to do so, you may have grown up with a deep sense of having failed her. As a result, you may unconsciously feel that you deserve to be chronically unhappy as well. It is all too typical that the child of a chronically unhappy parent will have great difficulty allowing himself to be happy in adult life.

Rotten to the Core

Deep inside, most of us have a sneaking suspicion that we are pretty unattractive people — weak, cowardly, mean, selfish, inadequate, or irresponsible. So the prospect of finding out more about our innermost motivations may appear unappealing at best. But once we realize that many of our problems are the result of profound feelings of responsibility for our loved ones, the process of unraveling these strands becomes considerably less distasteful.

Unfortunately, it is still not easy. As we work through our hidden guilt, we may discover a substantial reservoir of sadness — for the suffering of our parents and siblings, for our own suffering, and for our own self-imposed limits. In order to go forward we must acknowledge and experience this pain. We must face our own difficult family secrets. We must accept the fact that we have distorted and constricted our lives as adults in accordance with our unconscious beliefs. And we must become aware of the many ways in which we have passed over opportunities and subverted our own most cherished goals for love, friendship, happiness, and achievement.

The Curse of Omnipotence

As children, many of us are saddled with a problem psychologists call *childhood omnipotence* — an exaggerated sense of control of the feelings and behavior of others.[11] Although omnipotence sounds like a good quality, it is actually something closer to a curse. Since the child — and later the adult — is not really all-powerful, a child's so-called omnipotence usually comes down to a burdensome feeling of responsibility to make everyone feel good and make everything go right, without having the power to do so.

A child can come to suffer from omnipotence when parents give her a false sense of power. If quarreling parents each present their case to the child, as if the child were a judge or marriage counselor, she will unconsciously feel responsible for the success of their marriage. If an unhappy father complains to his daughter about how cold and mean his wife is, the child will unconsciously infer that it is up to her to cheer him up. If a frustrated parent tells a child things like "you make me so unhappy," "you drive me crazy," or "you have ruined my life" — the child may believe these things to be literally true.

A child may also feel responsible for any family trauma — death, divorce, alcoholism, or physical or mental illness. The young child can easily come to feel that such unfortunate events were caused by his bad thoughts or bad behavior. Once a child becomes convinced that his thoughts can harm others, he suffers from a particularly burdensome form of omnipotence — magical thinking.

Magical Thinking

Magical thinking is the child's belief that she has the ability to make things happen by simply thinking about them. When children feel this way about their positive wishes and hopes, it can be very reassuring. When they feel that their angry or hurtful thoughts can damage others, it can become a terrible burden.

One night when Hanna was eleven years old, she was angry with her father and refused to kiss him good-bye as he was leaving for a business trip. She never saw him alive again. His plane crashed and everyone aboard was killed. Today, twenty-five years later, Hanna is still troubled by the unconscious conviction that she caused her father's death, that somehow her angry thoughts caused his plane to go down. In the next chapter we will provide a detailed description of the problems this produced in Hanna's later life.

If You're Hungry, I Won't Eat

Because children have such strong feelings of responsibility for their parents, a person's ability to experience happiness, contentment, and psychological health is highly dependent on how happy his parents were. If Mom and Dad are happy, healthy, and successful, the child will feel that his actions — good thoughts and behavior — have kept his parent safe from harm. He will see himself as a positive influence in his parents' lives and will end up feeling good about himself.

But if things are bad — if Mom or Dad is physically or mentally ill, an alcoholic, unhappy, he will feel that he has failed in his responsibility. He may then unconsciously conclude that since he has caused his parents such harm, there must be something essentially malicious or inadequate about him.

Because we feel so responsible for our loved ones, we are not willing to be fulfilled or content if we feel that those closest to us are suffering. When my son Nick was seven years old, he watched a television program on world hunger. Afterward, he came into the other room and put his arm around me. "You know, Daddy," he said. "If you and Mommy were starving like those people in Africa, I wouldn't eat either." Nick's behavior provides a fine example of our natural tendency to share the same fate as other family members: If you do not eat, I will not eat. If you are not happy, I will not be happy.

But Are We Really Innocent?

We have asserted that children are *not* responsible for their parents' or siblings' unhappiness. Some readers may object. You may feel that you really *did* cause your parents or siblings great pain and unhappiness.

Some of us are fully aware that we were a burden to our parents. Some of us were unplanned. Some of us had serious physical or psychological disabilities. In some cases our care put inordinate demands on our family's emotional, physical, and financial resources. Our birth may have caused one of our parents to abandon a career or a lifelong dream. One or both parents may have stayed in an unhappy marriage for our sake. For some parents, taking care of one or more normally rambunctious children was simply more than they could handle. Parenting is difficult, and some people were simply not up to the task.

Yet even though such situations may have contributed to the suffering of our parents or siblings, it was neither our choice nor our intention to make them suffer. It is thus irrational for us to blame ourselves for that suffering. This is particularly obvious in the case of a child with a serious illness: although the illness does cause hardship to everyone in the family, the child did not cause himself to be sick.

The fact that you were too much for your parents — too active, too smart, too willful, or too different from their expectations — is not your fault either. Your parents did the best they could, but they were simply not capable enough or flexible enough to deal with you effectively. Being selfish, malicious, angry, or unmindful of the feelings of others is well within the repertoire of all normal children. Although we are each responsible for our own actions from the time we can tell right from wrong, it is ultimately up to parents to set meaningful limits.

The mere fact that your parents or siblings suffered does not mean that you were at fault. Life brings us all a measure of pain and suffering which is really no one's fault. It is quite irrational for us to take the blame for something that was not within our control.

Some of us *are* guilty of real transgressions against our close family members, such as being rejecting, cruel, exploitive, or sexually inappropriate with a younger sibling. If so, it is important to face up to these wrongs and to make what reparations are possible. If you can, talk to the family member concerned, acknowledge what you did, and apologize. If it is not possible to make direct amends because this person has died or will not speak to you, you may want to consider an alternative that will make you feel better: If you were rejecting toward your younger brother, you might become a Big Brother for a child who has been rejected by his own father. If you were abusive toward a younger sister, you might support a shelter for mothers and children fleeing from abusive situations. By balancing your own internal system of moral accounting, you may be able to reduce your unconscious drive to punish yourself.

Taking the Blame

Children from particularly chaotic, unloving, and neglectful families have another reason to repress their imaginary crimes: doing so helps them have the hope to go on. If one or both of our parents were cold, unhappy, mean, irresponsible, weak, or pathetic, we may tend to think of ourselves as the problem, not our parent.

It is psychologically easier and safer to blame ourselves than to face the distressing, shameful, and sometimes terrifying fact that we must depend on an incompetent, unaccepting, or unloving parent. Taking the blame may be less frightening than facing the truth. Also, in terms of the child's magical thinking, the mere act of admitting that a parent may be unhappy, impaired, unloving, or crazy is tantamount to making them that way.

Gaining Insight into Our Psychological Problems

Those who suffer from massive unconscious guilt may wreck their marriages, alienate their families, sabotage their careers, become chemically dependent, or may be afflicted with overwhelming feelings of anxiety or depression.[12] Those of us whose unconscious guilt is less overwhelming may punish ourselves in smaller ways — by fouling up a checkbook, unreasonably criticizing a spouse, or repeatedly "forgetting" to leave time for the activities that nurture us most.

As we shall see in the chapters that follow, we will not be able to fully understand our own psychological problems until we begin to identify the ways our own hidden guilt leads us to sabotage ourselves. Only then can we understand the ways this guilt is linked to our powerful altruistic concerns for our brothers, sisters, and, above all, our parents.

2

The Witch's Curse

Grim, Unconscious Beliefs Are Like Curses in a Fairy Tale

=========

*As long as things go well with a man, his conscience is lenient
. . . but when misfortune befalls him, he searches his soul,
acknowledges his sinfulness, heightens the demands of his
conscience, imposes abstinences upon himself, and punishes
himself with penances.*

— SIGMUND FREUD

From early in childhood we begin to develop beliefs about how the world works: If I touch the hot stove, it will hurt. If I cry, Mommy will come to comfort me. However, as children we are ignorant of the laws of cause and effect, and may at times come to irrational conclusions.

One of the most important things we need to learn is how our actions affect our parents. For all the altruistic reasons discussed in Chapter 1 — and because our very survival depends on maintaining parental ties — our connections with our parents are of paramount importance. We may therefore condemn any aspect of our personality which appears to upset them. We may reject any goals of which they seem critical. For we fear that if they are hurt or offended, they may withdraw the support, love, or protection we need to survive.

A lively child who senses that her rambunctious energy overwhelms her depressed mother may conclude that her liveliness is a bad and dangerous quality. As a consequence, she may curtail her playfulness and enthusiasm and may also become depressed.

Even if she maintains her liveliness, she may still carry the unconscious conviction that her exuberance is bad and will cause others hurt. The power of this unconscious belief may be so great that it makes her act in ways that will make these grim predictions a reality: she might speak without permission in class or act rebelliously at school, so as to be reprimanded by her teachers. Thus the unconscious ideas that we form in our attempt to maintain our ties to our parents can become self-fulfilling prophecies.

Beliefs That Don't Change

As very young children, some of our early theories of cause and effect were either partly or totally incorrect. However, as time went on we were able to test our mistaken assumptions and to refine our understanding of how the world works. Thus, as we got older, we developed a more and more accurate set of beliefs about the world.[1]

But some of our most problematic beliefs seem too painful or threatening to examine. And so rather than testing them, we simply push them out of consciousness. Unfortunately, once a belief becomes unconscious, it is no longer accessible to rational testing. Thus some of our mistaken childhood assumptions about the world go uncorrected. These uncorrected childhood conclusions can end up having a dreadful influence on our lives.

Control Mastery Theory calls these old, uncorrected childhood assumptions *grim, unconscious beliefs.*[2] They generally take this form: if I pursue X (a desirable objective), then Y (a terrible calamity) will happen to me or to another family member. We become convinced that by pursuing our own natural impulses, desires, or aspirations we will bring injury to ourselves or to those we love.[3]

Hanna's Grim, Unconscious Belief

As we saw in the last chapter, Hanna judged herself guilty of the imaginary crime of killing her father because she refused to kiss him good-bye shortly before his death. Hanna's mother was an unhappy, dissatisfied woman, who became even more disheartened after her husband's death. Her only pleasure seemed to come in controlling every detail of Hanna's life. If Hanna ever got angry at her mother's meddling, her mother would act terribly hurt. Instead of helping Hanna get over her feelings of responsibility for her father's death, her mother only reinforced them.

The unconscious conviction that Hanna had killed her father gave rise to a number of grim, unconscious beliefs. Since she considers herself a murderer, Hanna feels she deserves little in the way of pleasure or satisfaction, and she is unconsciously driven to sabotage her own happiness. And because she believes that her anger will cause the loss of those she loves, she is unable to express anger in her intimate relationships.

As a result, any close relationship poses a serious dilemma. If

Hanna freely expresses her thoughts and feelings, she feels she will lose the relationship. But if she doesn't, she becomes more and more resentful and eventually loses her warm feelings. As one might expect, Hanna has been unable to sustain a meaningful intimate relationship.

A Case of Self-Sabotage

Larry was a bright, personable thirty-four-year-old who worked as a low-level manager for a large chemical company. He was capable, well trained, and ambitious, but every time he came up for promotion, he would forget to mail a crucial letter, turn in a sloppy report, or provoke an argument with a superior. As a result, he was repeatedly passed over.

When Larry was a child, his father was a foreman in the machine shop of an automobile assembly plant. He was a good worker, but he had only rudimentary management skills. The young men he trained continually rose to higher positions while he himself was never promoted. As this scenario repeated itself again and again, Larry's father became extremely upset. Over the years he became a bitter, unhappy man who drank heavily and was highly critical of Larry. Sometimes, after a long drinking bout, Larry's father would heap abusive remarks on the younger, college-educated men who had received the promotions he wanted. Over and over, he would explain to his wife and sons how "those college boys had only book learning" and, in his opinion, weren't worth a damn.

Neither of Larry's two brothers were good students, but Larry was always at the top of his class. Larry's father and brothers resented his scholastic success. Sometimes, after Larry had received an academic award, his brothers would beat him up, explaining that the beating "served him right for trying to be such a smarty-pants." His father rarely interfered.

Larry's mother was a quiet, patient, mildly depressed woman, who had left a responsible and enjoyable job as manager of a large office when she married Larry's father. Even after Larry and his brothers were grown, her husband refused to let her go back to work. He was afraid people would think that he was not enough of a man to support his family. Larry was his mother's favorite and was the only one in his family who had ever attended college.

From an early age, Larry had the impression that his father resented him in the same way he resented the younger coworkers who were promoted over his head. His father clearly felt humiliated by being passed over, and Larry unconsciously felt that his father was equally humiliated by his own successes. Later on, when his father opposed his plans to go to college, Larry became even more convinced that his father didn't want him to succeed.

After he himself was repeatedly passed over for promotion, Larry began to suspect that he was sabotaging his own efforts to get ahead and decided to enter therapy.[4]

Seeing Our Success as Humiliating to Family Members

As his therapy progressed, it became clear that Larry believed his success at work would hurt every member of his family. He felt that he had already humiliated his father by going to college and getting a white-collar job. A promotion would only intensify the insult. Larry also felt he would be hurting his mother.

He would, after all, end up enjoying an executive position much like the one she had given up. Finally, Larry believed that by succeeding, he would be hurting his brothers, who had always resented his success.

Larry faced a terrible dilemma. He was a talented and ambitious young man, yet he could not bear the guilt of hurting his whole family by becoming successful. He resolved this dilemma by allowing himself to perform at a high level only when he was in no danger of being promoted. After spoiling his chances a number of times, Larry found that younger workers were being promoted over his head. Instead of outdoing his father, Larry ended up in a similar position.

Navigators Before Columbus

A person who harbors a grim, unconscious belief is like a navigator before Columbus. Even if such an explorer were skeptical of the theory that sailing west would mean falling off the edge of the earth, it would require great bravery to risk the terrible consequences, both to himself and to his crew, of being wrong. This analogy is particulary apt, as it illustrates that in failing to test our grim beliefs, we are concerned not only for our own welfare, but for that of others.

A grim belief is a kind of psychological curse predicting that dire consequences will follow from the pursuit of our desires. Psychotherapists have long been aware that we can suffer from unconscious guilt over being greedy, cowardly, selfish, enraged, having murderous thoughts, being aroused by taboo sex objects and other unpalatable goals and desires. What Weiss discovered is that we can be guilty about literally *any* trait, desire, or aspiration we have, no matter how worthwhile. As long as such aspirations appear to upset our parents, we can convince ourselves that pursuing them is tantamount to harming a parent.

- If your parent is clingy and needs you to remain dependent, the desire to be independent can become an imaginary crime.
- If your parent seems distant and burdened by your desire to be dependent and close, your desire for closeness can become an imaginary crime.
- If your parent seems upset by any expression of sadness on your part, feeling or acting sorrowful can become an imaginary crime.
- If your parent seems depressed and gloomy and does not appear to approve of happiness or high spirits, your desire to be happy can constitute an imaginary crime.

Wanting to be independent can be an imaginary crime in one family, whereas wanting to be able to depend on a parent can be a crime in another. There are even some parents who act hurt when their children want to go off and play with friends, but act burdened or rejecting when their children want to be taken care of by them. A child in this situation will feel guilty about both his desire for independence and his desire to be dependent.

Thousand-Repetition Grim Beliefs

Most of us acquire our grim beliefs through a slow and gradual learning process that takes place over a period of years. Larry developed *his* grim belief — that it would be both cruel and dangerous for him to become successful — as the result of his father's many small criticisms, his father's complaints about his job, and his brothers' comments and behavior. None of these childhood incidents was particularly noteworthy in itself, but taken together, they served to communicate a powerful and unmistakable message. Larry's belief that his success would injure his family members is an example of a *thousand-repetition grim belief.*[5] It is not based on a single traumatic incident, but on a series of interactions that took place again and again over a long period of time.

Some thousand-repetition grim beliefs come from negative parental messages. If a young boy is told over and over again that he will never amount to anything, he is likely to grow up believing that this is true. If a young girl's mother tells her over and over that you can't trust men, she may have a very difficult time forming a stable intimate relationship with a man. The effects of negative parental messages are described in more detail in Chapter 6.

Traumatic-Incident Grim Beliefs

Occasionally, grim beliefs are formed from a single powerful, shocking incident. Hanna acquired her grim belief — that if she withholds affection or defies a loved one she may harm that person or lose him forever — because her father died shortly after she refused to kiss him good-bye. A child who experiences the death of a parent or other close family member will almost always feel responsible.

Both children and adults struggle in the aftermath of a traumatic event — the unexpected death of someone close, an illness, accident, robbery, rape, natural disaster, or other misfortune. We all tend to hold ourselves responsible for these traumatic events, even if there was no way we could control them. If a friend commits suicide, we tell ourselves that we should have seen it coming, that we could have intervened. For children, this irrational assignment of self-responsibility is even more pronounced.

Some clients come into therapy hoping to find that single incident that will explain their problems. They almost never find it. That is because the vast majority of our problems is due to thousand-repetition grim beliefs. Traumatic-incident grim beliefs are much less common.

Separation and Other Traumas

Long separations from our parents — or separations that take place under frightening circumstances — can also produce grim, unconscious beliefs.

When Paul was two and a half, his older brother contracted measles. His parents worried that Paul might become infected as well. With no warning and little explanation, they sent Paul away to live with his aunt and uncle. The parents, who were struggling with overwhelming problems of their own, did not bring Paul back home until three months later.

At the time of separation, Paul was a lively and willful child. But when he returned three months later, he was quiet, tense, and almost too anxious to please. When he entered therapy at age thirty-two, Paul was not very different from the quiet, tense boy who had come back from his aunt and uncle's. He had unconsciously concluded that he had been sent away for being too lively and too assertive. For all the years that followed, he had subscribed to the grim, unconscious belief that such behavior would lead to rejection.[6]

Other types of childhood trauma can have similar consequences. These include accidents and illnesses (either your own or those of a family member), physical or sexual abuse, family financial distress, or a manic, depressive, schizophrenic, or alcoholic episode in a parent or sibling. The ways in which such continuing trauma within the family can give rise to grim, unconscious beliefs is discussed in greater depth in Chapter 10.

The Witch's Curse

These grim beliefs are like curses in a fairy tale. Sleeping Beauty was cursed by an angry witch who felt slighted when she was not invited to the royal birth. Just as Sleeping Beauty risked disaster as she was drawn to the fascinating spinning wheel, we unconsciously fear that we risk our own psychological doom by pursuing the attainments — independence, success, happiness — that are forbidden by our unconscious beliefs.

Those of us who carry this vague sense of doom feel that when things *are* going well, we are just temporarily cheating fate. It is as if we have been evading our taxes: we know that the authorities will catch up with us in the end. When this happens, all our back taxes, plus penalties, must be paid and we may face a jail term as well. When things go badly, either in major or minor ways, we feel that we have at last been overtaken by a horrible but inevitable fate. It seems to us that we were fools for ever daring to think we could be happy, successful, or fulfilled.

George, a high school dropout who had worked his way up to become a highly successful investigative reporter, was devastated when his antique Porsche was stolen. It confirmed his unconscious belief that he would never be able to hold onto anything he really cared about. For a period of several weeks, he was obsessed with the idea that he would lose his job and his girlfriend as well.

Many people with psychological difficulties carry the burden of a negative sense of fate. No matter what we do to try to stop it, the pattern continues.

Most of us at least occasionally have the feeling that we have been living our lives under a curse. The specifics of this sense of affliction vary greatly from person to person. Some people feel jinxed in *every* area of life. More frequently, a person's sense of being hexed is limited to one or two areas.

Some of us experience considerable success in our careers, but seem unable to maintain a satisfactory relationship. Some of us have satisfactory relationships, but are unable to achieve the professional success we crave. We may fear that we will never learn to put our financial affairs in order, that we will never be sexually satisfied, or that we will never be able to accomplish some other treasured goal.

Control Mastery Theory holds that our "curse" is often the result of our belief that we were hurtful, burdensome, or disloyal to our parents. Just as the witch punished Sleeping Beauty for a slight she had received from the king and queen, we curse ourselves because we feel we have injured our parents. The curse is our self-imposed punishment for our imaginary crimes.

Self-Fulfilling Prophecies

Many of us who feel doomed to failure have great difficulty in changing the behaviors and attitudes that cause our unhappiness. This is because we are unconsciously driven to make the curse come true.

• Michael, a businessman, suffered from the unconscious belief that no one can be trusted. Both of Michael's parents were unreliable alcoholics. He grew up never knowing whether a promise would be kept, whether he would be fed, or whether his parents would return home or stay out all night. He came to believe that he was a bad person who *deserved* such mistreatment. As an adult, Michael unconsciously made sure that he got what he felt he deserved by going into partnership with a known con man and by marrying a notoriously promiscuous woman.

• Charlotte was a bright, able, and unusually attractive woman. Her mother was a temperamental, unsuccessful actress. Her father was a kind, patient, and long-suffering attorney, who never divorced her mother in spite of her irresponsibility and occasional infidelities. Charlotte herself had been married three times to warm and supportive men. Each time she had wrecked her relationship by having affairs. Charlotte was driven by a powerful and self-destructive loyalty to her unhappy and irresponsible mother.

• Maria, described in Chapter 1, made sure that she would have a frustrating romantic life by constantly choosing a succession of inappropriate men — just as her mother had done.

Lifting the Curse

Some of us *are* eventually able to lift the curse. The encouragement of a special teacher, religious figure, coach, counselor, or mentor can sometimes help us free ourselves. A spouse or close friend who loves us and contradicts our deep sense of unworthiness can also make a tremendous difference.

The birth of a child, a new relationship, a severe illness, or a brush with death can make us feel that we have been given another chance. A religious conversion or other deep spiritual experience sometimes has the same result. Sometimes even the death of a parent can lift the curse. Once we realize it is no longer possible for us to harm a parent, we find that formidable life problems tend to diminish.

For many, however, this sense of doom remains surprisingly tenacious. We may validate those events that "prove" that the curse is true while ignoring those events that disprove it. A mentor's encouragement may be seen as misguided optimism. The warmth and caring of friends and loved ones are considered misplaced and unreliable. We are sure they will reject us when they discover what we are *really* like. Even escape from death may seem only a temporary reprieve. And after a parent's death, we may simply internalize the deceased, and come to think of him as "looking down from above," as disapproving and disappointed as ever. Many of us will find that we are able to lift the curse only with the help of group or individual psychotherapy.

The Misunderstood Payoff

Although our commonsense explanations for dysfunctional behavior may seem plausible enough — "I'm too selfish," "I don't really care about other people," "I'm lazy or undisciplined," "I'm afraid of responsibility," "I'm not smart enough" — they're almost always wrong, a cover-up for a grim, unconscious belief, e.g., "I'm a bad person and don't deserve success" or "If I'm successful, my parents will be hurt."

It is easy to feel that if we engage in repetitive, self-defeating behavior we must be "getting something out of it." We may thus attempt to explain our self-punishments in terms of a hidden payoff:

- Our failures will make others feel sorry for us.
- Our self-induced suffering will bring us attention.
- Our relentless self-punishments will allow us the masochistic "benefit" of self-pity.

Although there may be some truth in each of these ideas, they avoid the heart of the issue. When we say these things to ourselves, we are simply engaging in further self-punishment. A therapist who tells a suffering patient that she is wallowing in self-pity or making a bid for attention will, more likely than not, only make her feel worse.

Larry, for example, had his own explanation for why he always seemed to make a crucial mistake when a promotion was imminent. He thought he was afraid of failure and was thus avoiding the responsibilities a more responsible job would bring. While this sounds plausible, the real reason was that Larry was afraid that by becoming too successful he would embarrass his father and brothers.

Once he was able to identify his hidden beliefs, Larry became aware of the way they pervaded his life. As he began to let go of them, he found that he was able to stop sabotaging himself at work. He eventually received several well-deserved promotions.

The Roots of Self-Sabotage

Control Mastery Theory provides a new way to understand the roots of our painful, self-defeating behaviors, attitudes, and feelings. These beliefs were formed as a result of the particular traumas we suffered and the experiences we had growing up, and are therefore different for each of us. They have been with us for a long time and are part of a system of beliefs that we have depended upon to get us through life. However irrational they may be, they have allowed us to survive.

There is — and should be — a natural and understandable reluctance to drop our long-held unconscious beliefs. After all, our belief system is our road map to life. It is our guide to action. It is what allows us to survive. One should not expect a quick or easy make-over. Change often proceeds slowly and may take many months or years.

Simply understanding the importance of our grim, unconscious beliefs will not make them vanish. But it is an important first step. In Chapter 3 we will take a closer look at the belief that we have committed imaginary crimes against our parents and siblings and at the six common types of imaginary crimes.

3

Common
Imaginary Crimes

Understanding the Power of Guilt

By inflicting suffering on one's self, one can more easily deny that one has caused another to suffer. By a process of magical thinking, one becomes the victim and therefore not the offender.

— MICHAEL FRIEDMAN, M.D.

As we have seen, most people with psychological difficulties unconsciously believe that they are guilty of certain "crimes," even though these crimes are almost always based on false self-accusations and destructive messages from parents. But even though they falsely accuse themselves, they punish themselves as if their imaginary crimes were real.

Mike Snyder is a handsome, successful, thirty-nine-year-old plastic surgeon with a warm, easy manner. He sails San Francisco Bay in the summer and skis the Sierras and the Rockies in the winter. He has a beautiful home overlooking the bay and is well known for his elaborate and memorable parties. He is the quintessential eligible bachelor.

But behind the facade of his impressive lifestyle, Mike is desperately unhappy. Skiing and sailing have lost their charm. Entertaining has become a chore. He worries about hurting his friends by leaving them off his party list. Even his work, which he had always enjoyed, now seems far less satisfying. Mike has been forced to accept the fact that there is a major flaw in his seemingly idyllic life: although he would love to get married and have children, he finds himself destroying every promising relationship with a woman.

Mike has no trouble meeting eligible partners. But as soon as a friendship with a woman starts to become intimate, he begins to feel trapped and experiences an irresistible urge to end the relationship.

The women he dates find him warm, sensitive, perceptive, and caring — a kindly, affectionate father figure who seems to understand their feelings. True, he never talks much about his *own* emotions, but a lot of men are that way — or so his dates tell themselves. Each new woman friend gets more and more excited about her deepening relationship with Mike. But her dreams are shattered when, for no apparent reason, Mike gradually begins drawing away, and eventually disappears.

Mike is the oldest child of an alcoholic physician father and an overburdened mother. He was a model child. Like many children whose fathers are alcoholics, Mike has always felt responsible for taking care of his mother.[1] Mike's father died when he was eleven. After his death, Mike's mother went into a state of perpetual mourning. She made no effort to go out with other men. As the years went by, she seemed to withdraw from the world more and more.

Mike felt that since his mother was *already* carrying such a heavy burden of troubles, anything he did to add to them was especially unforgivable. He tried hard to be good. But even though he was extremely well behaved, his mother treated his occasional childhood misdeeds and adventures as horrible betrayals. When she heard that Mike had been reprimanded for being rude to a crossing guard at school, his mother threw herself on her bed and cried for several hours.

When Mike grew up he carried these childhood patterns over into his romantic relationships. He works very hard to be the perfect mate. But if he seems to be disappointing his partner in any way — feeling tired when she wants to make love, or needing time alone when she wants to see him — he is flooded with all the old guilt he used to feel toward his mother.

Naturally enough, this makes him feel terribly constrained as a new relationship begins to develop. Thus as each new relationship deepens, Mike feels a growing weight of responsibility. Thus as he grows closer and closer to his new friend, Mike becomes more and more determined that he *has* to get out of the relationship — because he is unconsciously afraid that if he stays he will only hurt his partner. And he punishes himself severely — bombarding himself with self-accusation and self-blame — after he breaks off the relationship.

Mike's childhood left him with a tremendous load of unconscious guilt. In spite of the fact that he was a very good child, Mike unconsciously believes that if he had only been *better,* perhaps his father might have stopped drinking. And since his father's death was partly due to his drinking, Mike feels indirectly responsible for his father's death. He also feels angry at his father and ashamed of the disgrace his father's drinking brought on the family.

Although Mike tried to help his mother in every possible way — cooking the meals, taking care of his younger brother and sister — Mike still feels that he was a great burden to her. He also feels guilty about being her favorite child. When his younger brother became an alcoholic, Mike felt responsible. He unconsciously believed that as his mother's favorite, he had gotten much of the love and attention his brother needed.

The Power of Guilt

Guilt can be an enormously powerful emotion. Many of us experience actual physical discomfort — a terrible sick feeling in the pit of the stomach, a feeling of tension throughout the body, a tightness in the chest, or difficulty in breathing. In addition, guilt can undermine our sense of self-esteem and self-worth. It can make us doubt our healthy instincts and question our good intentions. It can drive us to run away from situations in which we should stand up for ourselves. It can make us submit to unjust accusations or unmerited mistreatment. When we experience intense guilt we may be unable to sleep, unwilling to eat. If we feel guilty enough, we may even attempt to take our own lives.[2]

If we understand the source of our guilt, we may apologize, offer reparations, show repentance, or vow never to behave in certain ways again. But if our guilt derives from our imaginary crimes, we may, like Mike, be driven to sabotage our own fondest goals, even though we are unaware or only dimly aware that we consider ourselves blameworthy. Much of our self-defeating behavior is an attempt to escape the fury of our unconscious guilt.

• If, like Hanna (whose father died after she refused to kiss him good-bye), we feel that being independent or angry will cause a parent harm, we will give up our independence and anger. Hanna felt unconsciously guilty each time she became angry with a male friend. She suppressed her anger to avoid feeling this guilt.

• If, like Larry (whose father was continually passed over for promotions), we feel that our success will humiliate a vulnerable parent, we will give up being successful. Larry began to feel unconsciously guilty every time he was considered for promotion. He made his crucial "mistakes" on the job in order to avoid this guilt.

• If, like Mike, we believe that we will inevitably hurt those we are close to, we will find it impossible to allow ourselves to be close to *anybody*. Mike's unconscious guilt was activated whenever he began to get close to a woman. By withdrawing from the relationship he protected himself from that guilt.

We also may employ the unconscious strategy described by Michael Friedman in the quotation at the beginning of this chapter: we inflict suffering on ourselves so that we can see ourselves as the victim, not the offender. One of my clients believed that he had been a great burden to his overworked, depressed mother. To avoid the guilt for his "crime" he has arranged his life so that he, too, feels constantly overworked and overburdened. By focusing on his own victimhood, he no longer unconsciously feels so guilty of victimizing his mother.

Categories of Imaginary Crime

Most of us believe ourselves guilty of one or more of the six common imaginary crimes described on the following pages. As you read through this list, pay close attention to your own immediate emotional response. When you read the description of an imaginary crime that plays an important role in your own life, you may experience a visceral feeling of recognition.

Many people find that they feel guilty of two or more of these crimes. Others realize that they suffer from some guilt for each of the six crimes. But not all imaginary crimes fit into these categories. You may want to create your own categories of imaginary crimes.[3]

OUTDOING

The crime of outdoing can result from surpassing a family member in any way — becoming a college professor when your father was a factory worker, enjoying life when your mother was chronically depressed, or being attractive and popular when your sister was homely and friendless. The crime of outdoing stems from two irrational, unconscious beliefs. The first is that by having the good things in life (happiness, success, love and affection), you are using them up, not leaving any for your less fortunate parents or siblings. The second is that by achieving your occupational and personal goals, you are showing up those family members who were unable to achieve their own. Succeeding when a loved one has failed may seem cruel and unnecessary, like a football coach, already fifty points ahead, who still exhorts his team to run up an even bigger score.

But if outdoing is such a serious imaginary crime, how is it that many people seem to be able to outdo their parents without punishing themselves? A great deal depends on your parents' *reactions* to your success. If they take pride in your achievements — evidence that *they* have been successful as parents — then you are less likely to be troubled by the imaginary crime of outdoing. If, on the other hand, they appear to resent your success, or if they feel that they themselves did *not* achieve the level of success they aspired to, you may end up sabotaging your own accomplishments in order to avoid the crime of outdoing.

It is not your parents' *outward* success that counts so much as the *inward feeling* of success. If your father felt proud of his position as foreman of his factory's punch press shop, you will not feel guilty about becoming chief of cardiac surgery. But if your father felt like a failure because he was passed over for the presidency of General Motors, and ended his career as merely the executive vice-president in charge of nine western states, you may well find yourself sabotaging your own efforts.

Our sense of the seriousness of our crime of outdoing will also depend on its supposed effect on the "victim." If the family member we surpassed goes on to have a happy and satisfying life, we will realize that our crime did not inflict great harm. But if the family member we surpassed is unsuccessful, unhappy, mentally ill, or has a tragic life, we may unconsciously feel that our crime did great damage. And our self-punishment will be much more severe.

BURDENING

If either or both of your parents seemed weighed down by life, or drained by parental responsibilities, you may suffer from the imaginary crime of burdening. As the child of an overburdened parent, you may unconsciously feel yourself responsible for adding weight to an already heavy load. You may feel that if you had only been nicer, more loving, healthier, smarter, better-looking, more cooperative, more responsible, more disciplined, more successful, or somehow different, you might have eased the burden and made your unhappy parent happy.

Most often the parent's suffering has nothing to do with the child, and the child may in fact provide some solace from marital troubles, low self-esteem, or other life difficulties. But children unconsciously hold themselves responsible for the suffering of their parents.

In some situations, the parent does feel burdened by the process of raising a child. She may not be psychologically prepared for the rigors of parenthood, or other factors like poverty, the death of a spouse, or alcoholism may have compromised her ability to cope.

Recent research[4] suggests another important cause of parenting difficulties: a great disparity between the temperament of the child and that of the parent. If, for instance, two very active, highly energetic parents have a child who moves slowly and is contemplative, they may feel frustrated by the child's pace and approach to life. By the same token, two slow and deliberate parents may feel overwhelmed by their extremely active child.

This poor match between parents and child is sometimes set off by another sibling who is more in tune with the parents' natural preferences: two calm and deliberate parents might find their calm and deliberate daughter easy to care for, while their active and excitable son is a tremendous trial. You may be at special risk of convicting yourself of the crime of burdening if your parents had an easier time dealing with your brother or sister than they did with you.

But even though it may be true that your parents had a difficult time with you because of temperamental difficulties, you should not feel responsible for their struggles. Temperament is genetically determined. As a child you were no more responsible for your temperament than you were for your hair color.

Even without a temperamental mismatch, raising children is a challenging task. Kids are kids. They need a great deal of assistance, attention, and support. They need to play and to experiment with new behaviors. They need privacy. They need freedom to explore the world, to discover who they are. They need to test their parents' limits. They need to learn to assert their own preferences.

Unfortunately, many parents are never able to accept the idea that this is how children really are. Some parents treat a child's ordinary healthy behaviors as if they were terrible crimes or horrible betrayals. If one or both of your parents indicated to you that they struggled under the weight of child rearing, if you were given the impression that you were a difficult or ungrateful child, or if you were told that one or both of your parents were forced to give up a great deal for your sake, you may be at an especially high risk of convicting yourself of the crime of burdening. But even if you were *not* told that you were responsible for your parents' unhappiness, you may well feel responsible. It is not uncommon, for example, for children of divorced parents to feel that they were to blame for their parents' split.[5]

No matter how much trouble you were as a child, if your parents were happy and successful anyway, you will not feel that your imaginary crime of burdening was all that serious. However, if your parents had unhappy or tragic lives, you may unconsciously feel responsible for their suffering.

LOVE THEFT

Love theft is the crime of receiving the love or attention that another family member seemed to need in order to thrive. This imaginary crime is common among children who were favored over their brothers or sisters. If one of your less-favored siblings was or is unhappy, unsuccessful, or mentally or physically ill, the punishment you inflict upon yourself may be especially severe.

The underlying idea is that by competing for or accepting the love that your brother or sister needed but did not get, you stole from them the vital substance they needed to be happy, successful, or healthy. It is as if your mother gave you plenty to eat while starving your brother. Because you took the love or attention that your sister so badly needed you unconsciously hold yourself responsible for all her suffering and unhappiness. If your siblings are happy and successful in spite of the fact that you were favored, you may conclude that your crime is not a very serious one. But if they go on to live painful, tragic lives, you may conclude that your crime was very serious indeed.

Love theft can also occur if you felt that you and your mother had a warmer, closer relationship than she had with your father. Or if you and your father had a closer, warmer relationship than he had with your mother. By defeating one parent in the battle for the affection of the other, you become responsible for the defeated parent's troubles.

ABANDONMENT

Abandonment is the crime of wanting to separate from your parents — to have your own ideas, make your own choices, and, ultimately, to establish a separate and independent life. If your parents seem unhappy, or dependent on you for what happiness they have, simply distancing yourself from them — physically or emotionally — can make you unconsciously feel as if you are abandoning them. In addition, some parents act as if the whole process of growing up — thinking one's own thoughts, developing one's own identity, and eventually moving out of the parental household — is an unspeakably cruel and unfair thing for a child to do.

We do not mean to imply that adult children do not have a responsibility to care for their aged or infirm parents. It is natural and healthy to feel empathy for parents who need care, attention, or shelter. But there are parents, especially those who feel they have devoted their lives to their children, who expect their children to devote their lives to them in return. If these parents do not receive such devotion, their adult children can suffer from massive hidden guilt, which in turn, can cause substantial self-sabotage and self-punishment.

The children of such parents may suffer from powerful guilt feelings at pursuing their own independent lives.[6] Some adult children feel so guilty that they continue to live in the parental household and never really succeed in establishing independence. Others, who have moved away, punish themselves with a variety of symptoms to atone for their crimes. If one or both of your parents are or were accustomed to playing the martyr, you may find it especially hard to establish your own separate identity without carrying a substantial burden of hidden guilt.

DISLOYALTY

The crime of family disloyalty can result from breaking family rules or disappointing parental expectations. You may commit the crime of disloyalty by marrying a person of a different faith, race, or social class, or even by expressing different political, philosophical, or religious ideas. You may be considered disloyal if you did not join the family business. If you are the son or daughter of a family of doctors, you might be judged guilty of disloyalty if you were to become a carpenter. If you come from a family of carpenters, you might be judged guilty of disloyalty if you become a doctor. Any violation of your parents' hopes or expectations can be grounds for self-indictment on the charge of disloyalty.

Perhaps the most common kind of disloyalty is the crime of being critical of one's parents. In some families, a parent will act crushed if a child is the least bit critical. In others, one or both parents may quickly squelch any open expression of negative feelings, insisting that the whole family must be seen as uniformly wonderful by each of its members. But since it is only natural to feel critical of your parents or siblings, such demands leave children feeling disloyal. If one or both of your parents subscribed to the maxim, "If you can't say something nice, don't say anything at all," you are at high risk of the crime of disloyalty. And if you find yourself engaging in self-defeating behaviors even though you remember your childhood and your parents as perfect, you may be idealizing your parents to avoid committing this imaginary crime.

It is difficult indeed for us to face the fact that our parents were less than perfect. Many psychotherapy clients find the process of facing their parents' deficiencies and describing their parents' imperfections to someone outside the family extremely disturbing. For these clients, entering psychotherapy seems like an enormous betrayal, since psychotherapy inevitably includes a process of casting down an idealized image that the parents projected and the children silently agreed to maintain.

If you unconsciously believe you are guilty of the imaginary crime of disloyalty, you may find that the very act of reading this book makes you intensely uneasy. To the unconscious mind, thinking critical thoughts about your parents is nearly as bad as criticizing them directly.

BASIC BADNESS

Our basic sense of ourselves is determined, in large part, by the things our parents tell us and the way they treat us. If they say we are selfish, uncaring, unintelligent, unattractive, needy, lazy, crazy, or otherwise deficient, we may well grow up believing them. If our parents disregard us, neglect us, or show us little or no respect, we may grow up feeling that we do not deserve their attention and esteem.

Most of us have suffered to some extent from bad messages. As a result, we sense that we are somehow inherently flawed: depending on the messages we received, we may believe that we are not important, not worthwhile, not lovable, not attractive, not caring, or not intelligent. For some these feelings are mild, infrequent, and unimportant. For others they are a constant burden, a major factor in their lives. The more we were abused or neglected by our parents, the more severe our sense of being basically bad.

Children who were continually criticized, rejected, neglected, abandoned, or physically or sexually abused usually end up concluding that there is something deeply and fundamentally wrong with them. Why else would their parents treat them so badly?

Such treatment from seemingly all-powerful and wise family members is unconsciously taken as proof that you must have *deserved* it. The mistreated child thus grows up believing that no matter how nice she may seem on the outside, she is profoundly repulsive and horrible. The worse the treatment she received, the more grievous her presumed imaginary crime.

Basic badness is significantly different from the other five imaginary crimes. In the former, you believe that you have hurt or are in danger of hurting someone else. With abandonment, you hurt a parent or sibling by leaving them. With love theft you hurt a sibling or parent by taking the love they needed. And so on. With basic badness you feel bad about yourself not because of anything you did to someone, but simply because of who you are.[7]

We have stressed that favored children often suffer a burden of guilt for the crime of love theft. An unfavored child, on the other hand, may end up feeling that her parents' lack of attention and appreciation indicates that there is something basically wrong with her. As a consequence, she may go through life feeling that she deserves very little.

Mike's Imaginary Crimes

Let's now look back at the case of Mike, the plastic surgeon. On reviewing the foregoing descriptions of the six common imaginary crimes, we can see that he was guilty of at least four:

• Mike felt guilty of *outdoing* his father and brother by becoming more successful.

• Mike felt guilty of *abandonment*. Because he felt so responsible for cheering his mother up, he felt extremely guilty after he left home to enter medical school.

• Mike felt guilty of *burdening*. His mother felt so worn out and depressed at having to deal with his alcoholic father that she had little energy left to attend to the raising of her children. As a result, he felt that his very existence was a burden on her. And after his father's death, Mike felt that it was his mother's devotion to him and his brother that kept her from remarrying.

• Mike felt guilty of the crime of *love theft* because his mother favored him over his younger brother. When his brother became an alcoholic, he unconsciously judged himself responsible for his brother's tragic life. Mike also felt guilty of stealing love from his father: as his father turned to drinking, his mother turned to Mike. As his parents grew further and further apart, Mike and his mother became closer and closer.

Mike's case illustrates how many of us unconsciously believe ourselves guilty of a whole complex group of interlocking imaginary crimes.

Almost Anything
Can Constitute an Imaginary Crime

The most confusing thing about imaginary crimes is that they make us feel unconsciously guilty about impulses and aspirations of which we consciously approve. We all *want* to be independent, successful, and happy. We all *want* to have good relationships. But when we hold ourselves guilty of imaginary crimes, we unconsciously begin to feel that these healthy aspirations have caused others harm.

For some people, even being honest and law-abiding can be a crime. For most of us, criminal or unethical behavior causes us to feel guilty, but for those who grew up in families where criminal or unethical behavior was a way of life, acting honestly can cause unconscious guilt. In Richard Condon's novel *Prizzi's*

Honor, Charlie, a member of a Mafia family, wants to retire from his career as a hit man. But the thought of leaving the family business makes him feel intensely guilty. The father figure, the old Mafia don, plays on Charlie's sense of guilt by seeming hurt by Charlie's desire to leave the family. This intensifies Charlie's feelings of guilt. In the end he not only continues his life of crime but murders the great love of his life out of family loyalty. Here is a case in which murder, which one would normally think of as only guilt-*inducing,* was actually *motivated* by guilt. *Prizzi's Honor* provides an example of the fact that our unconscious desire to maintain family ties is so great that it can drive us to abandon our healthiest aspirations or sacrifice the things we value most.

I have seen a number of psychotherapy clients whose criminal or unethical behavior was motivated by guilt. Sometimes a patient felt guilty about outdoing or being disloyal toward a corrupt parent. These troubled clients were complying with a parental message: "You'll grow up to be a crook, just like your old man." In some cases the criminal or unethical behavior stopped once the client realized that he or she had unconsciously grown up believing that being honest was a crime.

Children Can Misunderstand

Serious imaginary crimes are most common among those with unhappy, unsuccessful, overprotective, overcontrolling, neglectful, or abusive parents. But it *is* possible for us to believe ourselves guilty of imaginary crimes even when both of our parents are reasonably happy, successful, loving, and sensitive to our needs. A restless, high-energy child may do much better if he grows up in the country, where he can run and play in the fields and woods, than if he is confined to a small welfare apartment in a neighborhood so dangerous that his mother cannot let him play outside.[8] A child whose father is working three jobs to make ends meet can come to feel rejected because his father has very little time and energy to devote to him. A mother who is overprotective because of her fears about a child can lead the child to unconsciously conclude that she will hurt her mother if she becomes independent and competent. A parent who constantly criticizes and yells at her child because she is ineffective at disciplining children can give the child the unconscious impression she needs him to act up because she likes to chastise him.

Just because your parents may have seemed unloving, uncaring, untrusting or in some other way harmful doesn't mean that was their predominant attitude toward you. The effects of emotional or financial stresses, temperamental mismatch, or even chemical dependence may have interfered with their best intentions.

It can be very helpful to develop an understanding of the forces that drove our parents to behave as they did, but we must first get a clear picture of how our parents *did* behave toward us. If, in this process, we discover that we were overcontrolled, neglected, exploited, or physically or sexually abused, we must face these facts. For it is only by understanding what happened to us as children that we can come to understand — and can begin to absolve ourselves of — our imaginary crimes.

4

Outdoing, Burdening, and Love Theft

Crimes of the Survivor

Survivor guilt . . . is based on a . . . person's belief that by acquiring more of the good things of life than his parents or siblings, he has betrayed them. The person believes that his acquisitions have been acquired at the expense of his parents and siblings.

— JOSEPH WEISS, M.D.

The imaginary crimes of outdoing, burdening, and love theft are all manifestations of a broader phenomenon, survivor guilt.

The term *survivor guilt* was originally used to refer to the irrational but powerful guilt feelings felt by the survivors after loved ones had died. It is the feeling that, It is unfair that I should be alive when my loved one is dead.

Judith Guest's extraordinary novel *Ordinary People* provides a dramatic example of survivor guilt. Conrad, the protagonist, a sixteen-year-old high school student, tries to kill himself after his brother drowns in a boating accident, which he himself survives. He is subsequently hospitalized until he is judged to be out of danger. It was primarily Conrad's guilt — survivor guilt — that triggered his crippling depression and drove him to attempt suicide.

As the story nears its conclusion, Conrad is getting much better. He is falling in love with a schoolmate, Jeannine, and has once again begun to feel that life is worth living. He then learns that Karen, a young woman he befriended at the mental hospital, has killed herself. Karen's suicide produces powerful new feelings of survivor guilt. It also reactivates the survivor guilt he feels toward his brother. Conrad once again feels that it is terribly unfair that he should remain alive, when those he cared about are dead. Fighting against his own suicidal impulses, he visits his psychiatrist where he finally blurts out that he feels responsible "for killing him. . . . For letting him drown!"

The psychiatrist tries to help Conrad see that these thoughts, though quite normal and understandable, are completely irrational: "You were on opposite sides of the boat. You couldn't even see each other. He was a better swimmer. He was stronger, he had more endurance. So, what is it that you think you could have done to keep him from drowning?"

"I don't know," Conrad answers. "Something."[1]

Conrad's illogical insistence that he should have been able to do something poignantly expresses the irrationality, persistence, and destructive power of survivor guilt. In spite of all evidence to the contrary, we often feel that we are somehow responsible for a loved one's death, even when we are totally blameless.[2]

Sophie's Choice

Many of the survivors of the Nazi death camps suffered unspeakable atrocities and almost inconceivable losses — parents, spouses, children, in some cases entire extended families. Even after their release, they continued to carry another terrible legacy of the Holocaust — survivor guilt.

William Styron's novel *Sophie's Choice* provides a dramatic portrayal of the plight of one concentration camp survivor. Sophie is a Polish expatriate who was liberated from Auschwitz after World War II. She arrives in New York and becomes romantically involved with a handsome, charismatic young Jewish man, Nathan, who is profoundly schizophrenic, living largely in a world of illusion. Nathan is wonderfully loving and tender during their first weeks together. But as the relationship progresses, his kind attentions begin to alternate with periods of abuse. He assaults Sophie both verbally and physically and falsely accuses her of infidelity.

The story unfolds through a series of flashbacks. Sophie and her two children, a boy of eight and a girl of four, are sent to the concentration camp for the crime of seeking food for Sophie's dying mother. When they arrive at the camp, a leering S.S. officer tells her that she will be permitted to keep only one of her children. The other will immediately be put to death.

Sophie refuses to choose. At last, as the Nazi soldiers are dragging *both* children away, she chooses to save her son. Her daughter is taken away to the gas chamber, her screams ringing in her mother's ears.

All Sophie's efforts thereafter are devoted to helping her son survive. She even attempts to become the mistress of the camp commandant, a man she despises. But despite her struggle, the boy is slain by his Nazi guards. Another flashback reveals that in spite of their pro-Nazi sympathies, both her father and husband were killed by the S.S.

The story is narrated by a young man, Stingo, who is secretly in love with Sophie. When Nathan loses his grip on reality and threatens to kill them both, Stingo and Sophie run away together and plan a quiet life in the rural South where Stingo has inherited a small farm.

But at the last minute, Sophie is overcome by guilt. If the insane Nathan kills himself, she will once again have to suffer the terrible survivor guilt that she experienced after the deaths of her mother, father, children, and fellow concentration camp inmates. She leaves Stingo, abandoning the pleasant life she could have had, and takes cyanide with the demented Nathan. Only then does her relentless survivor guilt come to an end.

Although Sophie felt that she was to blame for her children's deaths, she was not responsible. She *had* to choose one child or the other, or both would have been killed. It was the Nazis, not she, who murdered all of her family members.[3]

In the character of Sophie, author William Styron accurately depicts the plight of many concentration camp survivors.[4] As the story begins, Sophie is weak, depressed, pale, and incapable of joy — a condition common among those freed from the death camps. Even after they were cured of their disease and malnutrition and taken to safe and welcoming places, many concentration camp victims were plagued by powerful feelings of guilt. They felt that they had betrayed their dead friends and relatives by surviving, even though, like Sophie, there was really nothing they could have done to save them.[5]

In much the same way, *anyone* who has lost a mother, a father, a brother, a sister, or any other close friend or family member to disease, accident, injury, suicide, or other misfortune may experience feelings of survivor guilt. These feelings may continue to affect a survivor for many years, long after the anger, the denial, and the immediate pain of a loved one's death have passed away.[6]

Everyday Survivor Guilt:
A Broader Definition

Control Mastery Theory uses the term *survivor guilt* in a broader sense than those who use it to refer to the guilt brought on by a loved one's death. We use the term to describe guilt that arises as the result of having more happiness, success, or love than other family members.[7] In this sense, we can all experience survivor guilt, even if our loved ones are still alive, if they appear unwilling or unable to experience the joys of living. Everyday survivor guilt is usually less intense than that which arises after a death. But it can still be a frightfully destructive force. Control Mastery Theory holds that this guilt lies at the root of many of our most deeply ingrained psychological problems. It is survivor guilt that underlies the imaginary crimes of *outdoing, love theft,* and *burdening.*

- In outdoing, we feel we have achieved what other family members could not.
- In love theft we feel we have stolen the love and attention that a sibling or parent desperately needed.
- In burdening we feel we took up the time and energy that our parents needed to take care of themselves.

Outdoing, love theft, and burdening are all crimes that occur when we have gained access to certain necessities, pleasures, or satisfactions in life, but unconsciously believe that we have obtained these treasures at the expense of one or more family members.

Manuel: Master of Self-Sabotage

Manuel's immigrant parents ran a dry cleaning shop. They lived in a predominantly Mexican-American community and spoke very little English. They worked long hours and had little time to enjoy themselves. They seemed bitter and exhausted, and spent what little energy they had left after work squabbling with each other.

From time to time Manuel's parents would decide that their shop was in the wrong location. They would lease a new retail space and would move their business. There would be a brief period of hope and anticipation. However, as soon as it became clear — as it always did — that the new shop would do no better than the last, Manuel's parents would again lose their enthusiasm and would sink back into their harried, joyless existence.

For as long as he could remember, Manuel had been sure that he wanted no part of a vocation in which he would have to work long hours for very little return. He earned a degree in business, went into real estate, and after several years of hard work was able to buy an apartment building. By putting in many long hours refurbishing it himself, he was able to refinance and buy a second, slightly larger building. He worked long hours and made very little money, but he looked forward to the time when things would be better.

It wasn't long before trouble developed: Manuel found himself unable to confront his tenants who were behind in their rent. He would not inform his creditors when he had to pay a bill late and would avoid paying bills even when he had the money. After a year of this irresponsible behavior, the bank foreclosed on his loans and he lost both buildings. After a brief period of depression he cheered up, moved to a new city, and started all over again. At the time he entered therapy, at age thirty-four, Manuel had gone through this cycle four times: he would start a promising business, go broke, then move to a new city and start again.

It wasn't that Manuel consciously wanted to fail. He wanted to succeed in the worst way. But despite his best efforts, he inevitably ended up working long hours with little enjoyment and minimal financial reward. He had to admit that he had ended up repeating the pattern he found so deplorable. Like his parents, he was simply trusting that a new location would solve his problems. Like his parents, he was refusing to acknowledge or change his self-defeating behavior.

Manuel entered therapy because he was once again on the verge of being successful and "did not want to screw it up again." At first he focused on his problems with his business and his girlfriend, but from time to time he would speak movingly of the grim and joyless atmosphere that had prevailed in his home when he was growing up. He also talked about his brother, who at age thirty-seven still lived at home, had no girlfriend, and spent much of his time bickering with his parents. He described his own fruitless attempts to get his brother to leave home and to encourage his parents to take a vacation.

Manuel was well aware of the enormous contrast between his life and that of his closest family members: He was making a good living. They were just scraping by. He enjoyed his work. They hated theirs. He had a stimulating group of friends, including a woman he hoped to marry. His parents and brother lived friendless and isolated lives. His prospects were bright. Theirs seemed unremittingly bleak.

He felt intense unconscious guilt about having so much when they had so little. And the more he widened the gap between his life and theirs, the guiltier he felt. As therapy progressed, Manuel began to understand the ways he had attempted to narrow that gap by sabotaging his business and personal relationships. Once he understood this, Manuel was able to expand his business without sabotaging it. And he was eventually able to marry his girlfriend.

Manuel had unconsciously convicted himself of the three imaginary crimes based on survivor guilt: outdoing, burdening, and love theft. He felt guilty of outdoing because he was happier and more successful than any other family member. He felt guilty of burdening because he had unconsciously judged himself guilty of being an additional difficult responsibility in his parents' already overburdened lives. He felt guilty of love theft both because his mother had favored him over his brother and because his brother was so severely mired in his own destructive patterns.

If our parents, like Manuel's, lived lives of drudgery, martyrdom, and failure, then they lived in a sort of concentration camp of their own making. And whether our parents were oppressed by their own psychological problems or by storm troopers, we are still susceptible to powerful feelings of survivor guilt.

Since even the best of parents have some areas of insecurity, incompetence, and unhappiness, most of us suffer — at least to some extent — from survivor guilt. The severity of our guilt depends on two factors: 1) the extent to which we view our parents and siblings as unhappy, unsuccessful, and inadequate, and 2) our own aspirations and talents, and the opportunities that come our way.

For some people, survivor guilt is a minor issue. For others, it is so severe that it dominates their psychological life and greatly constricts their actions. In extreme cases, as with Sophie, it can drive a person to take her own life.

A Survivor Guilt Fantasy

Imagine that you are dining in a small restaurant. You and a group of your closest friends are sitting at a large, well-appointed table in the center of the room. Your parents sit at a small battered table in a dark corner.

The waiter brings large platters of beautifully arranged gourmet cuisine to your table: pasta, meat, fish, and fresh vegetables, all prepared with delicious sauces and served with expensive, carefully chosen wines. To your parents' table the waiter brings a chipped plate with a few morsels of wilted salad, stale bread, and moldy cheese.

You invite your parents to join your party but they refuse, insisting that they are doing just fine and don't wish to be a burden. But you can't help hearing them complain to one another about the meal.

Like most of us, you would probably find yourself so uncomfortable that it would be impossible to relax and enjoy the evening. In this fantasy scene, you might actually add to your parents' misery by having a good time, because they could easily feel envious and left out. In most real-life situations, however, the punishments we inflict on ourselves to assuage our survivor guilt do nothing to decrease our parents' or siblings' unhappiness or inadequacy. It is truly useless suffering.

This fantasy illustrates another important point: Even though you invite your parents to join you in partaking of the pleasures the restaurant has to offer, they refuse. And even though they are deliberately abstaining, you still feel guilty about enjoying your own meal.

It does not really matter whether your family members are denied life's satisfactions by outside forces (being confined to a concentration camp or a hospital bed) or by internal constraints (alcoholism or psychological problems). Whether they abstain from life's bounteous table because they cannot or will not partake, it is still difficult to enjoy your meal.

This restaurant fantasy is not as farfetched as it may seem. We all carry our parents around in our heads. We *do* feel unconscious guilt when we fill our plates with things our parents couldn't or wouldn't take for themselves. One effective way to handle that guilt is to dump our plates into the garbage as soon as they threaten to get full. This is essentially what Manuel did by sabotaging his business as soon as it began to become successful.

Case History: John

John was a successful thirty-five-year-old Seattle architect. He came into therapy complaining that he was depressed about his marriage. His wife complained that John cared more about his work than he did about her. She criticized him constantly. Their home life became so unsatisfying that John began staying at work to avoid coming home. From time to time he had affairs with younger women he met at work.

John was the son of a successful financier, a man reputed to be a financial genius. John's father had his own firm and served on the board of directors for several large corporations. One might well think that as the child of a particularly successful and famous parent, John would never suffer from survivor guilt. But he did.

John's mother felt neglected by her famous workaholic husband. She complained bitterly. His parents had terrible fights several times a week. It was clear to John that their marriage was painfully unhappy. Although he never left his wife, John's father consoled himself by bedding a succession of attractive young women.

Mother and son had a close relationship. As her confidant, John heard all the latest details of his famous father's unfaithfulness, immaturity, and irresponsibility. From an early age, John understood that his father was unable to maintain a mature and intimate relationship.

John did not worry about surpassing his father financially. He was working up to his capacity and was reasonably successful in his own right, but he had long ago accepted the fact that he was not the genius his father was. Yet in spite of his father's wealth and fame, John saw him as a pathetic man who could not have the most important thing in life — marital happiness. In the irrational logic of survivor guilt, John could not allow himself to have the one precious thing his father had *not* attained for himself. By doing so he would be commiting the imaginary crime of outdoing. In addition, John was punishing himself for the crime of love theft. He had unconsciously concluded that his close relationship with his mother had contributed to the rift between his parents.

In therapy, John realized for the first time that he was repeating the very aspects of his father's behavior he most deplored. He began to see how he provoked his wife's criticism by avoiding her, ignoring her, and taking her for granted. And he began to see how his extramarital affairs prevented him from achieving a satisfying intimate relationship with his wife.

John's case demonstrates that not even having notably successful parents necessarily protects against survivor guilt. Even if our parents were very successful in certain areas, we are well aware of the areas in which they felt disappointed or unfulfilled. And we may find ourselves unconsciously driven to deny ourselves the very satisfactions our parents were unable to attain.

De-idealizing Our Parents

For some of us, a major hurdle in our efforts to overcome our survivor guilt is our tendency to idealize our parents:

- If we were to see our parents' weaknesses and shortcomings clearly, we might feel guilty of the imaginary crime of disloyalty.
- If we let ourselves see how unhappy and unfulfilled our parents' lives really were, we might experience a great deal of sadness for them. We might also experience a painful sense of disillusionment.
- Our parents' shortcomings traumatized us and caused us great pain. Facing their deficiencies would thus require us to relive some of the sadness and suffering we experienced as children.

An extreme example of idealizing one's parents occurs in *Sophie's Choice*. As a young woman, Sophie thought that her father was the finest man in the world. It was only in the midst of typing one of his speeches — which called for the extermination of the Jews — that she finally admitted to herself what a rigid, cruel, uncaring man he actually was. She realized that she had unconsciously known this for a long, long time but had been unwilling to deal with the anger, sadness, and contempt she would have to experience if she faced the truth.

As part of going through a process of de-idealizing our parents, we may have to face the fact that although our own mothers and fathers may have been excellent parents in many ways, they may have been sadly deficient in others. In order to identify and accept our parents' imperfections, we may have to face powerful feelings of disappointment, sadness, and anger. But it is only by facing these painful, seemingly disloyal feelings that we can really understand our parents' psychological difficulties — and our own.

The process of de-idealizing our parents may involve a period of time when our relations with our parents become somewhat strained. We may experience powerful feelings of anger and disappointment and may be unwilling to play the roles that we have traditionally played in the family. (For more on family roles, see Chapter 10.) The very idea of making our parents uncomfortable may temporarily increase our guilt. But it is only by going through this process — facing, accepting, and understanding the injuries and humiliations of our childhood — that we can free ourselves of our own self-punishing patterns.

When Loyalty Becomes Pathology

Survivor guilt can be best understood as a kind of intense family loyalty gone awry. This can be confusing because family loyalty can be one of the most *positive* forces in human life, and survivor guilt is almost invariably destructive.

It is not pathological to want to help our parents and siblings. There is nothing wrong with making sacrifices for those we love. But it is quite illogical to suffer pointless misery and unnecessary failure in the irrational unconscious belief that we will be helping an unfortunate parent or sibling. Survivor guilt is a powerful example of how a deep and usually positive instinct to care for and help our family members can sometimes turn into a pernicious force in our lives.

Survivor guilt comes into play when our lives threaten to become "too good," when the gap between what we have and what other family members have becomes too wide. Understanding survivor guilt can help us to identify and head off impulses to sabotage our lives when things are beginning to go especially well. By learning to recognize these attempts at self-sabotage, and by identifying the family patterns that give rise to them, we can gradually learn to free ourselves of this powerful, destructive motive.

5

Abandonment and Disloyalty

Crimes of Separation

[Separation guilt] . . . is the child's belief, which he infers from his experiences, that if he becomes more independent of the parent he will hurt the parent.

— JOSEPH WEISS, M.D.

Our excitement at growing up and coming into our own is inevitably accompanied by at least some small measure of remorse and sadness at leaving our parents behind. Control Mastery Theory calls this feeling *separation guilt.*[1]

When we were young children, our parents stood at the very center of our lives. Our mothers and fathers were the wisest, strongest, most powerful people in the world. As we grew older, we found that these towering figures of our infant universe gradually became less central, less powerful, less all-knowing. Over time, we even found that there were certain ways in which we surpassed them. As we came into the full power of our adulthood and found our own opportunities expanding, some of us discovered that our parents' powers were failing, their opportunities gradually shrinking away.

There is an inherent dilemma in growing up and separating from our parents. We must each psychologically dethrone the king and queen of our childhood in order to create our own separate and authentic identities. To come into our own, we must sort through the beliefs and values they pass down, keep what suits us, and discard what doesn't.

This natural process need not in itself produce guilty feelings. If our parents support our steps toward adulthood and welcome our growing independence, we may well negotiate this important transition with no guilt. It is only when our parents appear to feel hurt or betrayed by our growing maturity and autonomy that we may convict ourselves of imaginary crimes.

If our parents depend on us for their own sense of self-worth and would be profoundly unhappy without us, we may feel unconsciously guilty of the imaginary crime of abandonment. If our parents are unable to accept the fact that we have different opinions, different preferences, different religious beliefs, or different political views, we may feel guilty of the imaginary crime of disloyalty.

Separation-Individuation: One of Life's Great Tasks

One of the great developmental tasks in each of our lives is to separate and differentiate ourselves from our parents. Psychotherapists call this the process of separation-individuation. It begins in our first year of life and continues for the rest of our lives.

At age two a child will briefly investigate the world, then return to the security of a parent or parent figure. A child may go and play with another child for a few minutes and then return to mother to check in.[2]

As a child grows older, she will check in less and less frequently. This process continues until she feels comfortable being away from a parent for hours at a time. Over time she gains judgment and experience and no longer feels the need for constant parental guidance. Indeed, at a certain age she will begin to consider parental guidance an intrusion.

Parents who are sensitive to changes in their child's needs continually adjust the mixture of freedom and limits. They prevent their children from attempting tasks that lie beyond their powers, while pushing them to accept challenges they may be avoiding out of shyness or fear. They may permit their ten-year-old son to make the long walk to school by himself, when at nine he would have dawdled or gotten lost. They may insist on a chaperone and curfews when drugs become a part of their daughter's high school environment, when without these dangers they would be less restrictive. They may revoke certain privileges when a child acts irresponsibly. Maintaining the proper balance between freedom and control can be one of the most difficult tasks of parenting.

Undercontrol
or Overcontrol

When a parent does not provide sufficient control, the child may feel uncared for and may later have difficulty controlling himself. He may act impulsively and may cause his parents so much difficulty by his irresponsible behavior that he can end up feeling guilty of the imaginary crimes of burdening and basic badness.

If, on the other hand, the parent is overly dominating or protective, the child may infer that the parent has a great need to control and care for him. Some parents, most often mothers, seem to base their whole identity on their parental status. Without that role, they feel lost and anxious. Some insecure parents, most often fathers, need to play the authority at all times, even when their children may not need their instruction or guidance. In such situations, the child's own need to care for and direct himself may cause him to feel unconsciously guilty of abandonment and disloyalty.

The Vulnerable Parent

Only very young children see their parents as consistently strong and invulnerable. As they grow older, children begin to develop a much more complex picture of their parents. They begin to notice that at times Mom seems frightened or overwhelmed, or Dad seems inconsistent, confused, or depressed.

This is not necessarily a problem. It is healthy and natural for children to learn that their parents have weaknesses as well as strengths. But if children, rightly or wrongly, get the impression that their parents are *chronically* weak, fragile, angry, helpless, or sad, then the stage is set for trouble.

We rarely imagine that children might view their parents as chronically vulnerable, weak, or out of control. Yet, they often do. Even when a parent is so dominating, critical, or physically violent that he inspires great fear in his children, they may also see him as brittle, damaged, and pathetic.[3]

If the child views her parent as incompetent, dejected, or weak, she may feel that she must stay home to take care of that parent. Instead of playing the normal child's role — being taken care of and nurtured — the child may unconsciously feel that she must assume the parent's role. When a parent seems too vulnerable, the natural process of separating may feel like desertion, and the child may unconsciously accuse himself of the crime of abandonment.

By the time she was seven, Lonnie was already cooking dinner for herself and her younger sisters — because Mom was drunk by the time she got home from school. At a very early age, Lonnie saw her mother as a fragile, impaired, incompetent woman.

George was raised in the mountains by his fierce and paranoid father, who allowed him very little contact with others. Although his father could hunt, fish, and was uncannily good at eking a living from nature, and although George feared and respected him, he also was aware that his father was crazy, lonely, and pathetically frightened of other human beings.

Jim's seriously disturbed father often went into towering rages. Jim was careful to stay out of harm's way, but basically viewed his father as ridiculous and pathetic.

Children of such disturbed parents often unconsciously understand that a parent's violence, criticalness, or domineering attitude is not a result of strength, but of weakness, of insecurity, of feeling overwhelmed by the responsibilities and challenges of life. Because of this, even though they may fear and want to avoid their parents, they can also feel unconsciously guilty for growing up and abandoning such insecure and out-of-control people to shift for themselves.

Even Good Parents
Can Cause Separation Guilt

It is clear that in extreme cases — like those of Lonnie, George, and Jim — children *do* see their parents as weak, damaged, or sick. Yet many of us come from situations in which our parents seemed reasonably intact and competent. Can we also suffer from separation guilt?

Indeed we can. Separation guilt can be an important factor even in families in which neither parent is seriously impaired.

What matters is what the child believes. If a child believes that she will hurt her parents by becoming independent, she will suffer from separation guilt.

Our Parents' Hidden Weaknesses

Even though a parent may appear strong, successful, and confident to an outside observer, the child may see things quite differently. Children frequently see aspects of a parent's life that are hidden from the outside world.

A father who is strong and independent in his social and work life may nonetheless give his son the impression that he is weak, needy, sad, or unhappy. A mother who is responsible and competent in many areas of her life may be unable to tolerate the idea that her daughter is a separate individual with her own ideas and her own life. Even parents who seem reasonably happy and capable may give their children cues that will make them feel guilty about becoming autonomous adults.

Marty's mom, a successful real estate agent, would not allow him to close the door to his room and told him there was no reason for family members to have secrets from one another. His father, president of a local bank, became obsessively concerned with Marty's high school football career. Occasionally, when a referee would make a bad call, Marty's father became so angry that he would run out onto the field and berate the unfortunate official, embarrassing Marty enormously. Although Marty didn't enjoy football, he remained on the team because he believed that his father would be terribly disappointed if he quit.

Because he was well aware of his parents' insecurities, Marty grew up believing that by thinking his own private thoughts and making his own choices he was hurting them. The community at large considers Marty's parents happy and successful. And in many ways they are. But Marty is still a likely candidate for the serious psychological problems that can stem from guilt over the crimes of disloyalty and abandonment.

Lisa's mother has an opinion on every subject under the sun — from the nuclear arms race to what colors Lisa should wear. She became hurt and angry any time her opinions were challenged. On several occasions she actually spanked Lisa for daring to disagree with her.

Lisa grew up believing that her mother derived vital satisfaction from controlling her life. As a result, Lisa felt very guilty about growing up and leaving her domineering but insecure mom. This intense, though unconscious, guilt over the crime of abandonment manifested itself as a lack of self-confidence and low self-esteem.

Each of these parents is a respected member of his or her community. None suffers from an incapacitating psychological problem. Yet the mild to moderate psychological problems they do have are sufficient to trigger profound feelings of separation guilt in their children.

Children Can Lack Perspective

Children sometimes see their parents as more fragile and needy than they really are. They may mistakenly infer that a parent would be hurt by their independence.

Jesse's mother lost her younger son when he dashed out between two parked cars and was run down by a delivery truck. She swore to herself that she would never allow Jesse to be endangered by a moment's inattention. She walked him to school and met him at lunch period when it was time to go home. She arranged to have him exempted from physical education class on a pretext because she was afraid he would hurt himself. She discouraged him from playing baseball and basketball with his neighborhood friends.

Jesse grew up a shy, bookish boy who spent most of his time in his room reading library books. In spite of being socially isolated, Jesse did very well in high school and received a scholarship to the state university.

After Jesse had been away at college for six weeks, he became intensely homesick. He called his mother and told her he had decided to quit school and come home. After conferring with Jesse's father, his mother called back. She told him that he must stay at school at least through the end of the semester. If he was still unhappy after that time, they could talk about the possibility of transferring at semester break.

After their discussion, Jesse found himself feeling oddly relieved. He had unconsciously interpreted his mother's protectiveness to mean she thought that the outside world was a terribly dangerous place. That part of his interpretation was correct. But he had also concluded that his mother would become extremely uncomfortable if he was not with her. That part of his interpretation was wrong. Although she was fearful and overprotective, she really *did* want Jesse to grow up, become independent, and become successful.

Once his mother refused his plea to come home, Jesse was unconsciously reassured that she could get along without him. His guilt over the imaginary crime of abandoning her was eased and he was able to vigorously pursue his own life. By the end of the semester, Jesse had made friends, was doing well academically, and had long forgotten his idea of returning home.

Why Children Worry
About Their Parents

Children are tremendously sensitive to their parents' emotional states and psychological vulnerabilities. Children depend on this psychological acumen to obtain the love and attention they need. As most parents are well aware, their children can employ this same sensitivity with great skill and sophistication to obtain treats and privileges.

But as a result of this perceptiveness, children may experience intense worry when a parent appears to be in pain. In the National Institute of Mental Health study we discussed in Chapter 1, researchers found that children between six months and two years of age frequently showed concern and even tried to help and comfort their mothers when they were sad or hurt. Here is one mother's description of Bobby, aged eighteen months:

> As I was vacuuming I began to feel a little faint and sick to my stomach. I turned off the vacuum and went into the bathroom, kind of coughing and gagging a little. Bobby followed me to the bathroom door and the whole time that I was in there he was pounding on the bathroom door saying, "OK, Mommie? OK, Mommie?" When I finally came out and picked him up, he looked at me with a very concerned, worried look in his eyes. I said, "Mommie OK." Then he put his head on my shoulder and began to love me.[4]

Bobby's instinctive concern and helping behavior can be a good foundation for the development of a caring and nurturing adult. But when a parent seems *constantly* hurt, depressed, vulnerable, or confused, the child's intense concern may lead to a continuous but often unconscious sense of worry. It is this sense of worry that is at the bottom of the imaginary crime of abandonment.

An extreme example of attempting to avoid the crime of abandonment is the person who grows up, dates halfheartedly, never marries, and never leaves home. This person may consciously feel he is too shy or too turned off by the hassles of the dating game. But in most cases he remains in the parental nest because of his unconscious worry that his parent would be devastated without him. Some clients have confided that they felt that if they left home their parent would have no further reason to live.

Can "Bad" Kids Suffer from Separation Guilt?

It is easy to see how well-behaved children, who value their parents' good opinion, might convict themselves of the crimes of abandonment and disloyalty. But what about rebellious and insolent children who seem as if they couldn't care less about their parents' feelings?

Many children who get into trouble at home, school, or with the law are currently referred to family therapists. Unlike some therapists, who would see the child alone, family therapists usually insist on meeting with the entire family. They have found that "bad" children sometimes get better much faster when the therapist points out the connections between the child's behavior and the parents' marital or psychological problems.

Family therapists have come to believe that many of their young patients' problems stem from unconscious attempts to create a distraction from the parents' problems.[5] It is not uncommon for a family therapist to discover that the parents of a delinquent child have serious marital problems or that one par-

ent is severely depressed. The child's delinquent or erratic behavior is unconsciously intended to draw attention away from
the parents' marital difficulties or to give the depressed parent a
focus for his attention and hostility. The child is unconsciously
attempting to hold the family together or to cheer up a troubled
or depressed parent. What seems to be disloyal, rebellious, and
hurtful behavior is actually the child's unconscious but loyal
attempt to reduce his parents' pain and unhappiness by making
himself a scapegoat.[6]

Is Worry Really Disguised Hostility?

Many therapists have been taught that clients who worry excessively about their parents were merely covering up their hostile
feelings: unconsciously they really want their parents to suffer
or die.

Control Mastery disagrees with this point of view. Most
clients who worry about their parents had parents who gave
them a lot to worry about: one or both of their parents were
sad, fragile, clingy, depressed, crazy, or suicidal. We all harbor
some resentment against our parents, but that doesn't mean that
we are not also deeply concerned about them. Our worry is
based on our belief that our parents are suffering or are in
danger of being hurt or of hurting themselves.

Case History: Ann

Ann is an attractive twenty-eight-year-old Chinese-American
lab technician. She is troubled by low self-esteem, constant

worry about her job, her marriage, and her parents. She is too fearful to drive at night or to venture into strange parts of town. Although she is well thought of at the university medical center where she works, she worries that she isn't doing a good enough job. She also fears that when her parents die she will be unable to go on.

Ann and her husband have dinner with her parents twice a week, even though neither of them enjoys it. Her parents insist on giving the couple advice on every aspect of their lives from where to buy a house (right next door) to when to have a baby (right away). Ann calls her mother at least once a day to talk. Her husband criticizes her for being so dependent on her parents and for constantly seeking their approval.

All through Ann's childhood her forceful father bullied her depressed mother into a bitter and resentful silence. Ann's mother worried compulsively: she worried about speaking up in groups, she worried about being in a traffic accident, she worried that harm would come to her children. She worried so much that she became nearly incapacitated. Although she was a bright and talented woman who wanted a career, she was too anxious and timid to seek a job after her children left home. As a result, she spent much of her time depressed and bored. She never learned to drive a car and she depended on her husband to get her places, pay the bills, discipline the children, and to make all the major decisions.

Ann's father, a pharmacist, doted on her. Ann enjoyed his optimism and high energy. Although she was close to both of her parents, her dad's enthusiasm was a welcome contrast to her mother's endless worries. But there was one area in which her father did not encourage her, and that was dating. Her father was so critical and unpleasant to any boys she brought home that he frightened off most potential boyfriends.

Ann suffered from guilt over the crime of abandonment toward both parents. Consciously, she felt she was totally dependent on them. But unconsciously she felt that it was *they* who needed *her*. Her parents were so unhappy with each other that it seemed to Ann that they only enjoyed life when she was there. She felt responsible for being their only source of pleasure, as well as the family peacemaker and go-between. Everyone counted on her to keep tensions down.

Ann entered therapy complaining of continuing feelings of anxiety and depression, and because she had begun to realize that she was overinvolved with her parents. In therapy she discovered that her tremendous need to be in touch with them stemmed from her feeling that they needed and were dependent on contact with her. This came as a surprise to her because she had always thought of herself, not her parents, as dependent and needy.

As her insights increased, Ann began to accelerate the pace of her separation, seeing her parents less often and not consulting with them even on major decisions. As a result, she had the paradoxical experience of feeling much better about herself while at the same time being assailed by all sorts of anxieties. She experienced brief episodes of intense fear that she would lose her job, would lose her husband, or would get cancer. These worries were particularly strange because she was doing much better at work, she and her husband were much happier than before, and she was in excellent health. As it turned out, she felt so guilty for abandoning her unhappy parents that even though she was now more able to separate, she had to punish herself by entertaining these grim scenarios.[7] As Ann began to understand the underlying reasons for her irrational worries, they subsided and she was able to enjoy both her job and her marriage without being obsessed with visions of disease and calamity.

In addition to her guilt over abandonment, Ann was also punishing herself for the imaginary crime of outdoing. She was outdoing both parents by having an intimate and mutually respectful relationship with her husband. And she was outdoing her mother by having a career.

The True Reason
for Overdependence

Why is it that some people are so chronically overdependent that they seem clingy, indecisive, and unable to assert themselves? Often they think that they are weak-willed, lazy, or stupid, but this is almost never the case. In my clinical experience, most overdependent people are like Ann. They suffer from unconscious guilt over the crimes of abandonment, disloyalty, and outdoing. It can be profoundly liberating to realize that our tendencies toward overdependence may be the result of this guilt.

We might spend our whole lives pushing ourselves to be stronger, braver, tougher, and more independent. But all the pushing in the world won't help if the real problem is that we cannot *allow* ourselves to be strong and independent because we feel that if we were, we would be abandoning our sad or foolish parents to a life of pain and unhappiness. Those who attempt to break out of this trap through the use of will power alone will doom themselves to an endless cycle like this one: trying to be stronger and more independent, succeeding for a while, slipping back, feeling hopeless, trying to be stronger again.

Most people who suffer from problems caused by separation guilt do not realize that they feel unconsciously guilty about being strong and independent. They feel that they are weak and frightened, afraid to face the challenges of life without the help of a parent or parent figure. This chapter carries a message of hope for such people: it tells them the task that they face is not the seemingly impossible one of becoming strong when they are basically weak. Instead, what they need to do is to free themselves from the irrational guilt of imaginary crimes, which causes them to hide and suppress their independence and capability.

While this is almost always possible, it is often not easy. The first step is to accept the fact that you are suffering from the grim, unconscious belief that by becoming independent, autonomous, and responsible, you would be hurting your parents.

Case History: Allan

"You're selfish and ungrateful. You've always been that way. We sacrificed for you and this is how you reward us. Really, Allan, how could you do this to us?"

This is how Allan's mother responded when he told her he was not returning to Chicago to join the family business. The message was clear and direct: if he chose to pursue his own career and his own life in another city, he was selfish and ungrateful. Allan's parents felt that he had no right to make his own choices.

As with all imaginary crimes, the unconscious guilt caused by the imaginary crime of abandonment is made even worse when it is reinforced by such hurtful, critical statements. We feel guilty enough about leaving our parents if they appear unhappy and seem dependent on us. We feel even *more* guilty if we are told that we are cruel and selfish for wanting to live our own separate lives.

Not all parents are as direct as Allan's. Many communicate their disappointment with actions and with body language. The humorist Dan Greenburg gives satirical instructions for inducing separation guilt: He advises his readers to tell their children the following kinds of advice — in a slightly sad tone of voice — as they are about to go out on a date. "Go ahead and enjoy yourself — but be careful." "Don't worry about me." "I don't mind staying home alone."[8] As these examples show, a parent can even make a pretense of encouraging independence while subtly engendering separation guilt. Although the apparent message is "Relax. Have a good time. Don't worry about me, I'll be fine," the real message is "Don't relax. Something may happen to you. Worry about me because I'll be miserable and alone, worrying about you."

Intense possessiveness on the part of a parent can also trigger separation guilt. Allan's parents were rude to every girl he dated. Each time he became interested in a young woman, they would make disparaging comments about her family, her looks, and her manners. Allan grew up feeling that he would hurt his parents by forming any meaningful attachment outside the family. This also contributed to the guilt he felt over his imaginary crimes of abandonment and disloyalty.

Case History: Michelle

The crimes of separation can sometimes cause us to sabotage our relationships. Michelle was a successful forty-four-year-old theatrical agent. She was married to Ian, a quiet and devoted British concert pianist, who loved her deeply. From time to time, however, she would go through periods in which she would miss her father desperately.

At such times she would criticize Ian for being too quiet and for not being affectionate enough. Sometimes she even said to him, "Why can't you be more like my father." Ian was not unusually quiet or particularly unaffectionate, but he *was* less demonstrative and talkative than Michelle's warm but very unhappy father.

Even though Michelle had left home at an early age, her guilt over the imaginary crimes of disloyalty and abandonment toward her father caused her to behave in ways that created a great deal of unnecessary unhappiness — both for her and for her husband.

There are many people, who, like Michelle, can never seem to find anyone as wonderful as one or both parents. The problem is not that Michelle's father was too good. No one suffers from having parents who were too perfect. The problem is that, as children, Michelle, and others like her, came to believe that their parents *needed* their closeness, love, and adulation. Of course, everybody likes closeness and appreciation from their kids, but Michelle's father's behavior led her to believe that he would be deeply hurt if she did not continue to love him above anyone else. When it came time for Michelle to make a primary connection with a lover or a spouse, she felt she was abandoning her father. She unconsciously chose to resolve the situation by being intensely critical of her husband.

How Guilt Can Make Us Avoid Our Parents

Although guilt over the crimes of abandonment and disloyalty can make some people cling to their parents, it may cause some of us to avoid our parents as much as possible.

Julie, a forty-five-year-old supermarket cashier, found that she became extremely depressed whenever she visited her mother. Julie had been the baby of the family. When she left home, her already unhappy mom seemed devastated. After Julie's father died, her mother withdrew from the world even more.

Julie felt particularly bad about the feelings of rage and depression that accompanied her rare visits home. She compared herself unfavorably to her older sisters and brother, who seemed to take her mother's subtle recriminations in stride. No matter how hard Julie tried, whenever her mom began talking about how lonely and neglected she felt, Julie became furious. By a certain point during most visits, Julie became so upset with her mother that she simply refused to have anything to do with her. Her guilt over the imaginary crime of abandoning her mother was so painful that she felt her only option was to avoid her mother altogether.

In therapy, Julie came to understand that she felt irrationally responsible for her mother's unhappiness. This insight allowed her to be more sympathetic toward her mother's pain and to confront her mother's recriminations calmly. Although she still found visits to her mother quite trying, she was able to see her without becoming angry and upset.

Separation Guilt Can Cause Us to Make Poor Choices

Some people deal with separation guilt by reproducing their old situations in new relationships. Paul, an unambitious counter man in a computer parts firm, lived with his critical, domineering mother until she died of cancer, when he was thirty-one. Two years later he married a critical, domineering woman who treated him very much as his mother had. Paul's unconscious sense that he should be loyal to his mother was so strong that he sacrificed the possibility of a happy and fulfilling marriage in order to unconsciously imagine that he was still with his mother.

Although many people who suffer from separation guilt appear to be weak and dependent like Paul, others seem quite strong and independent like Michelle and Julie. As these examples indicate, avoiding or doing penance for the crime of abandonment can lead to a wide variety of difficulties.

It's Not Necessary to Be Perfect

Luckily for those of us who are parents, it's not necessary to be perfect to avoid burdening our children with guilt over the imaginary crimes of abandonment and disloyalty. A few common-sense guidelines can help get us through:

• *Don't sacrifice too much.* Make sure you devote a substantial portion of your time and resources for your own pleasure. Do the things that nurture you. Do the things you love. For some this may mean reading, running, playing an instrument, listening to music, or taking long walks in the woods. For others it may be socializing with people you like, traveling to exotic places, or playing golf with your friends. If you devote your whole life to your kids they can easily come to feel that they, in turn, should devote their whole lives to you.[9]

• *Cultivate close friends and confidants other than your children.* Some clients have told me that their parents confided *everything* to them — including their most intimate fantasies and fears and their sexual problems. This degree of intimacy can be detrimental to children for several reasons. Young children may have great difficulty dealing with adult sexuality. And these inappropriate confidences may make them feel that their parents don't have close adult friends. These children may feel guilty if they want to devote their time and attention to their own friends.

• *Allow your child a reasonable amount of privacy.* Devastating as it may be for children to feel that their parents are not interested in them, it is equally harmful to give your children the feeling that they have no right to privacy. It suggests to them that they don't have the right to their own separate thoughts, separate tastes, separate friends. This may lead to a sense of disloyalty over the adult desire for a separate life.

• *Don't make your child feel guilty about growing up.* Avoid statements implying that your children are ungrateful or unloving because they want to pursue their own friends and interests. Although they may seem to ignore what you say, children can take these statements to heart.

• *Above all, be happy.* The best legacy you can leave to your children is the conviction that you are a happy person. A child who believes you will be happy with or without her will feel free to depend on you as much or as little as she needs to at each stage of her development. Being happy with yourself and your life is the best inoculation you can give your child against afflictions of guilt over abandonment or disloyalty.

This last suggestion can be the most difficult to follow. To do so, we may have to overcome our guilt over our own imaginary crimes. One important reason that many people do not allow themselves to enjoy the process of parenting is that by doing so they would be outdoing their parents. Their parents seemed burdened or uncomfortable raising them and they therefore feel unconsciously guilty about appreciating the joys of parenting themselves.

Those of us who feel guilty about pursuing happiness and fulfillment should remember that we are not doing it just for ourselves. We are doing it for our children as well.

Not All Separation Problems
Stem from Guilt

The imaginary crime of abandonment is the irrational belief on the part of the child that she has abandoned one or both parents. But what of the person who was physically or emotionally abandoned by her parents when she was a child?[10] What problems will she have? From what imaginary crimes will she suffer?

Lydia's parents were cold, brutal, and unhappy people. They were constantly fighting, both verbally and physically. They would sometimes ignore Lydia for days at a time. At other times, each parent would seek Lydia's allegiance in their endless conflict with one another.

Lydia left home when she was fifteen, supporting herself as a waitress. Although she was quite attractive, she dressed in a drab, no-nonsense way and exhibited a combination of coldness and sarcasm that kept potential friends — and suitors — at bay. She made her own clothes, repaired her own car, and spent virtually no money on herself. While supporting herself as a waitress, she built her first computer from a mail order kit.

When Lydia was nineteen she started college, working toward a B.S. and then an M.S. in computer science. She continued to work various jobs while at school. She was very thrifty and had no trouble paying the tuition.

As a child, Lydia came to the conclusion that people were undependable and irrational. She vowed she would never again expose herself to the hurt, fear, and manipulation she had experienced at the hands of her parents. She unconsciously determined that if she never again allowed herself to become close to another person, she would never feel so terribly rejected and abandoned. She set out to make herself completely independent of others.

Lydia was constantly suspicious of the motives of everyone

she met. She considered it extremely important to have an ample cushion of money in the bank because she wanted to feel free to quit her job at any time. Like others who have been neglected as children, Lydia felt that people were dangerous and unreliable and had to be kept at arm's length.

People like Lydia rarely seek help either from friends (since they avoid having them) or from professionals (whom they have great difficulty trusting). If they do decide to seek help, they often must work for many years to overcome the trauma of their early years.

So what is Lydia's imaginary crime? Unlike the other case histories described in this chapter, Lydia's main difficulty is not that she feels she abandoned a needy parent. She understood that *she* was the one who had been abandoned. But as we explained in the first chapter, the child always believes that everything that happens was somehow her fault.

Lydia unconsciously believed that she had been abandoned, abused, and treated like a pawn in the war between her parents because she *deserved* such treatment. In the world of the child, receiving bad treatment means you are a bad person. Thus Lydia unconsciously felt that she was guilty of the imaginary crime of *basic badness*. She felt that deep inside she was a worthless and unlovable person. Her early experiences were so painful that she had concluded that intimacy was simply not worth the price.[11]

In the next chapter we will examine Lydia's crime, basic badness, in more detail.

6

Basic Badness

Crimes That Result from Believing Bad Messages

━━━━━

Let your child hear you sigh every day; if you don't know what he's done to make you suffer, he will.

— DAN GREENBURG

Some of us are imaginary criminals out of a sense of *basic badness*. We may believe that we have inborn deficits of intelligence, morality, attractiveness, or lovableness. Or we may believe that we are cowardly, ugly, mediocre, or simply not important. This deep sense of being irretrievably flawed or insignificant stems from our parents' negative messages. We may have been told that we were stupid, shameful, or disgusting. We may have been treated as if we were unimportant, as if our feelings and thoughts didn't matter. We may have been treated without love or caring, as objects to be used for our parents' pleasure or convenience. Or we may have been verbally, physically, or sexually abused. As a result, we come to the deep and often unconscious conclusion that we are flawed human beings.

Unlike the crimes of outdoing, burdening, love theft, abandonment, and disloyalty, in which we believe that we have hurt other people, basic badness is a victimless crime. We feel bad because we believe ourselves to be shameful, disgusting, unimportant, disappointing, unattractive, unlovable, or unworthy. It isn't something we did or didn't do; it is something we *are*.[1]

Case Study: Joyce

Joyce was a tall, thin, forty-two-year-old office manager with an outgoing personality and an infectious laugh. She came to therapy complaining of being attracted to men who treated her badly. Time and time again she would fall in love with a man who criticized her, put her down, or took advantage of her. During these liaisons, Joyce had a hard time standing up for her rights. And she found it almost impossible to get out of these inappropriate relationships. She spent months or years with men she should have crossed off her list after the first date.

Joyce decided to enter therapy after finding her destructive behavior pattern described in alarming detail in Robin Norwood's book *Women Who Love Too Much.* "It was scary," she explained. "It made me realize I'd been blaming everything on the men in my life. Reading that book convinced me that my problems were the result of something *I* was doing."

Her family history helped shed some light on her problem: Joyce's father had flunked out of medical school before she was born. He had become a sales representative for a large drug company and found himself in the humiliating position of calling on men and women who would have been his colleagues if he had become a physician.

Joyce's mother, who had looked forward to being a physician's wife, was bitterly disappointed in her husband. He responded by drinking heavily, bickering endlessly with his wife, and criticizing and teasing his children. His nicknames for Joyce included Foghorn (because he felt she talked too loudly), Bones (because she was tall and skinny), and Crybaby (because his taunting frequently reduced her to tears).

Her mother, a bitter, dispirited woman, never protected Joyce from her father, agreeing and even seeming to enjoy hearing his ridiculing. She also criticized Joyce unmercifully for being self-centered, willful, and demanding.

Joyce's father often warned her that she would never be able to find a decent man — she was too tall, too loud, and too emotional. As her therapy progressed, Joyce realized that even though she had battled her father every step of the way, she had heard him repeat this dire prediction so frequently that she had come to believe it. Whenever she found herself in a dispute with one of her boyfriends, she concluded that she must be the one at fault.

These harsh self-blaming tendencies drove Joyce to do things that were fundamentally repugnant to her. When one boyfriend insisted that she sleep with a friend of his to enhance their sex life, she did. And even though she loathed the whole experience, she ended up agreeing with her boyfriend that she felt this way only because she was so uptight about sex.

Joyce did not feel capable of standing up for herself. Nor could she take the initiative to leave a relationship, no matter how unsatisfactory. She feared that if she were ever without a boyfriend, it would be impossible to find another. Joyce unconsciously felt that she was unattractive, unlovable, undeserving, and fated never to have a good relationship with a man. Her belief that she had been born that way and nothing she could do would change it was the direct result of her parents' cruel and critical treatment.

Why Parents Give Bad Messages

All parents give their children potentially harmful messages from time to time. But these messages are rarely given with any malicious intent. In most cases, parents are simply repeating the same critical, humiliating, or devaluing kinds of messages that they received from *their* own parents. Even Joyce's father, who sent his daughter a variety of extremely destructive messages, did not intend harm. He was, in most cases, simply responding to his own humiliations and frustrations by repeating *his* father's dysfunctional behavior patterns. Because of his own psychological problems, he frequently felt overwhelmed by the responsibility of raising a child.

When we speak of bad messages, we're not referring to things that happened only once or twice. Parents need not become unduly alarmed if they catch themselves occasionally snapping at their children in anger or occasionally saying something that can be interpreted as critical, devaluing, or humiliating. If this happens infrequently, and if the parent is able to apologize, such incidents are unlikely to produce any lasting harm. The messages most likely to create detrimental, unconscious beliefs are those that are repeated over and over again throughout childhood.

Our most important bad messages usually come from our parents, but we may receive bad messages from others as well. Such messages may come from our siblings or from parent substitutes: relatives, teachers, coaches, or religious leaders. Whatever their source, these messages can give rise to the imaginary crime of basic badness. And once these negative beliefs about ourselves take up residence in our unconscious they can be very hard to dislodge.

Direct and Indirect Messages

Some bad messages are unmistakably direct. These are the straightforward put-downs that curl your hair when you hear a mother say them to her child at the supermarket:

"You're dumb."

"You're crazy."

"You're stupid."

"You're worthless."

"Can't you do anything right?"

"Why can't you be more like your brother?"

"Shut up, or I'll *really* give you something to cry about."

But these insensitive denunciations, painful and hurtful as they are, are at least out in the open. They can sometimes be easier to deal with than less direct messages.

Other destructive messages are never stated directly, only implied. And since the child comes to negative conclusions about herself without being able to pinpoint the source, they are sometimes more difficult to correct.

• If a child is ignored, or if her own wishes and preferences are not considered, she is likely to conclude that she is unimportant or that her thoughts or feelings are of no consequence.

• If parents seem nervous, "walking on eggshells" whenever they are around him, a child may conclude there is something dangerous or terrible about him.

• If a child is dressed up, made to perform, and shown off, without regard to his own desires, he is likely to feel like a doll or an object whose only value is in how he looks.

• If a child is sexually abused or exploited, she may come to feel dirty and disgusting, and may conclude that she has no right to stand up for herself or to resist unwelcome attention.

• If a child is shamed for his natural desires and behaviors, he may come to have deep feelings of shame about himself.

• If a boy is told that his father is a bum and he is just like him, or a girl is told that her mother is a slut and she is just like her, these children are likely to feel doomed, flawed, and ashamed.

• If a child is constantly nagged and criticized, she will tend to feel that nothing she ever does is good enough, that she will inevitably fail in spite of all her efforts.

• If a child is treated like the golden child and expected to excel in everything, he may come to feel that no matter what he does he will never fulfill his parents excessive expectations. Thus in spite of considerable success, on the inside he may feel like a failure.

Guilt-Slinging Messages

These messages can be hard to identify because they often sound like the lament of an overburdened parent and imply that the parent is making tremendous sacrifices. A mother may complain that she gave up college or an artistic or professional career to care for her child. A father might confide that he stayed with a cruel and unloving wife because he felt it was in the child's best interests. A parent can deliver a guilt-slinging message by treating a normal childhood behavior — noisiness, lack of cooperation, or the desire for a reasonable amount of independence or privacy — as a flagrant crime. Or parents may communicate nonverbally, with sighs and exhausted expressions, that their children are a terrible burden.

Most guilt-slinging parents would indignantly — and quite truthfully — deny that they are consciously using these guilt-inducing techniques to control and constrict their children. In most cases, they are simply repeating the child-rearing practices they learned from their own parents.

When Parents Are Overwhelmed by Chemical Dependency

A parent who is overwhelmed by alcohol or drug addiction may give a child a variety of bad messages. Janet's mother had two separate personalities — one when she was sober and one when she was drunk. When sober she was responsible, apologetic, and mildly depressed. When she was drunk she was verbally and physically abusive. During her drinking binges she would accuse Janet of being a burden, being selfish and ungrateful, and of spoiling her chance for a professional career. As a result, Janet grew up feeling that she was the source of her mother's unhappiness. Her mother realized that her drunken outbursts were harming her daughter but was unable to quit drinking on her own and was ashamed to ask for help.

As an adult, Janet became a successful attorney specializing in divorce and child custody cases. Although she was competent and attractive, Janet was chronically depressed. She abused drugs and alcohol and suffered from extremely low self-esteem. Her marriage, on the whole a good one, was punctuated by bitter fights, usually preceded by Janet's drinking or drug use. Finally her long-suffering husband insisted that they enter marital therapy. In discussing their relationship with a therapist, Janet realized that she became extremely anxious when things were going well at home. She remembered that when things went calmly in her childhood home, it was only a matter of time before her mother would build up to another drunken rage.

Janet had received the unspoken message that it was dangerous to relax and expect good treatment. As an adult, she had short-circuited that painful anticipation by starting fights herself, thus precipitating the very confrontations she had dreaded as a child. And by behaving so badly, she confirmed her mother's opinion that she was selfish and ungrateful.

The bad messages we receive from a parent who was chemically addicted can be especially difficult to overcome. For more on these bad messages and how to deal with them, see Chapter 10.

From Generation to Generation

Many bad messages are passed down from generation to generation. Karen's father was a fundamentalist minister in a small town in rural Illinois. He and his wife had been taught that children were naturally lazy and sinful and should be allowed little or no pleasure or leisure time, lest they become spoiled. Karen was taught that she must keep herself constantly busy ("Idle hands are the devil's playground") and was forbidden to dance or sing. Dancing was too sexual and singing was reserved for hymns. She was constantly warned to avoid frivolous thoughts. Karen's mother acted as though taking care of her daughter was more than she could bear.

Karen came into therapy because she felt constantly worried and unable to relax. She was aware that she was causing her husband and children disappointment and unhappiness: she had never enjoyed sex with her husband, and every time the family scheduled a vacation, Karen got sick.

In therapy she began to realize what a pervasive effect her parental bad messages had had. They had convinced her that there was something basically sinful about her and that she did not deserve to be fulfilled. She had convicted herself of basic badness.

Bad Treatment as a Bad Message

A particularly destructive type of parental message is neglectful, uncaring, or abusive treatment. A child who is exploited, brutalized, or treated without affection usually comes to feel that he is unlovable and undeserving of good treatment.

Jay, a forty-five-year-old carpenter, six feet four, two hundred pounds, always believed that he had been a bad child because his father had frequently beaten him. As an adult he himself would at times become enormously angry and rage furiously around the house, frightening both his teenage son and his wife. He entered psychotherapy after his wife left him, threatening divorce after eighteen years of marriage.

In therapy Jay began to see his father as a bitter, frustrated man who, even as an adult, was criticized and verbally abused by his own father, who lived next door. When Jay looked back at the childhood offenses that had triggered his father's rage, they turned out to be nothing more than the ordinary misdeeds of childhood — taking pennies from his parents' dresser or getting his clothes dirty on the way home from school. Jay began to realize that he hadn't been a bad child at all. It was his father who had had difficulty being a mature, reasonable adult.[2]

Like many abused children, Jay never really faced the fact that he had been abused as a child. He minimized his father's misdeeds and continually tried to present his dad's behavior in the best possible light. Early in his therapy he commented that his dad had once really "knocked some sense" into him by administering a severe beating.

As therapy progressed, Jay began to see that the beatings he had experienced at his father's hand had left scars, not benefits. He saw his father as a troubled man who was unable to deal with his son's behavior in a mature, helpful way. Because he had never fully confronted the harmful nature of his father's critical, abusive behavior, Jay often found himself repeating his father's pattern by criticizing and verbally abusing his own wife and children.

Jay was able to make progress only after he accepted the fact that his father was a dysfunctional parent. He was then able to begin remembering what really happened when he was a child and to reassess the bad messages. As this process continued, he found himself becoming less and less angry with his wife and son. He is currently working hard at building better relationships with both of them.

How could it be that an intelligent man of forty-five could fail to recognize that he had been beaten unnecessarily, and that although he may have been an active, energetic child, it was his father, not he, who had the problem? Jay's father had repeatedly told him that he was being beaten because he was bad. Although they may consciously object, children in this situation almost always unconsciously accept any blame that is placed upon them. It is just too terrifying for them to think that their parents might be vindictive, unjust, or psychologically troubled.

A person who receives undue criticism or abusive treatment as a child frequently converts those experiences into a feeling of low self-esteem. The experience of being mistreated by a parent is so painful that most people "forget" where this negative self-image comes from. They are left with only the deep sense of basic badness and with self-defeating behaviors they struggle in vain to understand.

The "Aren't We Wonderful?" Bad Message

In some families, one or both parents consider it very important that all family members consider themselves part of a perfect family. These families may actually appear quite happy — at least from the outside. The children are often quite popular. They typically do well in school. They are frequently envied by their friends for having parents who seem "so easy to talk to."

Many such perfect families are reasonably healthy and well functioning. But in some cases, the parents' obsessive need to appear perfect one hundred percent of the time puts a severe strain on everyone. The hallmark of the perfect family syndrome is that it is very hard for the parents to handle criticism or conflict within the family or to tolerate disapproval from those outside. A child who is unhappy is not just a problem to be dealt with, but an embarrassment and an indictment — a living proof that not all is as perfect as it seems.

The troubled child of a perfect family may end up feeling particularly terrible about himself. His normal, angry, critical feelings may produce such family upset that the child may end up feeling intensely guilty. In addition, these children may feel ungrateful or crazy because they feel critical of parents who are praised and envied by all their friends.

Although some perfect families are not really all that bad behind their flawless exterior, the image sometimes hides much more serious problems — an alcoholic parent, sexual or physical abuse, criminal activity, a mild or severe case of mental illness, or a painful, empty marriage. In these cases, the child's sense of being bad and crazy can be particularly intense. Such children are at risk of developing severe psychological problems as adults. We will discuss such family secrets in more detail in Chapter 10.

Case History: Luke

Luke came into treatment complaining of long-standing depression, feelings of isolation, and a history of heavy drug use. At the time, he was not aware of any possible connections between his current state and his childhood circumstances. He described his parents as supportive and loving and blamed himself for his problems.

Over several years of therapy, a much different picture unfolded. Luke's parents had fought viciously. His mother was extremely overprotective. She favored Luke over his younger brother. Both his parents had been very critical of all his girlfriends.

One day, in the midst of a therapy session, Luke sat up in his chair and said: "You know, Lewis, it's not that my parents were really so perfect. It's just that they *told* me over and over again how perfect they were and how lucky I was to be their son."

Ordinary People

Judith Guest's novel *Ordinary People,* which we cited in Chapter 4 as an example of survivor guilt, provides a powerful and accurate portrait of a perfect family. Conrad's suicide attempt and subsequent hospitalization blows apart the image that his mother, Beth, had been striving to maintain. When Conrad attempts to tell his mother of the anger, hurt, and guilt he is feeling, she refuses to listen. She cannot bear to think of herself as less than perfect and is more concerned with what others may think than with what her son is feeling.

Conrad's mother rejects his attempts to share his feelings because she is intensely uncomfortable in dealing with human feelings of any kind. But Conrad has always interpreted his mother's rejecting behavior as meaning that he was a bad person who was not worthy of love. This rejection — combined with her apparent belief that his suicide attempt was nothing more than an attempt to embarrass her — only adds to Conrad's negative feelings about himself.

The loss of a child would be a difficult blow to any family. In this fragile, perfect family, in which the open expression of feelings is not permitted, it leads to a total breakup. When Conrad's parents split, their friends and neighbors are shocked. Everyone had always considered them the perfect family.

Societal Bad Messages

Although it is a complex subject to which we cannot really do justice here, it is important to mention that many of us have received negative messages from the media and from our society at large. Widely held negative stereotypes about women, older people, people who are overweight, Mexican-Americans, Jewish Americans, Afro-Americans, Irish-Americans, and other minorities have created great psychological burdens, making some stereotyped individuals feel incapable, unworthy, and doomed to failure. Sometimes positive messages from our families can overcome society's limiting stereotypes, but all too often the whole family is influenced by the same negative messages.

For example (although less common than in the past), in some families girls are treated as if they are less valuable than boys and are not expected to have careers. They are raised as caretakers with the idea that they will grow up to be good wives — and will perhaps work as secretaries, nurses, or schoolteachers until the babies come. The boys in the family get the attention, and it is made clear to them that they are expected to become doctors, lawyers, or executives.

Lu-Jean, a forty-six-year-old secretary, remembers vividly how her Chinese-American parents struggled to get her less talented, less motivated brother into a good college, but wouldn't even help pay her tuition to the local state college — in spite of the fact that she had earned straight A's, had won several high school debate tournaments, and had received strong letters of recommendation from her teachers. As a result, she never completed college, while her brother, a mediocre student at best, went on to become a successful physician.

Case History: Dwight

Dwight's father was an ambitious southern black man who moved to Detroit after World War II. With hard work and superior intelligence he worked his way up from a salesclerk to manager of a small department store. When the store was sold, the new owner, who was a bigot, told him that he was not about "to have no nigger running my store." He offered Dwight's father a job as janitor. In spite of his skill and experience, Dwight's father was unable to find a new position like the one he had lost. No other store would hire a black man as a manager. He was forced to take a series of dead-end, menial jobs.

A few months later, Dwight's mother, who had a stomach ulcer, suffered an episode of internal bleeding. She was turned away from a private hospital in an all-white neighborhood and died in an overcrowded county hospital emergency room. Dwight's father became a cynical and embittered man. He warned his son not to expect too much from life. Dwight's father probably hoped to protect his son from the crushing disappointments he had experienced. Instead he burdened his son with bad messages that proved a considerable handicap.

As an adult, Dwight took a job installing telephones. He was bored and felt sure he could function at a much higher level, but when it came time to study for the promotional exam, he would inevitably fall asleep, get sick, or become distracted. Dwight was referred to counseling by a personnel officer who felt that he showed great promise in spite of his failure to pass the promotional exam.

During his counseling sessions Dwight remembered the discouraging messages he had received from his father. He realized that although his father had meant them for his protection, his repeated dire predictions had made Dwight feel that he should not expect good treatment. He had convicted himself of basic badness and felt he did not deserve to be promoted.

Uncovering Your Own Bad Messages

Remembering the bad messages we received from our parents is understandably difficult, for it is distressing to think that the people we loved most in the world could have burdened us with such problems. This is particularly true if we have idealized our parents. But our golden memories of childhood all too often serve as a cover-up for a variety of humiliating and painful childhood experiences.

There are two ways to determine whether you received bad messages. One is simply to remember: Were you habitually put down or otherwise mistreated by a parent or parental figure? Were you repeatedly given any explicit negative messages like those in the list beginning on page 105? If you find yourself engaging in self-defeating behaviors even though you *cannot* remember any specific bad messages, ask yourself, "What kind of message could make me act this way?" For example, if you find yourself feeling nervous when things are going well, you may have received a message like "You'll never amount to anything" or "Good times never last." Or you might have received indirect messages that you were not worthwhile and don't deserve to have things go well.

Breaking the Chain

For those of us who are parents, the idea of bad parental messages takes on a special meaning. None of us wants to inflict our own bad messages on our children. Yet we may do exactly that unless we become aware of the negative messages that we have received from our own parents.

To correct these negative patterns is no minor undertaking. We may experience some strong resistance. By not passing on to our children the bad messages our parents passed on to us, we might become better parents ourselves. Thus, if we were to succeed in giving up our bad messages with regard to parenting, we might commit the crime of outdoing our parents. It may be helpful to remember that it is, by and large, unhappy parents who pass bad messages on to their children. The best thing we can do for our own young ones is to live the happiest, most meaningful and fulfilling lives we possibly can.

When it comes to letting go of our bad messages and forgiving ourselves for our imaginary crimes, our own interests and those of our children are exactly the same. For it is only by being as successful, happy, and fulfilled as possible that we can give our children the ultimate *good* message: "I know that you'll have a successful, fulfilling, and enjoyable life. Just look at how much I'm enjoying my *own* life."

COMMON BAD MESSAGES

Here are some of the bad messages you may have received as a child. If you find one or more statements that sound familiar — or if some of these messages make you think, That's no bad message, that's reality! — you have probably internalized those negative messages.

"You're Unlovable" Messages

- "I hate you."
- "I wish you were dead."
- "Get out of my life."
- "I'm sorry you were ever born."
- "You're no good."
- "You're just like your mother, a heartless, faithless whore."
- "You're just like your father, a mean, irresponsible bastard."
- Action: Cruel, insensitive, or neglectful treatment

"Don't Trust Others" Messages

- "Most people will screw you in a minute if you give them half a chance."
- "If you want it done right, do it yourself."
- Action: Parent repeatedly promises to come to a graduation, a big football game, etc., but fails to show up.

Sex Role Messages

- "Medical school is too hard for a girl. Be a nurse instead."
- "Having a career and being a mother just don't mix."

- "You'll never find a husband if you are too independent, too outspoken, or too smart."
- "Your brother will have to support a family someday, so we'll send him to college."
- "Big boys don't cry."
- Action: A father encourages his son, but not his daughter, to plan a college career. A mother encourages her daughter, but not her son, to share vulnerable feelings.

"You're Incompetent" Messages

- "Why can't you ever do anything right?"
- "You're so lazy and undisciplined you'll never amount to anything."
- "You're all thumbs."
- "You always find some way to screw up."
- Action: Constant criticism

"You're Crazy" Messages

- "You're just like your Uncle Jake [an alcoholic or hospitalized mental patient]."
- "You're nuts. You've always been nuts and you'll always be nuts."
- "Nothing's wrong with Daddy. Daddy's just not feeling well. But don't you dare mention this to anybody or Daddy will lose his job and we'll all starve." (when a parent is drunk)
- Action: A parent denies incest, violence, or verbal abuse.

"You Can't Trust the Opposite Sex" Messages

- "Men only want one thing — sex. And once they get it they'll dump you."
- "Women only want one thing — a meal ticket. A free ride. Once they get it they will tie you down and henpeck you to death."

- "You can't deal with a man directly. You have to learn to manipulate him."
- "You can't ever let a woman know you really care about her. If you do she'll manipulate and control you."
- "Men are bastards, but you can't get by without them."
- Action: Complaining constantly to a child about a spouse

"Succeeding Is Failing" Messages

- "The only way to get to the top is over the dead bodies of those on the bottom."
- "Money is the root of all evil."
- "It is easier for a camel to pass through the eye of a needle than for a rich man to enter the kingdom of heaven."
- Action: Criticizing anyone who is wealthy, successful, or famous

"It's Dangerous to Criticize" Messages

- "If you can't say something nice, don't say anything at all."
- "You'll destroy your mother if you imply she's got a drinking problem."
- "Don't say anything about your father's behavior. Just ignore it."
- Action: A distraught mother cries in her room for hours after her teenage daughter criticizes her.

"Don't Grow Up" Messages

- "You children are the only thing that gives my life meaning."
- "There's only one right way to do things, and that's *my* way."
- "You'll always be Daddy's [or Mommy's] little girl."
- "If you try something like that [to reach some cherished goal] you'll only be disappointed."
- Action: Stepping in to take over instead of letting the child learn to solve her own problems

• Action: Disapproving of a teenage child's attempts to date or withholding permission for dating until much later than is customary in their community

"Pleasure Is Dangerous" Messages

• "Idle hands are a devil's playground."
• "Masturbation will drive you insane."
• "Sex is nasty."
• "Sex will make you burn in hell."
• "Sex is only pleasurable for men. For women it is something to be endured."
• Action: Exhibiting anxiety whenever anyone else is having fun

"Don't Let Yourself Relax" Messages

• "If things seem good, disaster lies just around the corner."
• "Knock on wood [i.e., if you dare to say that things are good, they will surely go bad]!"
• "Don't be so cocky and full of yourself."
• "If you've finished today's homework you'd better start on tomorrow's."
• Action: Never relaxing

"Don't Take Care of Yourself" Messages

• "Be sure everyone else is taken care of before you serve yourself."
• "Don't be so selfish and self-indulgent."
• "You'd best stay away from doctors: if you're feeling bad the best thing to do is to ignore your symptoms and work right through it."
• Action: Parent refuses to let child stay home from school when ill.
• Action: Parent refuses to obtain necessary medical or dental care.

Martyr Messages

- "I had a very difficult delivery and almost died when you were born."
- "I gave up a promising career [on the stage, in business, as an artist, etc.] to take care of you."
- "You're my cross to bear. You always were."
- "I stayed with a monster for all these years for your sake."
- "Why do you make me suffer so?"
- "You don't care about anyone except yourself."
- Action: Never taking care of oneself, sighs, sad looks

7

The Lash of the Mind

Understanding Punishment Thoughts

═══════════

A person who suffers from . . . guilt . . . may, in his symptoms or in the course of his life, find a way of being tortured.

— JOSEPH WEISS, M.D.

In previous chapters we have described some of the actions people take to punish themselves for their imaginary crimes: Some destroyed their chances for promotion. Some chose to stay in bad relationships while others destroyed perfectly good ones. Some remained at home well into middle age. Some became addicted to alcohol or other drugs. Some made a mess of their financial affairs. But our actions are not the only way we punish ourselves. We also punish ourselves through our thoughts.

From her high school days in a small Texas town, Jean had always wanted to work for a leading national advertising agency and to live in a glamorous city. By age twenty-seven, she had made her dream come true: she was a highly paid, highly respected account executive at a major New York advertising agency.

Jean had been troubled by periods of mild anxiety and depression for as long as she could remember. She decided to enter therapy when her symptoms of anxiety and depression suddenly increased to the point where she felt she was having a nervous breakdown. She was so strongly affected by these feelings that she was forced to take a medical leave from her job.

In spite of her many successes, Jean felt secretly incompetent and feared that her bosses and coworkers would soon find her out. In spite of the fact that she had received excellent evaluations and a rapid series of promotions, she worried that she would be fired and that no one else would offer her a job. In the end, she would have to leave New York and go home to Texarkana to live with her parents.

Although she had previously been involved in a series of painful romantic relationships, for the past two years Jean had been involved with a successful graphic artist who was warm, loving, and extremely devoted. Yet she worried that her boyfriend would never want to marry her and she would never have the family she had always yearned for. She was plagued by an unending stream of memories of times she had hurt or disappointed others — stretching all the way back to a girlfriend she had rejected in the third grade.

Jean's prim mother and unpredictable hard-drinking father had always been somewhat unhappy with each other, but they had at least had a lovely home and a circle of close friends. Finally, a few months before Jean entered therapy, they had battled their way through a bitter, messy divorce. Because they were both so vengeful, both ran up immense lawyers' bills. After the divorce was final, they found themselves not only isolated but also greatly impoverished. They had to sell many of their favorite possessions, including the family home. In addition, her father had recently been fired, and at age sixty-one, his prospects were now particularly bleak. He was living alone in a small, studio apartment and was drinking heavily. Both parents called

Jean frequently to condemn the other and to complain about their unhappy lives.

In therapy, Jean came to see that she unconsciously felt guilty of the imaginary crimes of outdoing and abandonment. She was in a warm, supportive, respectful relationship, which her parents had never had. Although her parents were not financially destitute, their means were severely limited — and Jean was making more money than she had ever imagined. Both her mother and father were unemployed — and she loved her job and was considered a rising star in her firm. Her parents were old, frail, and bitter; their possibilities limited, their prospects bleak — and Jean was young, attractive, and talented, her future full of promise.

Jean's parents' divorce had triggered intense guilty feelings of outdoing. Since her parents were now doing so much worse, she now seemed to be doing much better by comparison. Her feelings of abandonment guilt also increased. Her punishment thoughts — that she would lose her job and have to move back to Texarkana — were related to her unconscious belief that the only thing that would make things easier for her parents would be for her to move back home.

Fortunately, Jean was not willing to make this sacrifice. But as a result of her guilt, she was plagued by irrational thoughts. This was her way of punishing herself for her imaginary crimes.

Punishment Thoughts: A Definition

Control Mastery Theory suggests that such irrational worries can be a way of punishing ourselves for our imaginary crimes.

All of us have been plagued, at one time or another, with similar bizarre, obsessive, depressing thoughts. Why is it that these thoughts seem to pop into our mind at some times in our lives, while at other times we are free of such nagging worries? In most cases, these thoughts arise when things are going extremely well — in fact, this is a telltale sign that our worries may be a form of punishment thoughts. Since we hold ourselves guilty of imaginary crimes, we feel that we do not *deserve* success or happiness. Whenever things do go well, our unconscious processes respond by producing punishment thoughts.

A punishment thought is a depressing or frightening idea or fantasy whose unconscious purpose is to make us feel bad. By feeling bad we can escape the unconscious guilt we would experience if we really allowed ourselves to enjoy our lives while family members were suffering. Thus the two events that are most likely to prompt punishment thoughts are the proverbial good news and bad news.

• Good news about you — success at work, in your relationships, good fortune, a substantial inheritance, a promotion, a raise, or other substantial achievement. Punishment thoughts occur when things go well because you feel unconsciously guilty for outdoing or being disloyal to family members who are not doing so well.

• Bad news about someone you love — hearing or being reminded that a family member or someone close is unhappy, unsuccessful, lonely, incurably ill, out of a job, on drugs again, getting divorced, in jail, or otherwise in trouble. Punishment thoughts occur when things go badly for others because their inadequacy or misfortune widens the gap between how well we are doing and how badly they are doing.

Case Study: Jack

Punishment thoughts can introduce pain and suffering into the most seemingly exemplary life. Jack was promoted to project manager of his computer company at age twenty-five. He and his girlfriend were very much in love. He had just moved out of his parents' house and into his own apartment. Jack was flying high. But his optimistic mood did not last long.

Jack began to dwell on the possibility of nuclear war. He reasoned that Silicon Valley would be a primary target. He became obsessed with images of nuclear devastation. As time went on Jack's concerns about nuclear war faded, but he began to worry that he would be reprimanded or fired at work. He compared himself to the firm's resident genius, one of the most famous and respected programmers in the world, and convinced himself that he was an undesirable employee. These ideas persisted in spite of good evaluations by his supervisor and a hefty raise.

As Jack continued to do well in the company, his concerns about being fired or criticized faded. He next began to worry about the possibility that he or his girlfriend might have AIDS. He began collecting magazine articles and reading books on the subject. The fact that neither he nor his girlfriend had a single risk factor for the disease did little to calm his worried mood. When his girlfriend finally got him to share his concerns, she arranged to have them both tested the next day. Both tests came back negative.

The things that worried Jack were all within the realm of possibility. Some are unlikely, such as the possibility of contracting AIDS. Some are hard to predict, such as the possibility of atomic war. But two things identify Jack's preoccupations as punishment thoughts — he began to have these thoughts soon after something favorable occurred and he was unwilling to take any constructive action regarding his fears. Despite his concerns about his work performance, Jack didn't check out his fears with his supervisor. Despite his fears of nuclear devastation, he did nothing to promote world peace. And despite his preoccupation with AIDS, he refused to get an AIDS test until his girlfriend bullied him into it. If a grim thought comes shortly after something good happens, yet you refuse to take constructive action, there is a very good chance that the grim thought is a punishment thought.

Why would Jack want to punish himself so relentlessly? To answer that question we will have to know a bit more about his family history.

As an only child, Jack was the one bright spot in his parents' otherwise dismal lives. His father worked as a carpet salesman and deeply resented the fact that he was never made manager. His mother spent most of her time taking meticulous care of the family apartment and worrying about Jack. Jack's parents rarely fought but they never seemed to enjoy life. Jack's father spent most of his time at home reading and watching TV. His mother did crossword puzzles or talked obsessively to Jack.

Jack's first imaginary crime was abandonment. He lived with his parents until age twenty-five, much longer than most of his friends. He told himself he was living at home to save money, but the real reason was that he unconsciously felt that his parents would be even more unhappy without him. When Jack finally did leave home, he felt as if he were selfishly and cruelly abandoning his parents. And by establishing a strong and satisfying relationship with his girlfriend he became even more separate from his family.

Jack's second imaginary crime was outdoing. By being so successful at work, he unconsciously felt he was humiliating his father, who felt unsuccessful and unappreciated in his own job. He was doubly guilty of this crime because he was so happy and excited about his life when his parents had become resigned to their bleak, joyless routine. Thus whenever he began to feel optimistic and excited, Jack also felt extremely guilty. He assuaged his guilt by, as he put it, "bumming himself out" with punishment thoughts.

By unconsciously punishing himself with thoughts of being

fired, being vaporized in a nuclear holocaust, or dying of AIDS, Jack was unconsciously able to feel that he wasn't so much better off than his parents after all. In this way he was able to pay for the crimes he had already committed and to avoid committing new ones.

Self-Critical Thoughts

One very prevalent type of punishment thought is irrational self-criticism. We put ourselves down in an amazing variety of ways. Some of us bombard ouselves almost constantly with self-accusations: we tell ourselves that we are lazy, stupid, selfish, shallow, hurtful, weak, cowardly, overdependent, socially inept, too fat, too thin, too ugly, or too afraid of intimacy. Some of us accuse ourselves of two, three, four, or more of these depressing characterizations. The most implacably self-punishing among us may accuse ourselves of virtually all of them. The following list includes some put-downs commonly used as punishment thoughts.

LAZY

One very common set of put-downs are self-accusations of laziness, lack of discipline, and weakness of character. We say to ourselves: "You just can't keep your nose to the grindstone, can you?" "You're a lazy bum, you'll never amount to anything." "What's wrong with you, anyway?" These thoughts make us feel discouraged or disgusted with ourselves. We feel small and defective. If we listen carefully to ourselves we can sometimes hear echoes of critical bad messages from parents or other important authority figures.

UGLY

Another very common self-criticism is the thought that we are physically unattractive: "My breasts are so big, I look like a cow." "My breasts are so small, I look like a boy." "I'm too fat." "I'm not handsome or rich, so no girl is going to want me." "Nobody takes a short man seriously."

STUPID

The notion that we are stupid, or at least not very bright, is another popular self-criticism. The key idea here is that because of our supposed lack of intelligence, no decent mate will want us, we will be constantly embarrassed, and we will never amount to much. Like attractiveness, the area of intelligence is a rich field for negative comparisons. "Everybody is thinking how stupid I am." "I never have anything intelligent to say." "Everybody seems so much brighter and more articulate than I." "Why would any woman be interested in a man who is not a good conversationalist?"

SELFISH

We accuse ourselves of selfishness when we want to do something for ourselves rather than for somebody else — if we want to stop listening to a tiresome acquaintance, if we don't look forward to a visit from Uncle Joe, or if we want to take some time from our obligations. This self-accusation almost always is an echo of a parental complaint. Although we can think we are stupid without ever being called stupid and we can think we are ugly without ever being told we are unattractive, the idea that we are lazy or selfish almost always comes from parents or other authority figures: "You really don't care about anybody but yourself, do you?" "I think I am incapable of real love." "I'm a terrible person and no one should care about me."

Not every thought that we are selfish is a punishment thought. Some such thoughts may serve as constructive criticism. But if these thoughts come with a painful regularity, if they seem to imply that our behavior makes us bad, unlovable people, and especially if they seem to come right after something good happens, they are almost certainly punishment thoughts.

Seeing the Worst in Ourselves

We all have our own characteristic personality traits: we may be more often cautious than bold, more often reserved than outgoing, or more often emotional than calm. When we seek to punish ourselves, we tend to characterize our own preferred tendencies in a particularly negative way. A neat and thorough person might thus describe himself as obsessive-compulsive. An emotional person may describe herself as hysterical. A trusting person may describe himself as gullible. And so on. If you find yourself habitually using the negative versions of such qualities, there is a good chance you are subjecting yourself to punishment thoughts.

Since the unconscious purpose of punishment thoughts is to make us feel bad, almost any type of criticism — no matter how irrational — will do. During an acute episode of self-punishment we can criticize ourselves for being obsessed with sex —

or for being asexual. For being too sloppy — or too neat. For being too independent — or for being overly influenced by others.

Here is a wonderful list of twenty-eight self-critical ideas that we can — and often do — use to attack ourselves. This list is adapted, with permission, from *After the Honeymoon: How Conflict Can Improve Your Relationship*, by Daniel Wile.

1. Thou shalt not be dependent.
2. Thou shalt not be self-centered.
3. Thou shalt not be jealous.
4. Thou shalt not be boastful.
5. Thou shalt not be withdrawn or withholding.
6. Thou shalt not be afraid of intimacy.
7. Thou shalt not be depressed.
8. Thou shalt not be overly sensitive.
9. Thou shalt not worry about things you can do nothing about.
10. Thou shalt not wallow in self-pity.
11. Thou shalt not run away from your problems.
12. Thou shalt not be unwilling to take risks.
13. Thou shalt not be a nag.
14. Thou shalt not be a wimp.
15. Thou shalt not be bossy.
16. Thou shalt not be defensive.
17. Thou shalt not feel turned off by your partner.
18. Thou shalt not have unrealistic expectations.
19. Thou shalt not fail to take responsibility for your actions.
20. Thou shalt not have a negative attitude.
21. Thou shalt not be frigid.
22. Thou shalt not be promiscuous.
23. Thou shalt not be a dirty old man.
24. Thou shalt always be eager and willing to have sex.
25. Thou shalt not fail to fulfill your potential.
26. Thou shalt not be a workaholic.

27. Thou shalt not suppress anger.
28. Thou shalt not express anger or even be angry.

Notice that many of these self-criticisms are contradictory, so that a negative characterization can be found for virtually any trait or behavior. (Incidentally, Wile's book is one of the best self-help books for couples we have ever read. We recommend it highly.)

As this laundry list makes clear, some punishment thoughts consist of little more than calling ourselves names. But we have more complex ways of punishing ourselves as well.

Negative Comparisons

Another common self-accusatory strategy involves comparing ourselves to others. We often use such negative comparisons to make ourselves feel lazy, dumb, unlovable, unattractive, or unsuccessful, or to devalue ourselves in other ways.

This self-punishment strategy can be pursued no matter how disciplined, creative, attractive, or brilliant you really are. If you are the number-two quarterback in the National Football League, you can compare yourself unfavorably with number one. And if you are number one, you can compare yourself to former greats or berate yourself that you have never lived up to your full potential.

Here are some examples of negative comparisons:

"He's the same age as I and he already runs a successful company, while I'm still just a middle manager."

"By my age Mozart had already written twenty complete symphonies."

"Jeff runs sixty miles a week. I'm lucky if I do fifteen."

Sarcastic Comments

Some of us keep up a running sarcastic commentary on our performance. If we do something poorly we say sarcastically to ourselves, "Great job, really terrific." If we do a good job at something we say to ourselves, also sarcastically, "Think you're pretty hot stuff, don't you?"

The Impostor Phenomenon

The impostor phenomenon is a condition in which a successful and capable person, like Jean, the advertising executive, feels that she is in constant danger of being exposed as a fraud. Such feelings are most commonly experienced in the workplace, but they sometimes extend to social and family life as well. This phenomenon is a common mode of self-punishment among successful people. A book about the impostor phenomenon, *If I'm So Successful, Why Do I Feel Like a Fake?* by Joan Harvey with Cynthia Katz, reached the best-seller list because so many successful people were relieved to discover that their secret feeling of being a fraud was so widespread.[1]

The idea that you are a fraud, and may at any minute be discovered, is a potent and painful punishment thought. Even though you may be the head of a corporation, a famous movie actress, or a successful cardiac surgeon, you may constantly feel tense, anxious, and in constant danger of being discredited and rejected by your friends and colleagues. Those of us who suffer from such fears can never really relax and enjoy our accomplishments.

Like all punishment thoughts, the idea that you are an impostor is a punishment for an imaginary crime. The crime, in this case, is being successful. Exactly *why* it should be a crime to be successful varies from person to person but it often has to do with outdoing our parents or siblings. Many of those who suffer from the impostor phenomenon turn out to have had an unhappy or unsuccessful parent or sibling whom they see as being humiliated or left behind by their own success.

Although the "impostor" seems very different from the chronic failure, they have a great deal in common. Both believe that success is a crime. Both thus unconsciously avoid the satisfying — and guilt-producing — feeling of success. The chronic failure avoids it by sabotaging his own successes, while the impostor assuages her guilt feelings by imagining that she doesn't deserve her success and by worrying that it may disappear at any moment.[2]

The Road Not Taken

This self-punishment strategy consists of thinking about the job you didn't take, the career you didn't pursue, the task you didn't do, the boy you didn't marry, the sale you didn't make, the real estate you didn't buy, and so on. Since there is always the possibility that things might have worked out better if you'd made different choices, this strategy can be used even when things are going well. And when things really *are* going badly, worrying about choices you did not make can make you feel even *worse*.

Not all such second thoughts are punishment thoughts. A man who feels remorseful after spanking his child may decide to develop other ways to handle unruly behavior. A woman who has gotten herself into financial trouble by overusing her credit cards may decide to cut up her cards, pay cash, and establish a monthly budget. To distinguish "road not taken" punishment thoughts from productive reconsideration, one must look at the results.

- Do these thoughts just make you feel bad to no good purpose?
- Do they concern something relatively inconsequential such as worrying that you paid a quarter too much for your toothpaste or twenty dollars too much for a set of tires?
- Are you regretting something that you couldn't have predicted, such as hitting an unseasonable series of rainstorms on a vacation trip?
- Do these thoughts seem to spoil things that you otherwise would enjoy?

If the answer to any of these questions is yes, chances are the thoughts in question are punishment thoughts.

Dwelling on Negative Experiences

The past is a gold mine of potential punishment thoughts. Some people, in the grip of such thoughts, may be unconsciously driven to spend hours combing through the past to relive unpleasant experiences.

- Jane, an attractive young travel agent, often thinks back over her life, recalling a long string of rejections and disappointments. These thoughts depress and discourage her and convince her that she has never been loved and never will be.
- Marcus, a successful middle-aged bachelor, endlessly recalls all the women he has disappointed and convinces himself that he does not deserve a good relationship.

• Jim, a hardware store owner, obsesses about the property he chose not to buy — which later quadrupled in value — to the point that he discounts the fact that his own business is thriving.

Learning from past mistakes is a very useful process. But it is quite a different thing from endlessly replaying old mistakes. The negative recapitulation of old misfortunes sets up the expectation of future failure. It is the painful and pointless obsessing that distinguishes punishment thoughts from fruitful self-examination. The same holds true for reviewing hurts you have caused others. If such thoughts lead you to make amends, or change your ways, they may be well worthwhile. If they simply repeat an unvarying message of self-castigation, they are punishment thoughts.[3]

Imagining Bad Outcomes

Some people are plagued with the idea that disaster lies ahead, that the future will inevitably be grim. We call these *bad outcome thoughts* and divide them into *general catastrophizing* (imagining bad outcomes for everybody) and *personal catastrophizing* (imagining bad outcomes for you or those close to you).

General catastrophizing can include worries about nuclear war, water and air pollution, a potential collapse in financial markets, overpopulation, the greenhouse effect, crime in the streets, and a number of other potential dangers. All these problems are real possibilities, and any thoughtful person will be concerned about some or all of them. But as we have already observed in Jack's case, these very real problems can be pressed into service for the unconscious purposes of self-punishment.

Personal Catastrophizing

Some people find themselves worrying that horrible things will happen to themselves or their loved ones. The two most common types of personal catastrophizing are:

- Imagining that you or your loved ones might come down with AIDS, Lyme disease, cancer, or some other life-threatening illness or injury.
- Imagining that you or someone close to you will be fired, that your business will fail, or that your livelihood will be taken away.

Again, to qualify as personal catastrophizing, it is necessary that there be no real justification for your worries. If you are a sexually active homosexual man living in New York City, who does not practice safe sex, it's quite reasonable to worry about AIDS. If your doctor has discovered a suspicious lump in your breast, it is quite normal to worry about cancer—at least until you receive the biopsy report.

Obsessing About the Sufferings of Others

Some people punish themselves with guilty thoughts about those less fortunate than themselves. Phil, a twenty-five-year-old law student, seemed to have everything going for him. He had won a prestigious scholarship to a highly respected school. His proud parents were only too glad to provide him with plenty of spending money. He edited the law review and was constantly near the top of his class.

But as his academic career progressed, Phil found himself feeling more and more guilty because his classmate Sonny had to wait tables at night and was doing badly in his classes. Phil found himself reflecting endlessly on how unfair it was that he had all those extra hours to study and relax while Sonny had to worry about hustling pizzas and Cokes. But no matter how upset Phil became, it never seemed to occur to him to find a way to offer Sonny a helping hand. Genuine concern over the suffering of others normally leads to efforts to help.

Like many people who torture themselves by thinking of the plight of others, Phil was really punishing himself for imaginary crimes against his family. Phil was favored by his parents over his sister who had been unpopular as a child and was now struggling with cocaine addiction. In addition, his mother felt unhappy and neglected by his father. Phil felt unconsciously guilty of the imaginary crimes of getting the love he felt his sister needed (love theft) and leaving and neglecting his unhappy mother (abandonment). By obsessing about the difficulties that his classmates faced, as well as having other punishment thoughts, Phil was able to relieve his unconscious guilt toward his mother and sister.

We do not mean to imply that it is inappropriate to be concerned with the plight of our fellow man. Far from it. Sympathy for the sufferings of others is the hallmark of a healthy, caring human being. Here again, the key to distinguishing true concern from punishment thoughts lies in the timing. If you find yourself preoccupied with, say, the suffering of those in the Third World *only when things are going very well for you,* you might well be engaged in self-punishment. To continue with this example, if you don't take any concrete steps to help those in the Third World, you would do well to consider the possibility that your preoccupation with Third World suffering is actually a punishment for your imaginary crimes.

How to Recognize a Punishment Thought

The following questions can help you tell the difference between a punishment thought and a legitimate concern. If you answer yes to one or more of the following questions, you should consider the possibility that your depressing or frightening thought is, in fact, a punishment thought:

- Has something *good* just happened? Have you been promoted, been given special recognition, begun a new relationship, or become newly successful in some other way?
- Are you beginning to think, hope, or dream about doing something that you that haven't done before?
- Have you just found out that a family member, a close friend, or even an acquaintance is doing poorly, while you are doing well?
- Does the painful thought depress and immobilize you — rather than move you to helpful action?

How Recognizing Punishment Thoughts Can Help

It would be nice to think that simply identifying a thought as a punishment thought would make it go away. Unfortunately, recognition is not usually enough. While some punishment thoughts may simply vanish after they are identified, others will persist. But their grip on you may considerably diminish. Let's look at an example of what can happen when a person realizes that certain bothersome fears are really punishment thoughts.

Case History: Dierdre

Dierdre was an up-and-coming M.B.A. who worked as a financial analyst for a young, rapidly growing corporation. She was a talented, responsible, ambitious employee, and her work was rarely criticized. One day at a staff meeting, a coworker was somewhat critical of a report Dierdre had prepared. Others at the meeting agreed that the report had not included some important information.

After the meeting, Dierdre began to experience nagging doubts about her own competence:

"I looked like a terrible fool in that meeting. No one will ever take me seriously again."

"Don't be silly. It wasn't that big a thing."

"They're on to me now. My days are numbered on this job."

"No they're not. You just got an excellent quarterly review. You made a mistake, that's all. Nobody's perfect. This is nothing to worry about."

This painful, obsessive internal dialogue went on until Dierdre went to her weekly therapy session. Her therapist was able to recognize her fears as punishment thoughts, and together they traced them to Dierdre's guilt about outdoing her mother.

Dierdre experienced a great sense of relief. Instead of feeling anxious about her own performance, she was able to experience her real feelings — sadness about her mother's constricted and unhappy life. Dierdre's case also illustrates that sometimes punishment thoughts operate by taking a real but small problem and blowing it up to monumental proportions.

That was not the last time Dierdre was troubled with punishment thoughts of this sort. But as time went on she became more and more able to stop her obsessive internal dialogue and instead to think productively about the imaginary crime for which she was punishing herself.

Beyond Positive Thinking

Many psychology writers have realized that negative, discouraging thoughts can keep us from attaining success, intimacy, or fulfillment. It is clear that our expectations have a great deal to do with whether we are able to reach our work goals, keep ourselves healthy, and make and maintain important social bonds.

A growing number of self-help books, tapes, and speakers admonish us to "think positive," and to "tune out negative thinking." To the extent that they can help people identify negative, self-destructive punishment thoughts, they may be of some help. But many of these programs merely attack the symptoms — our negative punishment thoughts — while ignoring the underlying process that gives rise to them. The success of such programs will be severely limited if they don't help us identify our imaginary crimes. Since it is our unconscious guilt that causes us to punish ourselves, we will continue to be plagued by punishment thoughts until we understand the origins of that guilt. Punishment thoughts are, after all, only one mode of self-punishment. We can also punish ourselves through the whole variety of self-destructive and self-sabotaging behaviors.

Why do we choose to punish ourselves in so many different ways? And how is it that we choose our own particular mode and style of self-punishment? For an answer to these questions, we must turn to the next chapter, where we will explore two powerful and helpful Control Mastery concepts — the ideas of identification and compliance.

8

Identification and Compliance

Making the Punishment Fit the Crime

Jill has a happy marriage, but suffers endless misery at work. Kevin has a dreadful marriage, but does beautifully on the job. Linda is unhappy with both her spouse and her job. Zack does well at work and has a great relationship, but repeatedly screws up his financial affairs. Alice has her job, relationship, and finances together, but is unable to relax and enjoy life.

We can unconsciously choose to punish ourselves in an incredible variety of ways. We can torture ourselves with punishment thoughts. We can choose from a wide variety of possible self-destructive, self-sabotaging behaviors. But how is it that we each receive our own unique self-imposed sentence for our imaginary crimes? How is it that we each choose our own distinctive form of punishment?

We punish ourselves in ways that are closely related to our imaginary crimes and that correspond to the way we came to adopt our negative behavior pattern in the first place. Control Mastery holds that there are two principal patterns of self-punishment: We may *identify* with an unhappy parent. Or we may *comply* with a parental bad message.

How We Identify
with an Unhappy Parent

If we grew up feeling responsible for the sufferings of an unhappy parent, we may punish ourselves by *identifying* with our parent:

- We may take on his worst qualities.
- We may imitate the very patterns that made her life unhappy.
- We may feel that our fate is the same as his, whether it really is or not.

Identifying with a parent is an unconscious strategy by which we avoid committing imaginary crimes of outdoing and disloyalty against that parent.

By repeating a parent's pattern of self-defeating behavior we can avoid the imaginary crimes of outdoing. For if we are just as self-defeating and in just the same way as they are, we are not outdoing them. As children we may have unconsciously felt that a parent's behavior was pathetic or absurd. However, being critical or contemptuous of a parent constitutes the imaginary crime of disloyalty. Therefore, we may find ourselves unconsciously driven to repeat the same absurd behavior, thereby blunting our contemptuous and critical feelings. In this way, we put ourselves in the position of the pot calling the kettle black. If we engage in the same self-defeating behavior as our parents, who are we to be critical or contemptuous?

Complying with Parental Bad Messages

If a psychological problem is not due to identification, it is often caused by our acting in obedience to a negative parental message (compliance). We comply with our parents' bad messages for many reasons: Because it allows us to maintain our ties to our parents. Because we tend to believe what our parents tell us. Because our parents are one of the major sources of information about life. Because these messages are drummed into our heads over and over.

But we also comply with parental bad messages to avoid the imaginary crime of disloyalty. Although we consciously wish to prove our parents' bad messages false, we unconsciously sabotage ourselves in order to prove them true.

- If parental bad messages made us feel we were a disappointment, we may act in ways that our parents would find disappointing.
- If our parents accused us of being selfish, we may behave selfishly.
- If they accused us of being lazy, we may behave in a lazy way.
- If they accused us of being an irresponsible, self-centered screwup, we may become exactly that.

- If they accused us of being unattractive, we may make ourselves unattractive.
- If they treated us as if we deserved little in the way of affection or material rewards as children, we may deny ourselves these things as adults.

The Control Mastery Therapist's First Question

When Control Mastery therapists see new clients, one of the first questions they ask themselves is this: "Is this person suffering from parental identification or a parental compliance — or both?" A client's problem, even the most mystifying or bizarre, will then often become readily understandable. This question can be profoundly valuable to ask of any psychological problem — either our own or those of others. Not every grim belief is an identification or a compliance. But since the majority are, asking ourselves this question often clarifies things greatly.

The Identifiers: Booker

In their influential book, *Black Rage,* psychiatrists William Grier and Price Cobbs tell of a black graduate student, Booker, working toward his Ph.D. in speech, who came into therapy complaining of three problems: His marriage had deteriorated because of his numerous affairs. He had gambled away most of his money. And in spite of his impressive intellectual ability and skills, his speech pattern remained that of a "rural uneducated southern Negro of seventy-five years ago." [1]

His therapist was struck by the fact that Booker, in spite of years of college and graduate school, still found it almost impossible to speak in the standard English required of a graduate student at a major university. The therapist was also perplexed as to why a man with a bright, attractive, and loving wife would engage in extramarital affairs and throw his money away gambling — activities that were clearly ruining his marriage.

As treatment progressed, the therapist learned that Booker's father had abandoned Booker and his mother for the life of a professional gambler — big cars, womanizing, and tricking the foolish out of their money. And in spite of many years in a large northern city, his father maintained an uneducated southern Negro speech pattern. In the course of therapy Booker came to realize that his speech problem and some of his relationship difficulties were "saying, in effect, that no matter what the price, it is important to me to be my father's son." In order not to be better or different from his father, he was sacrificing his career, his marriage, and his peace of mind.

The Identifiers: Sarah

Sarah, a thirty-two-year-old lawyer, entered therapy because she had been unable to succeed in her career. Although she was extremely intelligent and ambitious, and had landed a job at a top law firm, she frequently found herself procrastinating, making careless mistakes, and going into court unprepared. In addition, she developed an intense stage fright, and began to dread making the many court appearances her job required. Sarah had hoped that after a few years she would be named a partner. Instead, she was in serious danger of losing her job.

Her marriage was also in trouble. Her husband, a state legislator, had to be away at the capitol for weeks at a time. Sarah resented his absences and bitterly nagged him for being absent so much. She was so angry that married life became completely unsatisfactory to both partners. Although Sarah had never had any evidence that her husband was unfaithful, she imagined that he was out having affairs whenever he was away.

Sarah's mother had given up a promising law career to become the wife of a successful politician. Although she knew when she married him that a politician's life required frequent travel, she became bitter about her husband's business trips and complained to Sarah that he cared more about his career than he did about his family.

In the course of therapy Sarah came to realize that her intense identification with her mother lay at the root of her problems. She had chosen a man much like her father and was replaying the dysfunctional pattern of her own parents' unhappy marriage. She was sabotaging her success at work because she unconsciously felt guilty for pursuing a successful law career when her mother had abandoned her career. Her powerful, unconscious identification with her mother was literally wrecking her life.

As she explored these issues in therapy, Sarah resolved her work problems and she was eventually asked to become a partner in the firm. The problems with her husband were not as easy to solve. Once Sarah stopped attacking him and accusing him of infidelity, it became clear that prolonged intimacy with Sarah made him uncomfortable. Although the communications between them have markedly improved, Sarah is still not content with her marriage. Her husband has repeatedly refused to enter marital therapy. At present, Sarah is seriously considering divorce.

The Identifiers: Melvin

Melvin was a bright, able, hardworking but only marginally successful stockbroker who came into therapy because he found himself in constant conflict with his wife, clients, colleagues, and managers. His arguments with his wife centered on his habit of routinely going back on his word and on his extreme critical-ness. He also broke his promises to business associates, engaged in shady practices, and was slow in paying debts. As if to annoy his creditors further, Melvin always carried around a big roll of large bills.

One day when his therapist insisted he discuss why he was chronically late in paying his therapy bill, Melvin pulled out a big bankroll and paid off his balance. When asked why he carried so much cash around, Melvin recalled that his father had done the same thing. Melvin's father owned a small neighborhood bar, which was actually a front for a small-time bookmaking business. He was highly critical of his wife and children and loved to play the big shot. Melvin remembered being tremendously embarrassed as a child, when his father took him to bars, flashed his money, and told exaggerated tales about his accomplishments. He was shaken by the realization that he was repeating the very behavior he most detested in his father.

This realization was a turning point in Melvin's therapy. Although it was too late to salvage his marriage, Melvin became much more reliable and scrupulous in his business affairs and consequently became much more successful financially.

Booker, Sarah, and Melvin all came to understand that their serious problems were the result of adopting their parents' dysfunctional behavior patterns. Before they attained this insight, they had either been puzzled by their negative patterns or had adopted other, incorrect, explanations for their self-defeating behavior: Booker had been completely mystified by his inability to learn to speak standard English. Sarah had felt that her problems were caused by laziness and jealousy. Melvin blamed his wife and business associates for being overly critical and unforgiving. For each, the realization that the true cause of their problems was identification with an unhappy or unsuccessful parent was enormously useful.

The Compliers: Rachel

Rachel was a popular and attractive young schoolteacher who had a difficult time developing intimate relationships with men. Her father had repeatedly told her that she should never trust men because they were only after one thing — sex — and once they got it, they would leave. As soon as she became sexually involved with a man, Rachel would become so jealous and clingy that the man would immediately back off, confirming Rachel's belief that once she made love with a man, the relationship was doomed. He had gotten the one thing he wanted and would therefore leave her.

The Compliers: Lance

Lance was an entrepreneur who, instead of going to college, built his hobby, radio-controlled model cars and planes, into a very profitable mail order business. Although still in his early twenties, he worked fourteen hours a day, smoked too much, and was thirty pounds overweight. Troubled by a constant feeling that his business was going to collapse, in spite of all the evidence to the contrary, Lance was tense and unhappy and finally entered therapy.

His father was a nervous, hardworking department store executive. His mother was a schoolteacher who hated her job. Both parents repeatedly told their son that if he didn't get a college education, he would never get anywhere. His parents never seemed to have any fun and went many years without taking a vacation. "You can't have your cake and eat it too" and "Work first, play later" seemed to be their mottos. But in their case, the long-awaited rewards never came.

Lance thought he was escaping his parents' grim life by building his own around something he really enjoyed. But because he had accepted their dire predictions, he found himself unable to enjoy the life he had built for himself. He complied with their messages by working so hard and worrying so much that his dream had gone completely sour.

Lance and Rachel are examples of people who have an unconscious drive to prove that their parents' dire predictions were correct. Guilt from their imaginary crimes was driving them to prove the very things right that they most wanted to prove wrong.

Rachel consciously wanted to prove that men can be trustworthy and that relationships can be lasting and satisfying, but was unconsciously driven to prove that men are faithless beasts and that relationships are hopeless. Lance wanted to be able to enjoy the life that his talent and hard work had provided for him, but ended up toiling for so many hours that he was unable to enjoy either his work life or his leisure time.

In therapy, both Lance and Rachel began to see how actions that had appeared to be innocent oversights or random mistakes were actually a manifestation of their bad parental messages. Once they realized this, they were able to take steps to counter their parents' powerful curse: Rachel was able to stop her jealous, clingy behavior and begin a long-term relationship. And Lance was able to establish a reasonable quitting time and to enjoy regular weekends and vacations.

The Unsuccessful Rebel

Some children understood from an early age that their parents' psychological problems were what made them pass on bad messages. Because they didn't believe those messages as children, as adults they were able to successfully rebel against them. For example, Arthur, the owner of a successful machine shop, was told by his father, "You'll never amount to anything." He recalled saying to himself, even as a child, "Oh yes I will!" He went on to become quite successful. Unfortunately, many of us find that even though we do our best to deny our parents' bad messages, we may still be profoundly influenced by their dire predictions.

Robert is a thirty-seven-year-old filmmaker. He grew up in a middle-class family in which both parents worried constantly about money. Despite the fact that they were reasonably well off, they were incredibly frugal, depriving themselves and their children of even the smallest pleasures. Robert got this message from his parents: "Unless you live like a monk, work like a horse, and worry about money constantly, you will inevitably suffer financial ruin." Or, to put it another way, "It's OK to be successful and have money, but it's dangerous to take any pleasure in it."

Even as a child, Robert recognized the irrationality of his parents' ideas about money. He swore that when he grew up, he would not be excessively concerned with frugality. Over ten

years of hard work, Robert turned out a dozen modestly successful educational films. Several years ago, he reached the point
where he was making a good income, but his financial affairs
were always in a shambles. He had a long list of overdue bills,
all his bank accounts were overdrawn, and he had borrowed
substantial sums from several close friends.

Then one of Robert's films turned out to be much more successful than he had dared hope. He jubilantly told his wife and
children that they could now finally afford to buy the home they
had always wanted. The whole family went house-hunting.
They found the house of their dreams, and went to the bank to
arrange financing. To everyone's dismay, their loan application
was turned down because of Robert's horrible credit record.
The whole family was heartbroken.

As Robert pondered the unhappiness he had caused, he
vowed he would face and solve the financial problems that had
plagued him all of his adult life. His wife was too angry to be of
much assistance, so he asked a friend, the controller of a small
corporation, if he would help him work out a budget and a
financial management plan. Robert stayed on his budget for a
month, then found himself slipping back into his old, irresponsible, free-spending habits. At that point he decided to enter
therapy in order to get a handle on his financial problems. It
became clear that Robert's attempts to rebel against his parents'
bad messages about money were being undermined by an unconscious urge to prove their dire predictions true.

Robert's case is typical of many other unsuccessful rebels.
They refuse to follow the paths their parents laid down for them
— yet nothing seems to work out the way they had hoped. They
unconsciously sabotage their rebellions and eventually fulfill
their parents' dire predictions.

Identifications and Compliances: A Powerful Way of Looking at Our Psychological Problems

As we have seen, many psychological problems stem either from imitating our parents — identifications — or proving them right — compliances. Thus, when we become aware of a problem, we should ask ourselves:

- Is my problem similar to a problem my parents suffered from?
- Is it putting me in a painful situation similar to one they were in?
- Am I simply living out the discouraging picture of what they told me or implied I could expect in life?

Discovering that a self-defeating attitude or behavior is similar to a parent's can sometimes be a great help in modifying it. Very often, however, this is just the first step in an extended process of freeing oneself. There are two main difficulties that people experience in stopping self-defeating behavior after they have become aware of it.

- They find that they do not even realize that they are involved in the problem behavior until after it has happened.
- They know they are caught up in the problem behavior but feel that they simply cannot stop themselves.

Eldon became aware in the course of his therapy that he nagged and nitpicked his wife in much the same way his father had treated his mother. Even as a child he was aware that his father's continuous digs and put-downs had placed an enormous strain on his parents' marriage. Although he clearly recognized this negative pattern, he was completely unable to change his behavior. On some occasions, he was unaware that he was being critical. At other times he knew exactly what he was doing but simply could not stop himself.

Eldon used two principal strategies to help himself stop his criticism:

• He used his therapy sessions to explore incidents from his childhood and the grim beliefs he had formed from them. He recalled that his father had constantly criticized him as well as his mother and that he had unconsciously come to believe if you do not criticize someone you love, that person will become lazy and irresponsible and stop meeting your needs. Eldon realized that he considered his constant criticism a way of showing his wife and children that he loved them.

• He made a game of trying to catch himself being critical. He carried a small notepad in his shirt pocket and began to record each critical incident. In the beginning, he found that he could identify his digs only after the fact. As time went on, he learned to notice them more promptly. After several weeks, he found that he could frequently catch himself in the act, or even anticipate and stop a critical comment.

Although his wife and children had complained about his faultfinding for years, Eldon had never taken them seriously. But once he realized that by repeating his father's critical behavior, he was putting his loved ones through the same suffering he had endured as a child, he resolved to put an end to it. Eldon's decision to stop his critical behavior began a process that greatly improved his relationship with both his wife and his children.

Repeating Our Parents' Bad Patterns

Many of us have suffered at the hands of parents who were neglectful, intrusive, narcissistic, alcoholic, or who suffered from other moderate or serious psychological problems. We swore to ourselves that when we grew up the *last* thing we would ever do was to repeat the parental behavior that hurt or shamed us. But, to no avail, we find ourselves, over and over again acting in the very ways we most detested in our parents. Our conscious efforts to avoid being like them are opposed by our unconscious belief that by surpassing or disobeying them we will hurt and humiliate them.

Not Every Problem Is
an Identification or a Compliance

It is a major thesis of this book that many common psychological problems are actually self-punishments that come about as the result of either imitating our parents' bad patterns or believing their bad messages. But there is an important group of psychological problems that do *not* stem from self-punishment. They grow out of our irrational attempts to protect ourselves from being hurt in the same way we were hurt in the past.

Olivia, a highly paid legal secretary, entered therapy because she was very uncomfortable in any but the most superficial relationships. She dressed formally and was polite but distant in her work relationships. Olivia spent most of her spare time reading, sewing her own clothes, and taking walks around the city. Although she was an attractive woman, her prim clothes and aloof manner kept most potential suitors away. Over the years, her isolation had increased to the point where she was feeling depressed and suicidal.

Olivia's father was a cold, self-absorbed salesman who worked for a succession of fly-by-night real estate companies. He would sometimes take his daughter on business trips, leaving her abandoned in the car for hours while he drank with his buddies. Olivia's mother was an alcoholic. When drunk, she would alternate between being overly affectionate and physically abusive. She often beat Olivia on the legs with clothes hangers while the other children looked on in terror.

Although Olivia experienced some guilt over imaginary crimes, her major problems stemmed from her belief that it was not safe to trust anyone or be close to anyone. Olivia's primary problem was not that she unconsciously thought she might hurt someone. It was that she believed she herself was in danger of being hurt, as she had been in the past.

In the course of a therapy that lasted many years, Olivia came to understand that not everyone in the world would treat her as badly as her parents had. Through learning that her therapist was trustworthy and caring, she was able to begin to understand that there were some people in the world whom she *could* rely on. She was then able to join a local computer users group, where she met some women friends and finally, at age thirty-six, began to date men.

Like Olivia, most of us suffer from a combination of two types of grim, unconscious beliefs:

- Fear of hurting others by committing imaginary crimes.
- Fear of being hurt, rejected, shamed, exploited, humiliated, or abused by others.

If our parents rejected, humiliated, exploited, or abused us, it is not surprising that we fear that others will do likewise. Both therapists and laypeople have long realized that the fear of being hurt, rejected, humiliated, or exploited is the source of some of our most serious psychological problems. However, one of Control Mastery Theory's most important contributions is to tell us that for many, the fear of hurting others — by committing imaginary crimes — ends up being much more troublesome than the fear of being hurt.[2]

In the next chapter we will see how this intense concern for others can lead us to turn away from the very things we consciously believe we want most in life — intimacy, pleasure, and sexual fulfillment.

9

Running Away from Happiness

Why We Avoid Intimacy, Pleasure, and Sexual Fulfillment

═══════════

People occasionally fall ill precisely because a deeply rooted and long cherished wish has come to fulfillment. It seems then as though they could not endure their bliss.

—SIGMUND FREUD

Most of us have had at least one experience, however brief, of deep love for and openness to another person. Indeed, most of us seek a committed relationship because we see it as a pathway to such intimacy. But attaining and sustaining high-level intimacy is a tremendous challenge.

Nearly half of all marriages end in divorce. One study found that only about 20 percent of married couples felt they had attained truly intimate relationships.[1] The other 80 percent were categorized as:

- The Devitalized — Couples who had fallen out of love with each other.

- The Conflict-Habituated — Couples who fought constantly.
- The Passive-Congenial — Couples who had never expected marriage to be particularly passionate or intimate in the first place. They treated each other as friendly but detached roommates or business partners.

None of these relationships was truly intimate. None met the spouses' deep needs for closeness.

Some experts believe we expect too much out of our couple relationships. They say we shouldn't expect to maintain our feelings of intimacy and closeness through the daily struggles of job, kids, illness, arguments, money problems, sexual difficulties, preparing the meals, paying the bills, taking out the garbage, and all the other irksome problems of contemporary life.[2] But our desire for intimacy is so deep and so persistent that unless we attain it, most of us will continue to long for it.

If your parents were close and loving, you may well have learned, by observation and imitation, the difficult and complex skills that contribute to intimacy, and you should find it easier to maintain your own intimate relationships. If your parents had cold or hostile relationships, you may find it necessary to learn new intimacy skills on your own — or with the help of books, friends, or a professional counselor or therapist.

More Than Skills Are Needed

The skills of intimacy are difficult and complex, but they can be mastered by study and diligence, just like any other skills. There are a number of popular books that offer excellent guidance in the areas of good communication and negotiation, the most important couple skills.[3]

But if the whole problem was due simply to a lack of intimacy skills, a series of adult education courses could be instituted in local school systems, and divorce and marital unhappiness could be quickly eliminated. Unfortunately, it's just not that simple. Learning new skills is only part of the answer. Our imaginary crimes, our grim beliefs, and our unconscious guilt prevent us from having the satisfying, intimate relationships we desire. For most of us, the principal unconscious barriers to intimacy include:

- The beliefs we developed as the result of observing our parents' relationship.
- The beliefs we developed as the result of the bad messages we received from our parents.
- Our unconscious guilt over imaginary crimes of love theft, outdoing, abandonment, or disloyalty.

Training in communications and intimacy skills, although extremely useful, is often inadequate to restore real closeness to our relationships. Learning these new marital skills will not help us accomplish our goals unless we simultaneously learn to come to terms with our beliefs and to identify and forgive ourselves of our imaginary crimes.

We Avoid or Sabotage Intimacy for a Great Variety of Reasons

Maria, the successful restaurateur in Chapter 1, was attracted only to exploitive and unfaithful men. Her unconscious purpose in choosing such inappropriate partners was to avoid outdoing her mother, who had also chosen inappropriate men.

Mike, the plastic surgeon in Chapter 3, had grown up feeling responsible for his mother's happiness. He transferred this feeling of responsibility to the women he was dating. Because of this exaggerated sense of obligation, any intimate relationship soon came to feel claustrophobic.

John, the architect in Chapter 4, provoked trouble in his marriage by becoming overly involved in his work and by having affairs with other women. John had adopted this self-sabotaging pattern in order to avoid outdoing his philandering father.

Michelle, the theatrical agent in Chapter 5, bitterly and irrationally criticized her husband for being so unlike her father. Michelle unconsciously felt that she would become disloyal if her husband replaced her father as the number-one man in her life.

Paul, the computer parts man in Chapter 5, lived with his critical, abusive mother until she died. Paul then married a bitter, critical woman who treated him in much the same way his mother had. Paul was driven by separation guilt.

Lydia, the computer programmer described in Chapter 5, shunned all intimate human relationships. Lydia's experience with her brutal and undependable parents taught her that other people were dangerous and untrustworthy.

Joyce, the office manager in Chapter 6, became involved in a series of relationships that were neither intimate nor supportive. Joyce was obeying her father's bad messages, which implied that she was so undesirable that she would be lucky to get any man at all.

Jay, the carpenter in Chapter 6, had spoiled his relationships with his wife and son by uncontrolled expressions of anger. Jay had taken his father's beatings to mean that he was a bad kid and had gone on to adopt those aspects of his father's behavior he hated most.

These cases illustrate the wide variety of unconscious motives that may cause us to avoid, undermine, or destroy our intimate relationships. Guilt over outdoing or abandoning a parent; guilt over disloyalty to a parent; fear of hurting, or being hurt by, a partner; and the belief in a variety of bad messages can all make it very difficult for us to achieve satisfactory intimate relationships of our own.

Grim Beliefs About Intimacy Acquired from Experience

Our deepest and most profound convictions about the nature of relationships stem from our early experiences in our own family. In most cases, for good or for ill, our parents' interactions provide our basic model of the nature of long-term relationships.

We may fervently hope and solemnly vow *never* to have a relationship like our parents had. But that is exactly what many of us end up doing. It is difficult to rid ourselves of the conviction that our parents' pattern is real and that anything better is just a Hollywood fantasy.

Joyce, the office manager who received so much unjustified criticism from her father also witnessed fighting, sarcasm, and emotional cruelty between her parents all the time she was growing up. Once she *was* able to form a relationship with an empathic, loving, and supportive man, she became suspicious of her own happiness. She kept waiting for the fighting and the emotional cruelty to start.

Our Relationship with Our Parents

Our own relationships with each of our parents show us what it is like to be close to men and women. On an unconscious level, we expect *all* our relationships with men to be like that we had with our father. And we will expect *all* our relationships with women will be like that we had with our mother.

If we are close to both parents and they have a loving, intimate, and enduring relationship, we will grow up believing that we are lovable and valued by both men and women. We will also feel that marriage can be intimate, satisfying, and long-lasting. Those of us who come from such fortunate situations tend to have a relatively easy time with intimacy with both friends and spouses. Unfortunately, most of us grew up in family situations that were less than ideal, and end up with a mixture of beliefs, some of which help us in establishing an intimate relationship and some of which hinder us.

Case History: Sherry

Sherry's parents got along very nicely. Sherry had an intimate, warm relationship with her mother. But she never felt very close to her father. He was a traveling salesman and an avid fisherman. It seemed to Sherry that he was always gone, either on a sales trip or a fishing trip. On those rare occasions when he did notice her, he was impatient and critical.

As an adult, Sherry had no trouble forming satisfying, intimate friendships with women. But she found herself strongly attracted to men who were either critical or inattentive. She would no sooner leave one man because he criticized or ignored her than she would take up with another who treated her just as badly.

Sherry unconsciously believed that she *should* be criticized and rejected by a man — just as she had been by her father. But she also believed that in a long-term relationship each partner should treat the other well, as her parents had treated each other. With the help of her therapist, Sherry learned to overcome her deep conviction that men would put her down. Gradually she began to pick more accepting, less critical partners. Eventually she was able to establish a successful, intimate relationship.

Same Family, Different Patterns

As Sherry's case makes clear, the beliefs that make intimacy difficult have as much to do with how our parents treated us as with how they treated each other. Even two children from the same family may grow up with very different beliefs about marriage.

Sherry's brother, Paul, also had a close relationship with his mother. As an adult, he assumed that he would be liked and approved of by women and expected that his relationships with women would work out well. Paul too had a difficult relationship with his father. While this made it hard for Paul to relate to authority figures at school and on the job, it did not prevent him from forming and maintaining a satisfying intimate relationship with a woman.

Bad Messages About Intimacy

Not only do children draw negative conclusions about intimate relationships from what they see; they can also be profoundly influenced by what they are told.[4]

Joyce was criticized unmercifully by her father and was told that no man would ever want her. As a result, she never expected to be treated well by a man. Jay was told he deserved the beatings he endured from his father. As an adult he spoiled his marriage and relationship with his own son by ranting and raging just as his father had done. Such bad messages often have a profoundly destructive effect on our ability to maintain intimate relationships.

Leah's father was an unsuccessful insurance salesman. Leah's mother was bitterly disappointed in her husband in almost every way and criticized him constantly. He responded by spending most of his leisure time in bars and bowling alleys — or anywhere else he could go to get away from his angry, nagging wife. He had given up trying to please her shortly after they were married.

Furthermore, Leah's mother complained bitterly about her husband's sexual demands, his crudeness, and his insensitivity. "Life with your father is a nightmare," she often told her daughter, "but I suppose it's better than being a lonely spinster. I'd divorce your father in a minute if I thought I could do any better. But men are all the same."

As you might expect, Leah's intimate relationships were a disaster. She suffered from a sort of double whammy: Leah knew how difficult her parents' relationship had been. Yet her mother had assured her that without a man, things would be even worse.

Every time Leah found herself in a new relationship she would ignore all her boyfriend's positive qualities and nag him about his sexual demands, his crudeness, and his insensitivity. But as soon as one relationship ended, she felt desperate to find another.

Unconscious Guilt
Can Destroy Intimacy

It is widely recognized that one reason that people avoid intimacy is because they are afraid of being hurt. Each time we enter into an intimate relationship we risk rejection, betrayal, abandonment, or exploitation. These are terribly painful experiences. Those who have suffered from such bad treatment may be cautious about getting into another such relationship. But we may not have realized that guilt over our imaginary crimes can also keep us from achieving the closeness that most of us desire.

Unconscious guilt over *any* imaginary crime can cause us to avoid or sabotage intimacy. Love and closeness are essential to a sense of fulfillment for most of us. But if we unconsciously feel that we have committed a serious imaginary crime, we may feel that we do not deserve that fulfillment. Although unconscious guilt over *any* imaginary crime can make us deny ourselves intimacy, two common imaginary crimes are particularly likely to disrupt our relationships: outdoing and abandonment.

If we believe that our parents did *not* have a close and loving relationship, then by attaining such a relationship for ourselves we would be committing the imaginary crime of outdoing. The guilt we feel for outdoing our parents is a form of survivor guilt — guilt over having a full and happy life when our parents' lives seem constricted and sad.

In many troubled marriages, one of the unhappy parents forms a unique bond with one of their children. This special child may feel that his closeness and devotion is the only thing that prevents this parent from slipping into total despair. A boy may feel he is "Mama's little man." A girl, "Daddy's little girl." Or a child may have a special bond with the parent of the same sex.

When he grows up, he may unconsciously continue to believe that as long as that parent remains his primary love object, everything will be all right. However, if the parent is forgotten and someone else becomes number one, that parent will be lost. The adult child may feel guilty of the imaginary crime of abandonment if he becomes intimate with or makes a commitment to someone else.

Case History: Dorothy

Dorothy's father was a famous and successful criminal lawyer. He made a very comfortable living but worked late into the night on weekdays and devoted most of his weekend time to legal research. He took little if any interest in his wife and daughters. On those rare occasions when he *was* around, he was highly critical of Dorothy and was never a satisfactory father or husband.

Dorothy's mother was the center of a bustling household with four active girls. Although she was bitterly unhappy with her marriage, she kept up appearances and told no one except Dorothy about her pain and disappointment. Every night after the other children were asleep, Dorothy's mom would slip into her room and pour out her sorrows. "You are my first born," she would tell her. "If it weren't for you I don't think I could go on."

After graduating from high school, Dorothy attended a local city college and majored in radio and television broadcasting. She continued her long talks with her mother every night. She did a student internship at a local station and ended up marrying the assistant manager of the station, a talented and successful young TV executive. Soon after she was married, Dorothy began to telephone her mother every evening. They would spend hours commiserating about their two workaholic husbands.

This continued until Dorothy's husband lost his job and was unable to find work in any other local station. A few days later, he was offered a choice job at a higher salary — in Los Angeles, two thousand miles away. After several violent arguments, Dorothy decided that she would rather terminate the marriage than go with him, even though she too was promised a very attractive position. He took the job anyway and she moved in with her parents. That was the end of their relationship. Dorothy gave up her marriage and her independence to avoid the imaginary crime of abandoning her unhappy mother.

How We Avoid Intimacy

If you have had continuing problems with your relationships it can be quite valuable to identify your unconscious strategy for avoiding intimacy. We avoid intimate relationships in three principal ways:

• We avoid getting into relationships in the first place.
• We pick inappropriate partners.
• We pick good partners, but then spoil the relationship because we feel we don't deserve it.

Some people use just one of these strategies. Others use different strategies at different times in their lives. Individuals from very similar family situations may use different strategies to avoid the intimate relationships they feel they don't deserve.

Kevin's mother made his father's life miserable with her constant nagging and criticism. In order to avoid the imaginary crime of outdoing, Kevin developed the unconscious belief that he deserved no better fate than his father. He married a woman who was extremely critical. Kevin became so angry at his wife that all their initial warmth and closeness was completely lost. His wife felt disappointed and deprived and became even more critical. Kevin had unconsciously chosen an inappropriate partner. He thus was able to guarantee that he would not attain the intimacy he craved but felt he did not deserve.

Stuart's mother also nagged his father, but Stuart married a tolerant and supportive woman who was not prone to criticize or nag. Unfortunately, Stuart, like Kevin, had developed an unconscious sense that he did not deserve to have a loving, intimate relationship. After he and his wife married, he began to act irresponsibly — failing to fulfill his commitments, arriving home late without calling, and repeatedly scattering his clothing on the floor. It wasn't long before his formerly easygoing, sweet-tempered wife was nagging Stuart in much the same way as his mother had nagged his father. Stuart was unconsciously compelled to spoil a close, rewarding relationship to avoid the imaginary crime of outdoing.

Understanding our typical strategy for avoiding intimacy is an important first step to building and maintaining satisfying intimate relationships. If we sabotage our relationships by being irresponsible, we can make a special effort to avoid that behavior. If we torment our partner with criticism and put-downs, we can work to control this tendency.

But identifying our strategy of avoiding intimacy is only part of the solution. We must also identify the reasons we avoid intimacy in the first place:

- The imaginary crime for which we are punishing ourselves
- The grim, unconscious belief that is driving us
- The negative pattern we have adopted as the result of identifying with an unhappy parent
- The parental bad message we have chosen to obey

Suppose we realized we had been picking inappropriate partners and resolved to make more appropriate choices in the future. Unless we understood the reason we were driven to avoid intimacy, we might simply switch strategies. For example, we could choose a supportive and appropriate partner but indulge in fits of bad temper that eventually drove that person away. If we also understood that we unconsciously felt guilty of outdoing our ill-tempered father, we would be better able to try to avoid replicating his temper tantrums. Understanding both our strategy *and* our motive for avoiding intimacy thus provides the best hope for reversing this self-defeating pattern.

Why We Run Away from Pleasure

Why do we spurn pleasure? This is a great paradox of the human condition. We are biologically programmed to seek pleasure and avoid pain and discomfort. Yet many of us deny ourselves our portion of the delights and satisfactions of life. We may take only meager pleasure from our children, our spouses, or our work. We may never give ourselves the opportunity to appreciate the beauty of a sunset, a walk by the ocean, a perfect morning, a powerful film, or a moving string quartet.

Avoiding pleasure is not always irrational. The ability to postpone an enjoyable activity until important work is done is one of the hallmarks of a disciplined, mature adult. And avoiding potentially harmful pleasures — cocaine, extramarital sex — is also rational and desirable. But we may also avoid pleasure in order to punish ourselves.

Probably the most common reason for avoiding pleasure is to *avoid outdoing parents or siblings who have had very little pleasure in their lives.* We may unconsciously feel that experiencing pleasure when our loved ones did not is disloyal or hurtful. We act as if there were only a limited quantity of pleasure in the world. By taking some for ourselves, we would be depriving our closest family members.

We may also deny ourselves pleasure if we were treated badly as children. If we were abused, exploited, neglected, or relentlessly criticized as a child, we may judge ourselves guilty of the imaginary crime of basic badness and sentence ourselves to a life without happiness.

How We Learn That Pleasure Is Dangerous

• If we saw our parents become anxious, angry, or out of control shortly after they allowed themselves to relax and enjoy life, we may conclude that pleasure was dangerous to our parents and will be dangerous to us as well. Simon's parents would save their marital disputes for weekends and vacations, so Simon learned to associate vacation or weekend time with their bitter arguing.

• Anxious parents may be upset by the natural excitement and *joie de vivre* of their children. Each time Stephanie became enthusiastic or excited, her high-strung mother would warn her, "Don't get too excited. Somebody's going to get hurt." She soon learned to curb her natural girlish enthusiasm.

• A child can learn to associate relaxation with alcohol use and its consequences. Herbert's alcoholic father would become relaxed, affectionate, and indulgent after two drinks. But after five drinks he would inevitably turn into a snarling tyrant.

• Valerie's mother suffered from manic-depressive disorder. In her manic phase, she would become very excited and would make wonderful plans. But she would then become depressed and would forget all about them. Valerie grew up believing that planning pleasurable activities would lead only to frustration and disillusion.

• We may also learn that pleasure is dangerous from our parents' explicit warnings. Yvonne's fanatically religious parents repeatedly advised her that those who enjoy earthly pleasures will suffer in the hereafter. They scolded Yvonne each time they saw her playing or relaxing. As an adult, Yvonne found herself becoming anxious each time she began to have pleasurable feelings.

Grim Beliefs About Pleasure

Most of our grim beliefs about pleasure are unconscious, but there are some we may consciously believe to be true. If you are afflicted with one or more of the following beliefs, you may notice that you get extremely nervous when things are going well. This anxiety is a symptom of your unconscious guilt and fear. If this anxiety is strong enough, you may sabotage or avoid the situation that triggers these pleasant feelings.

• *This is too good, it can't go on.* On the face of it, this belief sounds like the simple recognition that what goes up must come down. But instead of simply being able to enjoy the good times until the bad times come, we may find ourselves becoming more and more anxious as the good times continue to roll. This anxiety may create in us a powerful urge to spoil things. This grim belief reflects the assumption that we are entitled to only a certain limited amount of good feelings, and if we feel too good or feel good for too long, we will be punished.

• *If I feel too pleased with myself, God will punish me.* Some of us have gotten the clear impression that God will punish those who are pleased with their lives. In order to avoid His terrible displeasure we may downplay our success, behave pessimistically, and worry compulsively. We may not allow ourselves to enjoy a sense of confidence and pride, even when these feelings are appropriate. We may torture ourselves with self-criticism, look for the worst in every situation, and worry constantly about the future.

• *If I relax and have fun, something bad will happen.* Brett's father was warm and fun-loving, but Brett's mother was prim and tense. His father frittered away the family fortune on ill-conceived and poorly managed business ventures, while continuing to live as though they were still wealthy. It all came to an abrupt end when the bank foreclosed on their properties and they were forced to live on the charity of relatives. His father didn't seem to mind, but the family bankruptcy was extremely humiliating to Brett and his mother. Whenever Brett began to relax and enjoy himself, and particularly when he spent any money, he unconsciously worried that he was becoming like his father.

• *It is dangerous or sinful not to be accomplishing something constructive at all times.* As children, many of us were taught, Work first, play later. Clean up your room, then you can watch TV. This lesson can be valuable. However, others of us were never allowed to play later. Our parents regarded life as an unending succession of tasks and gave us the impression that terrible things might happen if we ever took a break. As a result, some of us have become obsessed with being productive at all times. We can't go on vacation without bringing along a bulging briefcase. We get anxious on the weekend if we don't bring home work from the office, or at least devote ourselves to a long list of household chores.

Running Away from Sexual Pleasure

Society sends us many conflicting messages about sexuality:

- Sex is sublime.
- Sex is dirty.
- Sex is necessary.
- Sex is sinful.
- Sex is romantic.
- Sex is a wifely duty.
- Sex is disgusting and animalistic.
- Women are expected to be good lovers.
- Women are required to be virgins at the time of their wedding.
- A man should be ready for sex at every opportunity.
- A man should not be interested in a woman only for sex.
- A woman who has had a variety of sexual partners is a slut.
- A man who has had a variety of sexual partners is a man of the world.

All of these irrational, conflicting, or sexist messages can lead to the avoidance of sexual pleasure and to a variety of sexual problems. It is currently possible to get help for most of these problems either through sexual therapy or by self-help sex therapy. There are many very good self-help books for sexual problems on the market.[5]

Control Mastery Theory offers an important new insight into problems of sexual fulfillment: it suggests that *our guilt from our imaginary crimes can make us turn away from sexual opportunities and can even interfere with our ability to achieve sexual satisfaction.*

Some of us had parents whose relationship with each other seemed cold and nonsexual. Other parents made it clear that sex was a disgusting activity that repelled them. Still other parents gave us the impression that they would have liked an active sex life but could not obtain their spouses' cooperation. If you got the impression that your parents did not have sex or did not enjoy it, then you risk committing the imaginary crimes of outdoing and disloyalty simply by having a satisfying sex life. Our unconscious guilt can cause us to forgo or sabotage the sexual satisfaction that was denied to our parents.

Bondage, Sexual Masochism, and Imaginary Crimes

Some adults find themselves sexually excited by the thought of being beaten, punished, or restrained during sex. Some choose to include certain punishment and domination rituals as part of their sexual repertoire. Activities that would ordinarily be considered extremely unpleasant or even repugnant under other circumstances may be extremely pleasurable when they take place in a sexual context. Most of the adults who freely choose to engage in such sexual play encounter no problems with it. They do not require these practices to enjoy sex, and they engage in these activities in safe environments only with trusted lovers.

But some individuals may find that they are able to attain little or no sexual pleasure *without* being bound, hurt, dominated, or humiliated. Still others may find that their need for punishment is so intense that they are driven to employ dominating prostitutes or to get themselves into potentially dangerous situations. Control Mastery Theory offers some important insights into this need for punishment. These insights have proved extremely useful in treating a number of clients whose need to be controlled, hurt, or humiliated during sex was causing severe problems.

Case History: Ronald

Ronald, a forty-five-year-old automobile salesman, came into therapy complaining that when he worked hard and built up his sales, he would inevitably be overcome with an unnatural sense of fatigue that would almost incapacitate him. His sales would drop to half or a quarter of his former level, and only then would he be able to work vigorously again.

Though Ronald had never married, he had an active sex life. He found himself powerfully attracted to extremely domineering women who treated him badly. He found that he could become sexually aroused only when one of his lovers tied him up.

In therapy, Ronald recalled that when he was a child, his mother seemed depressed, fragile, possessive, and envious of his childlike energy and enthusiasm. Even as a very small child, he could make his mother feel helpless just by running around their small apartment. He felt that he was just too much for her — that by expressing his exuberance and making demands on her, he was hurting her. Unconsciously he felt both contemptuous toward his mother for her weakness and guilty of hurting and burdening her.

Ronald remembered being sexually excited on several occasions during his childhood when he was playfully held down by women. In adolescence and adulthood, Ronald's masturbation fantasies usually included being tied down by a woman. When he pictured himself restrained by a woman he was reassured that he could not hurt or humiliate her, and thus was able to feel strong and sexually excited.

He began to understand that as he became more and more successful at work and consequently began to feel powerful, he unconsciously believed his power and success endangered and humiliated his mother. At a certain point, his guilt about this irrational, unconscious conviction caused him to be overcome by a tremendous weariness. This malaise continued until his sales figures had slipped to the point that he no longer felt so dangerously powerful. Once that happened, he was free to get back to work again.

As Ronald worked through his fears of hurting his mother (and women in general) by being strong and sexual, his problem on the job became less and less severe and he began to go out with women who were strong but not rejecting. Although he was still concerned that he might hurt the women he was involved with, he no longer needed to reassure himself by finding women who would be emotionally hurtful to him.[6]

Case History: Stella

Stella was an attractive, slightly overweight, thirty-five-year-old newspaper photographer. She came into therapy after the breakup of a brief, unpleasant marriage to a sadistic ex-convict.

Stella's mother was an overbearing woman who would throw hysterical, abusive tantrums when she didn't get her way or when she was upset by any real or imagined misdeed that her mild-mannered husband might have committed. As Stella was growing up, her parents' marriage deteriorated further and further. At last, things got so bad that her father stayed away from home as much as possible to avoid his wife's abuse, hysterics, and emotional blackmail. Stella felt angry at her mother but hesitated to criticize her for fear of triggering her wrath. And she felt sorry for her father, with whom she maintained a very close and loving relationship. As she grew into adulthood, Stella came to hate her mother for consistently abusing her kind and gentle father.

While supporting herself as a news photographer, Stella earned a Ph.D. in art history. She met a variety of people through her work and found herself attracted to a series of abusive, domineering, poorly educated men. She found that she became extremely excited when she was held down, tied up, spanked, or humiliated before or during sex. Eventually, she became a kind of sexual slave to a succession of extremely unsuitable boyfriends.

In therapy, Stella began to understand why. By arranging to be treated badly, she was preventing herself from hurting and humiliating her partner — as her mother had. She unconsciously felt that she was very strong and that men were very fragile. She thus feared that she could easily dominate and humiliate them — as her mother had humiliated and dominated her father. By casting herself as the victim, Stella was avoiding the role of the persecutor and identifying with her passive, submissive father.

From Punishment to Pleasure

Control Mastery suggests that when someone feels a strong urge to be humiliated, hurt, or tied down during sex, the underlying motive is often to avoid hurting the partner. People with this sexual pattern unconsciously feel guilty over imaginary crimes — either those they committed in the past or those that they are about to commit by experiencing powerful sexual feelings. They experience the pain, humiliation, or physical restraint as a deserved punishment.

As soon as the punishment begins — whether it is real or only in fantasy — their guilt is decreased and their pleasure intensifies. It may thus *appear* that the punishment causes sexual pleasure. Actually, the bondage or punishment only frees them to enjoy the sexual pleasure they would normally experience were they not burdened with the guilt of their imaginary crimes.

In addition to helping us handle fears of hurting our partners, bondage fantasies are a way of dealing with the unconscious guilt many of us have about being sexual at all. Sex has been portrayed as shameful, sinful, and dirty. And even though as sophisticated adults we may reject these characterizations, unconsciously they may still have considerable force.

By having fantasies of being taken by force, or by allowing ourselves to be physically held down or punished during sex, we assuage the unconscious guilt and anxiety that would otherwise oppose our sexual feelings. These rituals and fantasies allow us to think, I'm not really responsible. I'm not really to blame. Someone else is making me do it. I have no choice but to have sex.

The Parental Ceiling on Intimacy, Pleasure, and Sexuality

Each of us places limits on our intimacy, pleasure, and sexual fulfillment in different ways. Some of us have an extremely difficult time with *any* type of intimacy or pleasure. Others of us take the edge off intimacy or pleasure to the point where we allow ourselves only a discounted version of life's joys. Or we may deny ourselves certain kinds of intimacies and pleasures altogether while allowing ourselves unlimited enjoyment of others.

We may find that we permit ourselves only those kinds of intimacy and pleasure we saw our parents allow themselves. Our impression of our parents' level of happiness represents a kind of a ceiling on the level of happiness in our own lives. It is only by absolving ourselves of irrational, unconscious guilt and by freeing ourselves of our grim beliefs that we can lift that ceiling.

10

Family Secrets

Adult Children of Alcoholics and Other Dysfunctional Parents

━━━━━━━━

"This is what makes me crazy in this family, Dad. I don't care that you hit us. I really don't. That's over and there's nothing any of us can do about it. But I can't stand it when I state a simple fact about this family's history, and I'm told by you or Mom that it didn't happen."

— PAT CONROY,
The Prince of Tides

Few of us make it through childhood without experiencing some trauma. Many of us have had to endure frightening or upsetting incidents as children. But trauma itself does not make a family dysfunctional. In what we are calling the dysfunctional family, there are severe and often repetitive traumas, combined with *a prohibition against talking about the feelings and beliefs that those traumas trigger.*

Parents may become dysfunctional when their parenting is impaired by alcoholism, chemical dependency, sexual addiction, compulsive gambling or eating, criminal behavior, severe physical or mental illness, or other serious impairments. But whether or not these factors are present, if there is physical, emotional, or sexual abuse of a child, or if a child is severely neglected or is not provided with the nurturing and understanding she needs to grow up psychologically healthy, then one or both parents must be considered dysfunctional.

Children have a remarkable ability to undergo hardship and to recover from early trauma — *provided that they are allowed to talk about the traumatic experiences with helpful parents or parental figures.* But in the dysfunctional family, the imaginary crime of disloyalty is considered the worst betrayal: Dad's alcoholism or physical abuse, Mom's mental illness or sexual infidelity, is treated as if it did not exist or at least cannot be talked about. The underlying assumption is that if the truth were to come out, the reputation of the family would be compromised. Family appearances are placed above the needs of its members.

Children of a dysfunctional family do not, at the time, usually realize that their family is dysfunctional. Children assume that the way things are in their family is the way things should be. It is often only years later, as adults, when they are trying to come to terms with their own confusing psychological problems, that the children of dysfunctional families come face to face with the notion that one or both of their parents may have been moderately or severely dysfunctional.

The Adult Children of Alcoholics Movement

The adult child of an alcoholic is a person who has grown up with a parent or primary caretaker whose dysfunctional pattern involved the abuse of alcohol. The Adult Children of Alcoholics movement, or ACA, is the largest and most influential of a growing number of support groups.[1] For more information, see Appendix III, "Finding or Starting a Self-Help Group."

If one or both of your parents were heavy drinkers or were addicted to alcohol, you will benefit from sharing the insights developed within this movement.[2] But even if alcohol was not a specific problem, you will benefit from learning about these insights because all dysfunctional families have many elements in common.

Links Between Adult Children of Alcoholics Theory and Control Mastery Theory

The concepts of imaginary crimes, unconscious guilt, and grim, unconscious beliefs can be extremely helpful to the adult children of any dysfunctional family. They dovetail nicely with the concepts of the Adult Children of Alcoholics movement and can offer a new but highly compatible vantage point from which adult children of alcoholics can view their problems.[3]

Although Control Mastery and the Adult Children of Alcoholics movement have developed independently, there are a number of striking parallels. The most basic point of agreement is the notion that *the traumatic experiences of childhood give rise to powerful irrational beliefs that cause our most distressing psychological problems.*[4]

Unfortunately, some therapists have dealt with their clients' memories of childhood trauma by considering them either imaginary or unimportant. Both the Children of Alcoholics movement and Control Mastery consider childhood trauma the basis for most psychological problems. But it is difficult to recover from childhood traumas if everyone insists that they never happened. When family members, professionals, and society at large deny or downplay the existence or severity of our traumatic experiences, it becomes even more difficult for us to change the beliefs that arose from them.

Other important areas of agreement between Control Mastery and Adult Children of Alcoholics theory include the following:

• Adult children of alcoholics — and of other dysfunctional families — often feel irrationally responsible for their parents' problems. They thus suffer from guilt over many imaginary crimes.

• They frequently suffer from guilt over the imaginary crime of outdoing, as the result of having a better life than a profoundly unhappy parent.

• They frequently suffer from guilt over the imaginary crime of abandonment, leaving a profoundly unhappy parent behind.

• When they choose to break away from their parents' dysfunctional patterns, they are often plagued by guilt for the imaginary crime of disloyalty.

• Adult children of dysfunctional families frequently suffer from guilt over the imaginary crime of burdening. Since both the impaired parent and the nonimpaired spouse are frequently overwhelmed by the enormous problems the dysfunction creates, these children are likely to feel that the additional stress of parenting causes an intolerable burden on their parents.

• They frequently suffer from guilt over the crime of basic badness. Physical, emotional, and sexual abuse are more common in chemically dysfunctional families. And the victims are likely to conclude that they are unlovable people.

Are You the Adult Child
of a Dysfunctional Parent?

Because the children of dysfunctional parents will almost always feel unconsciously responsible for their parents' problems, be they alcohol, violence, or physical or psychological illness, they may inflict a bewildering variety of self-punishments upon themselves: They may torture themselves with chronic depression, anxiety, or guilt. They may remain overinvolved in family difficulties. They may themselves become alcoholic or chemically dependent, or may form primary relationships with partners who are addicted. They may engage in a variety of other self-defeating behaviors.

Identifying yourself as the adult child of a dysfunctional family can be a painful step to take. It involves the recognition that one or both of your parents were so impaired that, as a child, you were exposed to damaging, traumatic experiences in a situation in which you not only could not protect yourself, but did not even feel free to question your parents' behavior. Just as most dysfunctional parents find it difficult to face the fact that they have a serious problem, their children find it very difficult to admit they grew up in a partly or totally dysfunctional family.

But facing the fact that one or both of your parents may have been partly or totally dysfunctional can be the first phase in recovering from the damaging effects of your childhood. It can help you understand the sense of being different, frightened, or undeserving that may have plagued you all your life. Facing these difficult facts can be the beginning of a long process by which you can free yourself to have a full and satisfying life.

Adult Children of Alcoholics: Common Characteristics

Although every adult child of an alcoholic is unique, many share the feelings and behavior patterns in the following list.[5] Virtually all of these characteristics are also common in adult children of other types of dysfunctional families:

- I have an exaggerated sense of responsibility.
- I have difficulty beginning and maintaining healthy, intimate relationships.
- I have an excessive need to control others.
- I have an excessive need to control myself.
- I sometimes feel isolated, lonely, and deeply sad.
- I have a great wish for closeness but I also fear it.
- I have low self-esteem.
- If people really knew me they wouldn't like me.
- I try very hard never to disappoint other people.
- I deny or suppress deep feelings.
- I am particularly afraid of anger in myself and others.
- I have difficulty asking for what I want and standing up for my own needs.
- I am uncomfortable around alcohol.
- I have had trouble with addictive behavior (alcohol or other drugs, food, shopping, working, etc.).
- I tend to see things in black-and-white, all-or-nothing, terms.
- I frequently overreact to personal criticism.

This list includes such a wide variety of common human problems that almost every reader will identify with some of it. However, children of alcoholics — and the children of other dysfunctional families — often find that *many* of these items are serious concerns. If you can claim a substantial number of them yourself, there may be important ways in which your family was dysfunctional.

It is also possible that your family suffered from an alcohol-related dysfunction even though neither of your parents was obviously an alcoholic. One of your parents could have been a secret or recovered alcoholic. In some families, dysfunctional alcoholic-like behavior patterns were passed down from an alcoholic *grandparent,* even though neither of the parents abused alcohol. In addition to the direct effects of alcohol, it is the dysfunctional family's patterns of relating — particularly the rigidity and denial — that are so destructive to the family members involved, especially the children.

The Varieties of Alcoholic Families

There are a great many types of alcoholic families, and a variety of patterns of other types of dysfunctional families as well. Each may injure a child in a different way, but they are all harmful:

- Alcoholism may cause repeated job loss and the resulting loss of income.
- An alcoholic parent may function well (or at least adequately) on the job and confine his dysfunctional behavior to the family circle. Indeed, many alcoholic parents are able to pursue successful and prestigious careers, for example, as judges, generals, or the heads of large corporations.
- Either the father or the mother may be the alcoholic. Or *both* parents may abuse alcohol.
- The alcoholism may have been there from the beginning or may have slowly developed over the years.
- The alcoholic may still be drinking heavily.
- The alcoholic may not have had a drink for many years.

Because of these tremendous differences, the effects of growing up in an alcoholic family may vary greatly. Just because you are the child of an alcoholic parent does not necessarily mean that you have all the problems that typify children of alcoholics. *At the same time, don't fall into the trap of believing that the alcoholism in your family was so mild that you were unaffected by it.* That belief may simply represent the massive denial of the alcoholic family carried over into your own thinking.

Having an alcoholic parent is inevitably traumatic. If one or both of your parents had a serious drinking problem, understanding how that trauma affected you is a necessary step in the process of solving your own psychological problems.

Case Study: The Clark Family

Pat Clark, a district sales manager for a large Florida real estate firm, was a friendly man with a ready supply of good jokes. He was popular and successful at work and was a favorite buddy of most of the men in his neighborhood.

But Pat was also a seriously troubled alcoholic. Over the past few years, his drinking had become so compulsive that it had begun to affect his health. His doctor finally warned him that his liver already showed early signs of alcoholic cirrhosis. As his drinking increased, Pat's home life began to deteriorate. Within the past few years, Pat's wife, Joan, had seen him change from a man who *liked* a drink now and then to a man who constantly *needed* a drink.

Luckily for Pat, his old boss, who had never confronted him about his drinking, retired. The new office manager, Steve, was himself a recovering alcoholic. He told Pat that if he did not stop drinking he would be fired. He encouraged Pat to join

Alcoholics Anonymous and to make a commitment to abstinence. Pat's life had become so disorganized and confusing that he could no longer deny he was an alcoholic. He agreed to give Alcoholics Anonymous a try.

Pat was extremely nervous as he accompanied Steve to his first Alcoholics Anonymous meeting. But once he arrived, he felt surprisingly comfortable there. The others at the meeting were simply men and women whose situations were very similar to his own. Pat had always thought of alcoholics as hopeless derelicts. Now, looking around the table, he realized that the derelicts were the ones who lacked the courage to admit their problem and to seek help.

Joan Clark was a devoted wife and mother who, in addition to caring for her four children, kept the house spotless, headed the local PTA, and served as den mother for her son John and a dozen other Cub Scouts. She was a capable, perfectionistic woman who gave up her job as head nurse at the local hospital when Mary, her oldest daughter, was born. Joan had always been cheerful and energetic, but as Pat's behavior began to deteriorate, the strain began to show.

It was Joan who routinely called in to tell Pat's boss he was too ill to come to work when he was actually suffering from a gigantic hangover. She helped him avoid the confrontation that might have led him to an alcoholism treatment program. She was the one who kept the children quiet, knowing that if Pat was awakened with a hangover, there would be hell to pay. Joan had given up many of her own needs in order to protect Pat from the consequences of his behavior. She had had good training for this role: she was herself the adult child of an alcoholic. Her father drank himself to death when she was nineteen years old.[6]

Joan exhibited many of the characteristics of the codependent spouse. Although she did not abuse alcohol herself, she was just as preoccupied with drinking as her husband. She watched him anxiously at social events, dropping desperate hints not to drink too much. She rode in terror as he drove home drunk, afraid to say anything lest he become angry and drive even more erratically. She tried to avoid arguments about Pat's drinking, but as time went on, it became harder and harder for her to avoid a confrontation.

When Pat finally quit drinking Joan found the transition every bit as difficult as he did. As a child she had watched her mother take complete control over all the activities in her alcoholic family. She had felt very comfortable doing likewise, and became quite depressed when Pat started to insist on being involved in decisions about the children and the household. She unconsciously feared that things might fall apart if she relinquished her tight rein. Joan also experienced both disloyalty and outdoing guilt each time she did dare to relax and share control with her newly sober and responsible husband. As part of her own transition, Joan entered individual therapy and also joined a support group for people with alcoholic parents.

The Codependent Spouse

Codependent behavior was first described by researchers and clinicians who noticed that the spouses and other close family members of alcoholics typically developed a recognizable behavior pattern to cope with their alcoholic family member.[7] Paradoxically, the codependent's attempts to rescue the alcoholic can actually serve to put off the day of reckoning when he must deal with his drinking. In addition, this codependent behavior pattern has a destructive effect on the life of the codependent herself.

The codependent syndrome often continues whether or not the chemically dependent person stops using alcohol. Thus, in recent years, alcohol treatment programs have begun to include the nonalcoholic spouse and other close family members in the alcoholic's treatment plan.

Alcoholics Anonymous recognized this many years ago. As a result, they established Al-Anon, an organization that offers support groups for the family members of alcoholics. Most drug and alcohol treatment programs now offer family therapy and groups for codependents, as well as referrals to Al-Anon.

Characteristic Problems
of the Dysfunctional Family

The Clark family illustrates some characteristic problems of many dysfunctional families:

DENIAL

Perhaps the most harmful characteristic of the dysfunctional family is massive denial. Pat and Joan's actions often implied that there was no problem whatsoever. This was very confusing to their children, who sensed that something was wrong, but were repeatedly told otherwise. In a situation like this, a child soon comes to feel that *she* is the one with the problem. *Something* is obviously wrong because the child feels so sad, scared, worried, and angry. Since the parents insist that nothing is wrong with either of *them*, it must be the child who has a problem.

EXAGGERATED RESPONSIBILITY

When the parents of a dysfunctional family repeatedly deny that a problem exists, the child may assume that anything that goes wrong is his fault. In some cases, parents give this message directly: "Before you came along, your Mom and I were very happy" or "If it weren't for you, your father wouldn't drink." The children of dysfunctional families frequently end up with the unconscious belief that they are bad, selfish, unworthy people, who are responsible for the pain and disappointment of everyone around them.

OVERSENSITIVITY TO CRITICISM

If you are the child of a dysfunctional family, you may find it very difficult to deal with any kind of criticism, direct or implied. Since you already unconsciously feel so guilty and responsible, you may react to criticism with extreme defensiveness — to acknowledge *any* imperfection would make you feel intolerably guilty. This defense can be intensified if you identify with a parent who couldn't tolerate even the most mild-mannered reproach. In order to avoid criticism, the child may strive — at least in some ways — to be so perfect that no one will ever have occasion to criticize. As a result of these perfectionistic tendencies, the children of dysfunctional families often make excellent employees.

MOOD SWINGS

Many chemically dependent and mentally ill parents are subject to extreme mood swings. Take Pat's behavior on Saturday mornings: He typically awoke late, depressed and hung over. After a few Bloody Marys he became amiable and affectionate and might go out and play basketball with the boys or work in the yard. Later on, if he had a few too many, he might become angry and authoritarian. His children never knew what to expect. The need to cope with these abrupt shifts makes the children of dysfunctional parents extremely vigilant and sensitive to the moods of others — so much so that they frequently become extremely adept at reading other people. They may also learn to ignore their own needs — so much so that they may lose touch with what it is they really want.

UNDEPENDABILITY

The children of many dysfunctional parents grow up believing that other people simply cannot be relied upon emotionally. At times Pat was a model parent. He attended all of his son's basketball games the year Evan's team won the championship — all except the final game, when he was passed out drunk at home. Evan told his friends that his Dad had a terrible case of the flu, but he was heartbroken. It can be very difficult for children like Evan to trust their partners — or potential partners — to maintain a reasonable emotional consistency. As a consequence they may seek to avoid any kind of emotional dependence — or, like Joan Clark, they may attempt to stay in total control of their relationships at all times, making it difficult or impossible for them to develop a mutually supportive, mutually respectful relationship.

INABILITY TO EMPATHIZE

In many cases, a dysfunctional parent's ability to understand fully and empathize with her children is impaired. The child may then grow up feeling that even though her material needs were met, the parent was frequently distant or emotionally out to lunch. The child may come to believe that she is unlovable, not worth another person's close attention. She may also conclude that others are not compassionate and will not take the effort to understand or to provide for her needs. Both of these beliefs can make it difficult for the child to develop her own successful intimate relationships.

GUILT TOWARD THE NONDYSFUNCTIONAL PARENT

The spouse of a dysfunctional partner is often so overwhelmed and overburdened that a child can easily get the feeling that her own demands are simply too much. Thus the adult children of many dysfunctional families suffer from the imaginary crime of burdening the nonimpaired spouse. Such children may feel especially guilty of the imaginary crime of abandonment when they leave home. To leave Dad alone with Mom, who is seriously mentally ill, or to leave Mom alone with Dad, who is an alcoholic, can seem terribly cruel.

INCREASED LIKELIHOOD OF ABUSE

Dysfunctional parents are much more likely than other parents to abuse their children. One study indicates that daughters of alcoholics were twice as likely to become incest victims as girls in nonalcoholic families.[8] Mothers in an alcoholic home were four times more likely to be violent, and fathers were more than ten times more likely to be violent than their counterparts in nonalcoholic families.[9]

Roles in the Dysfunctional Family

Because of the uncertainty and chaos within most seriously impaired families, most children of dysfunctional parents adopt rigid roles. In the Clark family, Joan, the mother, acted out the role of the codependent spouse, the long-suffering saint. Mary, the oldest daughter, was the family hero, the perfect little child who would grow up to be so successful that the whole family would be proud. Her sister, Evelyn, was the spaced-out, lost one. Mary's older brother, John, played the family clown. Her younger brother, Evan, was the black sheep.

In healthy families, such role assignments are flexible and are not usually taken terribly seriously. They can even help the child develop a sense of his own unique and valuable identity. But in many dysfunctional families, these roles are rigid and constricting and may prevent the child from realizing his full potential.

Many children of alcoholics, like most of the children in the Clark family, might easily have been taken for model children. Contrary to what one might expect, these are not the kids who typically come to the attention of school, medical, or legal authorities.[10] They were aware that the family placed a premium on looking good. They understood that to look bad was to commit the crime of disloyalty. Many children of dysfunctional families, like Mary and John, are academic stars. But inside they are frightened, confused, burdened, and lonely. They are thus at special risk of developing serious psychological difficulties as adults.

THE FAMILY HERO

Mary Clark is a good example of a family hero. She reacted to the chaos caused by her father's drinking by turning herself into a responsible little adult at an early age. It is usually an older child who adopts the hero role. Mary did everything she could to ease her mother's burden — both out of concern for her mom and with the recognition that while Pat was drinking, Joan was the only dependable adult in the family.

As in Mary's case, the family hero may identify with and imitate the long-suffering nonaddicted spouse in order to avoid the crimes of abandonment, disloyalty, and outdoing. By trying desperately to be the perfect child — just as Joan tried desperately to be the perfect wife and mother — Mary developed a number of her mother's dysfunctional patterns, including constant anxiety and a tendency to ignore her own needs. The hero-child will often develop competency far beyond her years. A nine-year-old girl may prepare dinner for the whole family or supervise her younger siblings in cleaning the house. Such family heroes, superboys and supergirls, are often a source of great pride to their parents. And their extreme competence and reliability may serve them well in later life.

But the hero-child may never experience a true childhood. He can take care of others, but he cannot allow anyone to take care of him. Because he was forced to grow up so quickly, he may have real difficulties being spontaneous and having fun as an adult.[11]

THE FAMILY BLACK SHEEP

The black sheep serves as the family scapegoat. By getting in trouble, he diverts attention from the central problems in the family: the father's drinking, his mother's mental illness, or the parents' painful marriage. In addition, he may repeat the impaired or addicted parent's behavior. This child unconsciously avoids outdoing the impaired parent.

This child may be angry or antisocial. He or she may do poorly in school or even engage in criminal behavior. Children of dysfunctional families — especially the children of alcoholics — tend to be at increased risk of chemical dependency. But the black sheep may be at the highest risk of all.

THE FAMILY LOST ONE

The lost one is the invisible child. She deals with the pain and chaos in the family by withdrawing into herself. She is quiet and well behaved and does moderately well in school — but not so well as to attract attention. The motto of the lost one is, "To get along, go along." The lost one will avoid all strong opinions and all intense connections with others.

The lost one is protecting herself from the crime of burdening. While the hero reacts to the strain in the family by trying to help, the lost one tries to ease strain in the family by making no demands and staying out of the way.

THE FAMILY CLOWN

Like the black sheep, the clown tries to relieve the tension in the family by drawing attention away from the dysfunctional parents and directing it toward himself. He does it by joking, laughing, doing outlandish things, and by generally making a fool of himself. He is attempting to avoid the crime of burdening and disloyalty by cheering everyone up and diverting everyone's attention away from the impaired parent.

As an adult, the family clown may have trouble taking himself seriously, being successful, or focusing his attention. In many cases the clown will suffer from intense anxiety and may resort to tranquilizers or alcohol to calm himself down.

THE FAMILY PLACATER

The placater is extremely sensitive to the feelings of others. She makes it her job to keep things peaceful and to smooth over open conflicts. She suffers from the grim, unconscious belief that it is her responsibility to avoid friction or problems between family members. And she is so good at it that her irrational belief is often confirmed.

Like the hero, the placater gets lots of positive reinforcement from parents, teachers, and other authority figures for being so caring and so unselfish. As an adult, she can never rest until everyone else is taken care of. And she suffers from a tremendous need for approval. She may also have great trouble getting her own needs met, since she always chooses to put off caring for herself to take care of others.

The child of a dysfunctional family may combine two or more roles, for example, being both the hero and the clown. A child may also switch roles. Such a role change may develop gradually over time or it may occur abruptly when there is a change in family composition. When the family hero leaves for college, the black sheep may suddenly take on the hero role and start doing well. When a black sheep leaves the family, the placater may begin using drugs and getting into trouble.[12]

It Is Not Normal to Grow Up with a Dysfunctional Parent

In treatment, children of dysfunctional families will often insist that their family wasn't so bad, that everybody's family has some negative patterns. By admitting how bad things really were, they risk committing the imaginary crime of disloyalty. And they also risk having to face a variety of painful memories.

One of the most important contributions of the Adult Children of Alcoholics movement is its insistence that it is *not normal* to grow up in a dysfunctional family. As Claudia Black writes, "If this is not understood, children of alcoholics grow up believing that the unpredictable, chaotic, and destructive family system is the normal state of affairs." [13]

Family Secrets

In many dysfunctional families, the key problem — alcoholism, drug addiction, incest, mental illness, adultery, divorce — is considered a terrible secret, a source of shame. Family members are supposed to pretend that the problem does not exist. The fact that *Dad gets drunk every night, Mom is mentally ill, Dad is having an affair, Mom and Dad despise each other, Brother killed himself,* or *Dad had sex with Sis* is known or suspected but rarely acknowledged. Children with such family secrets grow up feeling that they are somehow different. Many of us who were the children of dysfunctional parents grew up with an intense sense of shame and confusion.

The denial in some of these families is so strong that many people begin to realize that they themselves are the adult children of dysfunctional parents only through more objective outsiders — by reading about such families, seeing a therapist, or attending a support or therapy group. Discussing their secrets openly in an accepting, supportive group made up of children of other dysfunctional families has given many the sense of being understood for the first time in their lives.

By sharing our feelings with others who have had similar experiences, we can help relieve the oppressive sense of loneliness that almost inevitably afflicts those of us who grew up with such secrets. Just to know that many of the things we have felt and believed are a natural consequence of our family situation — and that millions of others have similar feelings — can be tremendously liberating. Through this sharing process we can begin to loosen our deep conviction that we were to blame for our families' problems.

Although being in a group composed of other adult children of dysfunctional families is a particularly powerful experience, even reading books in the appropriate area — children of alcoholics, incest survivors, abuse survivors, children of divorce — can be enormously helpful. For specific suggestions, see Appendix II, "Recommended Reading."

Adult Survivors of Child Sexual Abuse

Perhaps the most "shameful" family secret of all is child sexual abuse. If the secret of alcoholism comes out there may be embarrassment for the family and at worst, job loss. If sexual abuse comes out there is the possibility of incarceration for the offender, taunts and humiliation for the victim, and even the permanent breakup of the family. Because of this danger, the abused child may be pressured not to tell what really happened. She may even be told that she merely imagined the traumatic episodes.

Many children who were sexually abused have repressed the experience so deeply that they have become totally unaware of it. It may be helpful to ask yourself the following questions. When you were a young child or teenager, were you: [14]

- Touched in sexual areas? Fondled, kissed, bathed, or held in a way that made you uncomfortable?
- Made to pose for sexual or seductive photographs or forced to listen to sexual talk?
- Made to look at sexual organs or pornographic materials?
- Made to perform sexual acts?

- Made to listen to or read graphic descriptions of terrible sexual experiences (gang rape, etc.) in the guise of helping avoid them?
- Raped, penetrated, forced to masturbate, or to engage in oral sex?
- Forced or seduced into any other sexually oriented activity by a parent, caretaker, or older or stronger sibling?

Even if you have no specific memories but just the vague sense that something abusive happened to you as a child, there is a significant chance that it did. It is not uncommon for survivors of child sexual abuse to suddenly remember previously forgotten incidents of molestation or sexual abuse only after months or years of therapy.

For many victims, a parent's sexual abuse has become their major imaginary crime. They feel that they caused it, that they should have stopped it, or that they somehow deserved it. This is true even when the experiences were horrifying and repulsive, but it is particularly true if the victim experienced sexual pleasure. It is easy for a child to assume that because she found some aspects of a molestation pleasurable, this makes her responsible for its occurrence. If children are not given the opportunity to talk openly about these experiences, they will frequently assume responsibility. Even worse, in many abusive families they may be explicitly told that they initiated or deserved whatever happened.

Sexual abuse gives rise to a variety of problems: low self-esteem, anxiety, depression, sexual difficulties, and difficulty in trusting others. Even seemingly minor and isolated incidents of sexual abuse can be profoundly traumatic for the young victim. As Ellen Bass and Laura Davis, authors of a guide for sexually abused women, write, "A father can slip his fingers into his daughter's underpants in thirty seconds. After that the world is not the same." [15]

Other Dysfunctional Family Patterns

Physical abuse is only beginning to be recognized as serious and widespread. In fact, there is a deep conviction in some families that being beaten is beneficial for children (and wives). "Spare the rod and spoil the child" implies that we are derelict in our duty if we do not beat our kids.

The children of parents with major mental illnesses such as chronic depression, manic-depressive disorder, and psychosis grow up in a terrifying, unpredictable environment. They realize that their parent is out of control and they feel very endangered. They are also likely to assume that it was something they did — or did not do — that made their parent crazy. If a mentally ill parent requires hospitalization, the child may feel that he caused these traumatizing separations.

The Importance of Friends, Family Members, and Support Groups

Control Mastery Theory and the leaders of the adult children of dysfunctional parents movement agree that even under the best, most therapeutic circumstances, changing our irrational, unconscious beliefs is a gradual process. But even though these patterns cannot be changed quickly or easily, they *can* be changed.

Don't be discouraged if you can't work through these problems in a week or a month, or a year. And don't hesitate to reach out for help. It is often a part of the dysfunctional families syndrome to feel that you should be able to do it all yourself and should not depend on anyone else.

If you find that certain sections of this book seem to speak directly to you, ask a friend or family member to read the sections you indicate and to discuss them with you. When an opportunity arises, share the experiences and insights you have had as a result of your reading — as well as those you have developed in discussions, or from your own thinking. You may find that several people close to you are dealing with very similar issues.

Most experts recommend working on your own psychological material through a combination of techniques: reading and thinking, discussions with family and friends, participation in one or more formal support or therapy groups, and perhaps individual therapy. A group, whether it is a self-help group or one led by a psychotherapist, can be tremendously helpful in showing us that we are not alone. Individual therapy allows us to focus more intensely on our own problems.

The best approach may vary from person to person and from community to community. Some people make remarkable strides working on their own. Others work intensively with a spouse, friend, or family member. Many make their most important breakthroughs in a group or in individual therapy.

Ending the Conspiracy of Silence

Most adult children of dysfunctional families were victims of a conspiracy of silence by parents, relatives, schools, and society at large. The fact that one or both parents suffered from a serious addiction or psychological problem or that one or more of the children were repeatedly abused was never spoken about either inside or outside of the family.

The conspiracy of silence has several effects:

• It allows the impaired parent to continue his negative pattern without confronting his problem.

• It contributes to the child's sense that her feelings of sadness, anger, and fear were unwarranted.
• It makes many children of dysfunctional families feel isolated and crazy.
• It makes children of dysfunctional families feel that all the bad things that happened were their own fault.

An important message from the Adult Children of Alcoholics movement to all of us — children of alcoholics and nonalcoholics alike — is that we must all stop participating in this conspiracy of silence.[16] The whole subject of family dysfunction is coming out of the closet. As a society we are beginning to face the truth about dysfunctional families, particularly those plagued by the problems of alcoholism, chemical dependency, and child abuse. We are beginning to acknowledge the enormity of the problem and are beginning to seek solutions.

Although this process may be intensely painful, uncovering family dysfunction is extremely helpful to those of us who are adult children of such families. But perhaps most important, this growing awareness will help us to protect and treat those children growing up in dysfunctional families now and in the future.

11

How
Psychotherapy Works

The Importance of Testing

If . . . the analyst is able to see in his patient's behavior the active reenactment of a situation passively endured in childhood, he will ask himself how the parents treated this child and whether the patient's behavior may not be telling the story of the totally dependent child, which lies so far back in the past that the patient cannot tell about it in words but only in unconscious behavior.

— ALICE MILLER

I f you were to enter individual therapy, you would probably meet with a therapist at least once a week for a period of months or years.[1] You would do most of the talking. She would listen attentively and ask questions, encouraging you to fill in certain details. From time to time she would offer interpretive comments.

It is hard to understand how, by merely listening, asking questions, and interpreting, your therapist could help you overcome distressing feelings and change behavior that may have troubled you for many years. Yet this is exactly what happens in success-ful therapy. After more than twenty years of study, Control Mastery researchers have developed some powerful insights into how this process works.

Our Unconscious Plan
for Psychological Health

Control Mastery researchers have concluded that *a client comes into psychotherapy with an unconscious plan for mastering his psychological problems already in mind.* As they studied the transcripts of hundreds of therapy sessions, they discovered that each client appears to have an unconscious plan to overcome his constricting inner convictions.[2] Among other things, our un-conscious plan sets out *to use our close relationships — with a therapist, spouse, mentor, or friend — to free ourselves from our grim, unconscious beliefs.*

This discovery that people with psychological difficulties have an unconscious plan to get better can be enormously helpful — to individuals with psychological problems, to the friends and family members of such individuals, and to therapists. It is en-couraging for us as individuals because it assures us that we have within us a strong sense of what it will take to solve our problems. Its help to friends and family lies in how they can best support a loved one. And it can be useful for therapists because it suggests that their role is to attempt to understand the client's unconscious plan and then to act in ways that support that plan. Since every plan is unique, that means that the therapist must tailor a different approach for each client.

Our unconscious plan for mastering our psychological prob-lems includes:

- The goals we would like to accomplish (for example, to become more independent or less driven).
- The unconscious beliefs (including imaginary crimes) that block the achievement of these goals.
- The insights that would help us overcome our internal obstacles (for example, that we feel irrationally guilty about being independent).
- The way we would like our friend, family member, or therapist to respond to the requests, demands, or provocations that we unconsciously plan to present to them.

A Client's True Goals

There is sometimes a great disparity between a client's professed conscious goals and his unconscious goals. Furthermore, although some clients have a remarkably clear idea of what is holding them back, others do not. Their conscious plan for therapy may be quite different than their unconscious plan. When the two are in conflict, the therapist must align her actions with the client's unconscious plan.

Vicki came into therapy asking her therapist to help her adjust to her depressing marriage with a cold, distant, uncaring husband. As her sessions continued, it became clear to her therapist that Vicki's real mission was to overcome her belief that she should stay with this man even though she realized he had no interest in trying to change. She talked about how her mother had stayed with *her* unresponsive husband and had ended up a bitter, unhappy woman. Vicki unconsciously felt that by leaving her unsuitable spouse and finding a man who was warm and nurturing, she would be committing the crime of outdoing. In the course of her therapy, Vicki was able to leave her husband and find a more satisfactory partner.

The Key to Effective Psychotherapy

After studying dozens of therapists over a period of twenty years, Control Mastery researchers discovered that regardless of their training, when therapists are working effectively they all have one thing in common: they are acting in ways that support their clients' unconscious plan to get better.

Dan was the director of a successful tennis club. He came into therapy complaining that he was having trouble with making a commitment to marry his girlfriend. Dan told his therapist, Dr. H., that he wanted help in overcoming his fear of intimacy. He explained that he had caused his girlfriend, Jeanie, a great deal of suffering because he had been unable to make up his mind. Jeanie was convinced that they would be happy together if Dan would only get over his reluctance to commit to the relationship. On several occasions Dan had told Jeanie that he wanted to call the wedding off once and for all. Each time, she had responded by becoming hysterical and threatening suicide.

Dan's father had died when he was ten. His mother never really recovered from that tragic loss. Dan showed a flair for sports at an early age, and his mother, an excellent tennis player herself, began teaching him the fundamentals of the game when he was little. She told him that from the day he was born she had expected him to be a tennis champion. She managed his tennis career and encouraged him every step of the way. As a high school senior, Dan won his first state championship.

All through his childhood and adolescence, Dan's mother made all his decisions for him — everything from what clothes to wear to what girls to date. If he ever disagreed with her advice, she seemed so hurt and upset that he soon acquiesced.

From his history and the description of his current difficulties, it seemed clear that Dan suffered from the imaginary crimes of abandonment and disloyalty. He believed that by making his own choices and acting independently he would hurt his mother or others like her (Jeanie, for example). Dr. H. inferred that Dan's unconscious plan was to have his therapist help ease his guilt about being independent. Once Dan felt less guilty, he would be able to make a free choice to leave or stay with his girlfriend.

Dr. H. decided that one way he could ease Dan's guilt was to express skepticism at his notion that he was being cruel to Jeanie by not marrying her. Sure enough, when he did so, Dan appeared greatly relieved. His therapist's attitude contradicted his grim belief that disappointing Jeanie's expectations was a cruel and dangerous thing to do. As time went on he was able to be more honest and assured in expressing his needs and feelings.

Dan repeatedly asked Dr. H. for advice. Since he suspected that Dan unconsciously hoped that instead of telling him what to do, he would encourage him to make his *own* decisions, Dr. H. would repeatedly tell Dan that *he* was the one who must make those decisions. Even though Dan complained that his therapist was refusing to be helpful, Dr. H.'s unwillingness to direct his behavior did help. By refuting his grim belief that authority figures didn't want him to be independent, it allowed Dan to become noticeably more decisive and assertive.

One of Dan's beliefs was that it was cruel and dangerous to make his own decisions or to assert his own needs, especially if a woman would be disappointed. Dan's therapist was able to help him overcome this belief both by his interpretations and his behavior.

Control Mastery research provides powerful support for the idea that most clients, like Dan, unconsciously hope the therapist will demonstrate both by *word and deed* that their grim, unconscious beliefs are untrue.

Many Therapists Would Have Done the Same

Although his therapist's understanding of Dan's unconscious plan allowed him to treat Dan successfully, many other experienced therapists, even those who have never heard of Control Mastery Theory, might also have been quite helpful to Dan. They would have recognized that they should not encourage Dan to accede to his girlfriend's suicidal threats. And many therapists make it a rule not to give advice. As long as his therapist did not agree with his girlfriend that he should be more committed, and as long as his therapist did not make his decisions for him but instead encouraged him to make his *own* choices, Dan would have made positive therapeutic strides.

If the therapist acts in accordance with the client's unconscious plan for psychological health, that client will be helped. Fortunately, many of the attitudes and behaviors that are common to most therapists are helpful to a wide variety of clients. That is why most therapists are able to help most clients get better, even though they often have very different conceptions of their role.[3]

Let's consider Dr. A., an experienced classical psychoanalyst, who has been trained to sit quietly and listen intently to her clients, delivering interpretations sparingly and only after great consideration. This attentive, restrained behavior will be a very positive experience for many of her clients. Just being listened to, respectfully and attentively hour after hour, day after day, week after week, can give a client a sense of being important and worthwhile — especially those clients who have an unconscious belief that they do not deserve respect and attention.[4]

Many experienced therapists, like experienced teachers or parents, often acquire an intuitive appreciation of the special needs of their clients and act accordingly. A therapist can be excellent, even outstanding, with no formal knowledge of the client's unconscious plan. But by incorporating the notion of the client's unconscious plan into his practice, we believe that he may become an even more effective therapist.

Unlike other schools of psychoanalysis, Control Mastery holds that there is no need for the therapist to force the client to work on his problems or to attempt to break down the client's defenses. The client will let down his defenses just as soon as he feels it is safe to do so — and not before.[5] Many clients come into therapy with their goals and aspirations thwarted by their unconscious fears of hurting others or being hurt themselves. Rather than pushing the client, the therapist must strive to understand what those dangers are and to make the situation feel safer so that the client can muster the courage to test his fears. A therapist who makes the therapy situation even *more* threatening may actually impede progress.[6] Therefore, Control Mastery holds that it is the therapist's job to create an atmosphere in which the client will feel safe.

In order to accomplish this, the therapist must understand the client's unconscious concerns. If a client was smothered by a needy and intrusive mother, the therapist may need to maintain a cool, professional distance to make that client feel safe from being taken over. But if a client's parents were cool and aloof and gave the child little attention or assistance, then the therapist may need to be warmer, more open, and more actively involved in the therapeutic discussion. No single approach is right for all clients. Control Mastery's plan concept can thus be of great help to a psychotherapist. While a therapist may intuitively adopt an approach that is of considerable help to her client, understanding the client's plan can allow her to treat that client with more consistency and precision.

Therapy as War

Early in my training, one of my professors commented that "the neurotic does not want to get better. He merely wants to become a better neurotic." This is a common view among psychotherapists, one with which Control Mastery emphatically disagrees. Such assumptions imply that the therapist must be on guard at all times to stop the client from subverting the therapy process. They also imply that therapy is war, that the therapist must be careful to protect himself from the client's efforts to subtly undermine and attack him. If the client improves, the therapist wins. But if the client does not improve, the client wins because he resists positive change and succeeds in making the therapist feel frustrated and impotent. Inherent in this antagonistic view is the idea that the client would rather make the therapist feel bad than make progress toward psychological growth.

Control Mastery assumes that all clients truly wish to get better, both consciously and unconsciously. This view is positive, but it is not based on naive optimism. Rather, it is supported by many years of rigorous research.[7]

It is a tremendous advantage for the Control Mastery therapist *not* to feel that he is at war with his client. To be sure, there are times when therapy is a painful struggle. But since the client genuinely wants to get better and the therapist truly wants this, too, both client and therapist are ultimately fighting on the same side.

Do Clients Really Want to Get Better?

It is not hard to see why some therapists might believe that some clients do not really want to get better. Clients frequently do things that frustrate their therapists. Some will ask the therapist for suggestions, then belittle or reject any advice. They will complain about their life situation but will take no steps to improve it. They will accuse the therapist of not caring enough, yet will reject any demonstration of caring. At times these clients seem to cling to their unhappiness as if it was their most treasured possession.

All of us have at one time or another tried to help a friend or family member with a psychological problem. Our attempts to help are sometimes frustrated by the seeming unwillingness of that person to let go of his problem. At one time or another, all of us have probably thought to ourselves, This person really *wants* to be miserable.

Control Mastery holds that even though it may sometimes appear that way, *nobody really wants to be miserable.* People who are trapped in such self-defeating patterns are suffering from grim beliefs that tell them it is dangerous to be happy or to do the things that would make them happy. They believe that they have committed imaginary crimes and thus do not deserve good things in life. Or they unconsciously believe that letting go of their problems would cause terrible things to happen — either to themselves or to others.

Testing and the Client's Unconscious Plan

Control Mastery Theory asserts that clients in psychotherapy often intentionally attempt to provoke their therapist. The client is testing the therapist to determine whether his (the client's) own grim, unconscious beliefs are really true. Thus, in Control Mastery Theory, the word *testing* has a very special meaning.

Dan, the tennis club owner, was testing his therapist by repeatedly asking him for advice. But he did not really want the advice he asked for — if Dr. H. had acceded to his requests by telling him what to do, it would have confirmed Dan's grim belief that he would only hurt others by making his own decisions. By refusing to offer advice, Dr. H. helped contradict Dan's predictions. In the long run, this helped Dan free himself of those unconscious beliefs.

Transference Tests

One type of test that clients offer their therapists is called a *transference test*. In a transference test the client invites or provokes the therapist to treat him in the same negative way that he was treated by his parents.[8] If the parent was critical, the client invites the therapist to be critical. If the parent was controlling, the client invites the therapist to be controlling. If the parent was sexual toward the client, the client invites the therapist to be sexual toward her. And so on. To pass these tests, the therapist must refuse these invitations.

The client does not really want to be criticized, controlled, or sexual with her therapist, even if she appears to want such treatment. What she unconsciously desires is for the therapist to demonstrate that he will not criticize her, reject her, control her, or sexually exploit her — even if given the opportunity. In this way she can overcome her unconscious beliefs that she deserves these indignities. If the therapist *does* respond by criticizing, rejecting, controlling, or sexually exploiting her, the client's grim, unconscious beliefs will be confirmed. Her symptoms may get worse and she may be damaged instead of helped by her therapy. This is one important reason why it is so harmful for therapists to have sex with clients, even those who actively attempt to seduce them.

A transference test is a client's attempt to answer three questions:

- "Are you (the therapist) going to traumatize me like my parent(s) did, *or* will I be able to have a new, more positive experience with you?"
- "Am I really a bad person, an imaginary criminal who does not deserve to be treated well?"
- "Are other people all unavailable, abusive, or undependable the way my parents were?"

Case Study: Mark

Mark was a bright and capable young college graduate who was having trouble keeping his job as a waiter. After being in therapy with Dr. L. for several months and making good progress, he began to come late, pay his bill late, and seemed unable to understand what Dr. L. was telling him.

When he was a child, Mark's parents had repeatedly told him that he was dumb and irresponsible, and he had come, unconsciously, to believe them. In addition, he unconsciously believed that his parents — and other authority figures — wanted him to remain that way, that they needed to criticize him in order to feel better about themselves.

During his first year of therapy, Dr. L. didn't understand Mark's grim beliefs. She told Mark that his irresponsible behavior represented indirect hostility toward her. Mark took this response as a criticism. He became even more anxious and depressed and began to have even more trouble at work. He had unconsciously concluded that his grim, unconscious belief was true — is therapist, like his parents, wanted him to be an irresponsible screwup so that they would always have someone to criticize. As a result, Mark continued to believe that if he acted competently, he would be committing the imaginary crime of disloyalty. Dr. L. had failed Mark's transference test.

But Mark's lack of progress caused Dr. L. to consult a supervisor, who advised her not to interpret Mark's acts as hostility, but instead to suggest that Mark was giving her an excuse to be critical of him — because Mark unconsciously believed that she, like any authority figure, would *want* to criticize him. Once Dr. L. followed this suggestion, Mark resumed his therapeutic progress. His depression lifted, and he eventually was offered a much more responsible job. Dr. L. was now passing his test by helping him learn that it wasn't really a crime to be competent and successful after all.

Passive-into-Active Tests

For many therapists, the most difficult part of their job is enduring the times when a client acts in a hostile, critical, or guilt-inducing way. Very often this kind of behavior is an example of the second type of test, a *passive-into-active* test. For this test, the client mimics his parents' behavior and treats the therapist in the same way he was treated as a child. He *actively* inflicts on the therapist — or other friend or helper — the same abusive behavior that he *passively* endured as a child. If a parent was critical of the client, the client will be critical of the therapist. If the parent accused the client of being selfish and uncaring, the client will accuse his therapist of the same things. If a parent was depressed, hopeless, and inconsolable, the client will copy this behavior. If the parent went into uncontrollable rages, the client will do likewise. If the parent blamed the client for the parent's own problems, the client will blame the therapist for his.

In posing a passive-into-active test, the client is attempting to answer the question, If I treat my therapist the same way my parent treated me, will she (the therapist) assume something is wrong with *her* as I assumed that something was wrong with *me?* To pass a passive-into-active test, the therapist must be able to endure the traumatic treatment that the client is dishing out, without being traumatized by it.

If the client is critical, the therapist must avoid being defensive or overly apologetic. If the client is rejecting, the therapist must avoid being hurt. If the client is threatening, the therapist must avoid acting frightened. If the client acts in a guilt-inducing way, the therapist must avoid feeling unduly responsible.

If the therapist is able to pass a passive-into-active test, the client will gain strength from the therapist's example. The client will then unconsciously think to himself, If my therapist doesn't feel responsible for the bad treatment I give her, maybe *I* don't have to feel responsible for the bad treatment *I* received as a child.

So once a therapist — or a friend or family member — passes a passive-into-active test, the client is able to use her as a kind of role model — a role model who does *not* suffer from irrational self-blame. Observing the therapist successfully passing a passive-into-active test helps weaken the grip of the client's grim, unconscious beliefs, which can help him absolve himself of his imaginary crimes.

Case Study: Edwina

Edwina was a thirty-nine-year-old insurance adjuster. She came into therapy complaining of depression, disliking her job, her inability to maintain friendships with either sex, and feeling deep discouragement about life.

When her therapist, Dr. D., suggested she look for another job, Edwina replied that she was just too depressed to do so. She would complain for hours on end, imploring Dr. D. to help. But whenever he offered a suggestion or interpretation, she would respond incredulously as if to say, "For *this* I'm paying seventy-five dollars an hour?" She frequently accused him of not caring about her and of being interested only in making money. Dr. D. began to dread seeing her.

Edwina's father was a workaholic dress manufacturer who was rarely home while she was growing up. When Edwina was eleven, her father left her mother for a much more pleasant woman. Edwina's mother was an unhappy, demanding, sarcastic woman who seemed to expect her daughter to make up for her husband's absence. Each day when Edwina would come home, her mother would greet her eagerly at the door but would soon act disappointed, as if Edwina wasn't sharing enough or being entertaining enough, and would rapidly slip back into her normal, chronically depressed mood. Edwina believed that she was a disappointment to her mother and was therefore responsible for all her mother's unhappiness.

In spite of the difficulty of working with Edwina, her therapist did not allow her false accusations, guilt-slinging, sarcasm, and criticism to undermine his sense of competence and integrity. Nor did he take responsibility for the fact that Edwina was unhappy. He realized that Edwina was treating him very much as she had been treated as a child. In fact, because of the way she treated him, Dr. D. was able to form a surprisingly accurate picture of Edwina's childhood long before Edwina was able to talk about it.

Dr. D. passed Edwina's test. As a result, Edwina began to feel less guilty of the crimes of disloyalty and abandonment toward her mother. Whereas at first she told her therapist that her mother was "the best mother a girl could have," as therapy went on, she began to remember how painful their relationship had actually been — the way her mother had always been disappointed in her, how sarcastic she had been, the unfair accusations she had made, and all the ways in which she had rejected and belittled her.

Although Edwina's therapy was long and difficult — both for Edwina and for Dr. D. — over time she came to understand that she was not really responsible for her mother's unhappiness. As a result she became noticeably less depressed, she was able to stop sabotaging her friendships, and she eventually found a job she enjoyed.

Because Dr. D. recognized Edwina's seemingly abusive behavior as a passive-into-active test, he was able to understand how she needed him to react. And it was in large part because Edwina gradually learned about her need to treat others as she had been treated, that she became aware of situations in which she was repeating her mother's negative behavior patterns and eventually learned to control them.

A Two-Edged Sword

For the therapist passive-into-active tests can be a two-edged sword. On the one hand, because they expose the therapist to the same traumatic behavior that the client received as a child, they can be a difficult and painful experience. This is especially true if the client's parents were particularly angry, critical, guilt-inducing, or cruel.

On the other hand, a passive-into-active test can give a therapist tremendous insight into her client. This insight consists not only of an intellectual understanding of what it was like for the client growing up, but a gut level experience of how it must have felt. As Alice Miller writes, "the manner in which the client treats the analyst offers clues to the way the parents treated him as a child — contemptuously, derisively, disapprovingly, seductively, or by making him feel guilty, ashamed, or frightened." [9] These clues can allow the therapist to develop for herself a much fuller picture of what the client's parent was really like. They are particularly valuable when the client has few conscious memories of his childhood, or if the client has idealized her parents and can remember only the good times.

A Guidepost for Therapists

Much of the time, the response to a passed or failed test is immediate. If the therapist has successfully passed the test, the client will immediately become less anxious, will think more clearly, will feel more expansive and more capable, and will be more likely to remember relevant childhood material. [10] But if the therapist *fails* the test, the client will become more anxious, will think less clearly, will feel less capable, will be less likely to remember relevant childhood material, and will feel more despairing about the future.

So the therapist, by carefully observing the client's response, can usually tell whether he has passed a test. If he fails, he can change his response the next time the test is offered. Many tests are offered repeatedly in different forms as the client works to disprove his grim beliefs. Even if the therapist fails a test the first time, he will usually get another chance.

All therapists must make difficult decisions in the course of therapy: whether to be silent, ask a question, offer advice, or accede to a client's requests. The therapist who is aware of the testing process is able, by taking careful note of her client's reactions, to obtain helpful feedback that allows her to continue when she is doing the right thing and to change her tactics when she is not.

Insight and Interpretation

Clients in therapy make progress in two ways: One is by testing. The other is by attaining insight into their own psychology.

If a therapist passes a client's tests, even inadvertently, the client will get better. His grim, unconscious beliefs will be challenged and at least partially disproved. This can occur with no conscious understanding on the part of the client. In fact, Control Mastery asserts that progress can occur even if *both the client and the therapist are completely in the dark as to what is really going on*. But this does not mean that insight is irrelevant.

Insight is extremely helpful to us all, particularly in our ability to carry on our own self-directed therapeutic work without therapy, outside of therapy, or after we have completed therapy. It gives us a structure of ideas to refer to when we feel confused, out of control, or overwhelmed. Even though it is sometimes possible for us to resolve major psychological problems without understanding their root causes, it is almost always easier if we do have an understanding of them. Understanding our grim beliefs can thus provide us with a powerful tool for managing our psychological difficulties.

Interpretations That Harm

Interpretations that are consistent with a client's unconscious plan can be of great help to the client. But interpretations that run counter to a client's plan may actually be *harmful*.[11] These interpretations can stop or reverse progress by reinforcing our destructive, unconscious beliefs.

In addition, some interpretations are virtually never helpful and often harmful to clients. This is because they tend to reinforce common grim beliefs, and thus will almost always run counter to a client's plan:

• Suppose a client reports that she remembers being sexually molested as a child. Her therapist responds by telling her that in all likelihood, the molestation didn't really happen, that she only *wished* that it had happened. The therapist has failed to validate an important part of the client's own experience. Furthermore, a client who already feels irrationally responsible is made to feel even more responsible. The same thing occurs when a client is told that it doesn't really matter whether a traumatic event really happened, that the only thing that matters is how the client feels about it. When a painful childhood memory is not given its proper importance or is labeled a fantasy, the client is harmed.

• Suppose a client is excessively polite and restrained. Her therapist responds by telling her that she only appears cooperative and agreeable, that she is actually sitting on a huge storehouse of rage. The therapist goes on to insist that the client is actually full of murderous impulses. This interpretation may reinforce the client's irrational belief that she is a time bomb waiting to go off. People who avoid confrontation at all costs usually feel that it is terribly *dangerous* to express anger. They unconsciously fear that their anger will damage others terribly, that they will lose control and go crazy, or that they will be viciously attacked or abandoned by those they love if they show any signs of anger. It is not helpful to suggest to such clients that they are walking powder kegs. These clients need to understand that their fears are irrational or greatly exaggerated. They need to be helped to see that although anger is indeed a difficult emotion, it is possible to learn to express it in a constructive way. They need to learn that the fact that they *do* have angry feelings is not a crime.

• Suppose a client reports intense worry about a parent's health or happiness. His therapist responds by telling him that he unconsciously wants his parent to be ill or unhappy. The therapist may even tell the client that he unconsciously wants to murder his parent. While it is true that everyone harbors some anger toward their parents, when a client expresses worry about family members it is almost always real. Such clients typically have parents who are depressed, lonely, ineffectual, or who treat each other badly — in short, parents who give them good *cause* for worry. Such a client usually suffers from survivor guilt or separation guilt. He already feels that he has been cruel to his parents merely by becoming happy, successful, or independent. If he is told that he secretly wishes his parents unhappy or dead, his survivor and separation guilt may become even more intense.

• Suppose a woman client habitually expresses angry or competitive feelings toward men. Her therapist responds by telling her that she is suffering from *penis envy* — because she feels that a woman's genitalia are somehow inferior to those of a man. Not only is this inaccurate, it is almost always harmful. Such sexist interpretations imply that any competitiveness or anger a woman might feel is pathological whereas the same feelings in a man would be signs of assertiveness and healthy ambition.

• Suppose a client is severely depressed. His therapist responds by telling him that he actually enjoys making himself miserable. The therapist goes on to explain that the client enjoys being unhappy because it allows him to collapse, to make no efforts on his own behalf, and to get attention without having to put out any effort, insisting that the client derives unconscious masochistic gratification from his suffering. Control Mastery holds that people are *not* miserable because they are lazy or because of unconscious masochistic desires. People are miserable because they are blocked from being happy by their unconscious beliefs.

Testing in Everyday Life

Our efforts to disprove our grim, unconscious beliefs are not limited to psychotherapy. We may use testing in our relationships with the most significant figures in our lives — spouses, parents, teachers, bosses, coaches, and mentors. We will be particularly likely to use testing in those relationships in which we feel most secure.

In testing our spouses, friends, or bosses, we may use either transference tests or passive-into-active tests. If we use transference tests, we will behave in ways that will provoke these people to criticize, humiliate, manipulate, or reject us — just as our parents did. However, we are unconsciously hoping that they will not, because if they don't, it will help free us from irrational guilt over imaginary crimes.

If we use passive-into-active tests, we may find ourselves being critical, angry, guilt-inducing, depressed, or rejecting — or we may repeat *any other* parental behavior that made us feel responsible or guilty as children. When we use this type of testing with a boss, a colleague, a friend, or family member, we hope that our behavior will *not* make the people we are testing feel guilty or bad about themselves — as *we* did when our parent treated us in the same way. If *they* don't respond by blaming themselves, it can help us to stop blaming *ourselves* for the bad treatment we received as children.

Thus, some of our seemingly self-defeating behaviors may have two unconscious purposes:

• They can serve as a punishment for our imaginary crimes.
• They can provide us a way to test our grim beliefs.

We will sometimes unconsciously attempt to sabotage our own success, intimacy, or happiness, while at the same time unconsciously hoping that our spouse, friend, coworker, family member, or therapist will not allow us to do so.

Case Study: Joyce

Joyce, the office manager who was attracted to men who treated her badly because she had been relentlessly criticized by her father (Chapter 6) eventually developed a relationship with Orville, a man who was very loving and tolerant. Joyce had been in therapy for some time and had begun to feel much better about herself. Over a period of years, she had been going out with progressively more acceptable men. After she had been with Orville for several months and things had been going very well, she unconsciously felt safe enough to give him a number of excuses to be critical of her.

She began to act irritable and depressed. But instead of responding by being critical, as her father had, Orville would pamper her. She began to make careless mistakes, but instead of being critical, Orville would point out that her goofs were minor — which they always were — and would encourage her not to worry. Orville's respectful and compassionate behavior was the exact opposite of Joyce's treatment by her father and her earlier boyfriends.

One day when she ran out of gasoline far from the nearest service station, she telephoned Orville for help. By neglecting to stop to buy gasoline, Joyce was unconsciously attempting to provoke Orville into criticizing her. But he arrived promptly and was warm and sympathetic. Orville passed Joyce's test and helped her dispel her feelings of badness, of deserving all the put-downs she received as a child. Once Joyce realized that Orville did not intend to bark at her, she found herself sobbing uncontrollably. What a shame it was that she had had to experience all that humiliation from her father for so many years. How sad that she had wasted another dozen years running after men who were just as critical. How lucky she was to have found, at long last, a truly kind, compassionate man.

After she saw that Orville was able to pass test after test, Joyce began to feel better about herself and became much more optimistic about the future. She began to get along much better with her other friends. After some time, she found that she was no longer unconsciously driven to make the small, provocative mistakes she had used with Orville to test her conviction that she deserved to be criticized and treated badly.

At work, Joyce tested her boss in a similar way. She performed most of her duties as office manager very effectively: she maintained extremely high morale, managed complicated scheduling issues, was willing to work late when necessary. But she always left a few small but important things undone. She forgot to fill in her time sheets. She didn't complete certain forms. She continually forgot several small duties. As a result, her boss was always slightly frustrated and irritated with her. Because he recognized how valuable she was, he did not confront Joyce about these small errors. But his resentment built up nonetheless. He occasionally became unduly critical on some unrelated matter.

Orville was able to pass Joyce's test, but her boss wasn't. He would have to have been able to praise her good work at the same time as he insisted that she complete the small things she typically left undone. Her boss's snappish attitude toward her confirmed her belief that she deserved to be criticized.

In therapy, Joyce came to recognize that she was testing her boss. But she also came to realize that the fact that she provoked her boss did not mean that she was a bad person who deserved to be put down. It was only then that she was able to stop the small provocations that had kept her boss on edge. Once Joyce began to do the little things that were important to him as well as the other aspects of her job, he gave her uniformly high performance ratings and became consistently warm and supportive.

Some Tests Are Very Difficult to Pass

If we are completely convinced that our grim, unconscious beliefs are true, our tests may be virtually impossible to pass. Or we may continue to choose inappropriate people to test. If this is true, we may find it very difficult to make progress without the help of a therapist.

Control Mastery Theory views the ideal therapist as *a professional skilled in passing even the most difficult tests*. The therapy situation is structured to make it much easier for the therapist to pass tests than it might be for bosses, lovers, friends, and other family members: the therapist has no personal stake in obtaining the affection or approval of the client, making him much less vulnerable to criticism or to threats of rejection.

Case Study: Veronica and Norton

Veronica, a thirty-two-year-old city planner, and Norton, a thirty-six-year-old clerk at the municipal court, enjoyed a whirlwind romance and the first year of their marriage. Then Veronica's behavior changed. She began to treat Norton in extremely critical, nasty, and unreasonable ways.

Veronica's mother had henpecked and verbally abused her husband, an eminent physician. She was also extremely critical and controlling of her children. Veronica was repeating the same behavior she had hated in her mother.

Norton had been raised in a cool, polite family. He endured Veronica's abuse without fighting back or responding in kind. He was patient and forbearing with Veronica — in much the same way that Orville was patient with Joyce. But as time went on Norton gradually became more and more depressed and withdrawn. While Orville had passed Joyce's tests, Norton failed to pass Veronica's.

Ironically, it was at Veronica's urging that Norton went into psychotherapy. Once he began to explore his own feelings, he realized that Veronica's unjustified attacks made him angry —

but that he was forcing himself to repress his anger. His therapist supported him to stand up for himself.

When Norton began to confront Veronica and insist that she stop her controlling and critical behavior, she initially intensified her nasty behavior. She verbally attacked his therapist and insisted that Norton discontinue his therapy. Norton remained firm. He told Veronica that now that he understood what was happening, he was no longer willing to put up with her constant criticism. He told her that if she was unable to stop her undermining treatment of him within a reasonable time, he planned to divorce her.

Veronica was forced to accept the fact that she had taken on her mother's hurtful, negative behavior pattern. This insight made it easier and easier for her to cut back on her abusive behavior. As she did, Norton felt his depression begin to lift. Both became warmer and more responsive. Their relationship improved dramatically.

Veronica suffered from guilt over outdoing her mother and was spoiling her marriage in the same way that her mother had spoiled hers. Veronica had also been traumatized by her mother's overcontrolling nature and abusive verbal treatment. She was inflicting on Norton the same abusive treatment — with the unconscious hope that he would be able to stand up to her, and not be beaten down by it, as *she* had been as a child. Veronica was giving Norton a passive-into-active test. If he could pass the test, she would be less guilty for being the bad girl her mother said she was and could allow herself to deserve a good marriage.

Until he got into psychotherapy, Norton failed Veronica's test repeatedly and she continued being the bad girl. But when Norton stopped accepting her angry accusations and stood up to her, it actually helped her immensely: she was able to feel less guilty. She realized that she had been sabotaging her marriage just as her unhappy mother had sabotaged her own. Even though considerable damage had been done over the years in which Veronica's destructive behavior went unchecked, her relationship with Norton has been getting better and better and both are enjoying it more than ever before.

We would like to be able to say that most everyday testing produces positive results. Unfortunately this is not the case. Our grim, unconscious beliefs are all too frequently *confirmed* by our experiences as adults, and we end up feeling even more guilty of our imaginary crimes. We frequently choose to associate ourselves with partners or with authority figures who share many of the same difficulties our parents had. We do this partly out of family loyalty — we feel we don't deserve a happier life than our parents had. But there is also a healthy motive — we are attempting to master the trauma we experienced in childhood. We may involve ourselves with someone very similar to one of our parents, then try to get them to treat us better than our parent did. We unconsciously believe that if we can only get this new person to treat us well, it will help disprove our grim, unconscious beliefs.

Breaking Our Negative Patterns

Clients frequently come into therapy complaining that they are repeating self-destructive behavior patterns again and again. They may sabotage their success at work. They may get involved in painful and unproductive relationships. They may be troubled by irrational anxious or depressed feelings. Whatever their specific pattern, its most striking feature is the way it repeats and repeats — in spite of all their efforts to break the negative cycle.

We repeat our negative behaviors for two reasons. The first and most powerful reason is the primary focus of this book:

punishing ourselves for our imaginary crimes. But as we have seen in this chapter, we also repeat for another more positive reason, with the unconscious hope of proving that our grim beliefs are false.

In the next chapter we will describe a number of ways in which you can begin to understand your own personal unconscious plan for psychological health.

Absolving Ourselves
of Our Imaginary Crimes

Finding Our Own Way
to Psychological Health

But first there had to be a time of renewal, time to master a fresh approach to self-scrutiny. I had lost nearly thirty-seven years to the image I carried of myself. I had ambushed myself by believing, to the letter, my parents' definition of me. They had defined me early on, coined me like a work they had translated on some mysterious hieroglyph, and I had spent my life coming to terms with that specious coinage. My parents had succeeded in making me a stranger to myself. They had turned me into the exact image of what they had needed at the time.

— PAT CONROY,
The Prince of Tides

In reading through the earlier chapters of this book, you may well have had some realizations about your own life. The key elements of Control Mastery Theory — grim, unconscious beliefs, imaginary crimes, identification and compliance — may have already begun to provide some insights into your psychological patterns. For some readers, this will be enough. Others may wish to continue this process of self-exploration by completing the exercises in this final chapter.

When Control Mastery researchers study a client in therapy, they prepare a detailed written document, which outlines that client's unconscious plan for psychological growth. This document is called a *plan formulation*.[1]

You may wish to use the four steps of the plan formulation as a way of identifying your own plan for psychological health. To do so, you will examine — and, if you wish, write out — four elements of that plan: your *goals, obstructions, tests,* and *insights.*

• *Goals* — the things you would most like to accomplish in life. These can be divided into long- and short-term goals. For example, a person with a long-term goal of having a successful and satisfying executive career may have a short-term goal of learning to feel comfortable and perform well during a job interview. A person with a long-term goal of building intimacy and reducing conflict within her marriage may have a short-term goal of learning to listen to her partner in a nondefensive, non-accusing way.

• *Obstructions* — the barriers that stand in the way of achieving your goals. These are the dangers, both to yourself and others, that you unconsciously believe you will unleash if you dare to pursue your most important goals.

• *Tests* — in the Control Mastery sense, these are behaviors designed to disprove your grim, unconscious beliefs through interacting with others. If others fail your tests, you will continue to have these beliefs. But if they pass, you will gradually be able to accept the fact that your grim beliefs are false.

• *Insights* — any understandings that can help you absolve yourself of your imaginary crimes or overcome your grim, unconscious beliefs: understanding the connections between your present behavior and your experiences as a child, understanding your identifications with one or both of your parents, or understanding the ways in which you have complied with a parent's bad messages.

Once a Control Mastery therapist understands these four aspects of a client's plan, she is able to make more helpful interventions. Similarly, the more you understand about each of these four aspects of your plan, the more you will be able to make sense of your own most troublesome thoughts, feelings, and behaviors. As your understanding increases, you may find it easier and easier to avoid getting caught up in your old self-punishing, self-defeating patterns. But before we take you through the steps of completing your own plan formulation, let's see what an actual plan formulation looks like.

Larry's Unconscious Plan

Let's look back at Larry, the chemical company executive described in Chapter 2, who sabotaged his own success at work by forgetting key tasks each time he was considered for promotion. Larry unconsciously felt that by accepting a promotion himself he would be outdoing his father. Larry also unconsciously felt guilty of love theft toward his brothers. In addition, he found himself provoking unnecessary fights with his girlfriend by being overly critical and domineering. In therapy, he was saddened and surprised to discover that he was treating his girlfriend exactly as his father had treated his mother.

What were the elements of Larry's unconscious plan for psychological health?

Larry's Long-Term Goals
• To be able to have a fulfilling and satisfying work life
• To get married and have a family

Larry's Short-Term Goals
• To stop his inexplicable lapses and other self-sabotaging behavior at work
• To stop provoking senseless fights with his girlfriend

Larry's Obstructions
• Larry felt he would be guilty of disloyalty toward all the other members of his blue collar family if he became a successful executive.
• Larry felt that if he was promoted, he would be guilty of outdoing his father and brothers.
• Larry felt guilty of love theft toward his brothers because he was so obviously favored by his mother.
• Larry felt that if he allowed his relationship with his girlfriend to strengthen, he would be guilty of abandoning his mother, whose closeness to him was so essential for her well-being.
• Larry felt that by having a warm, close, conflict-free relationship with his girlfriend, when his parents' relationship was always tense and full of conflict, he would be outdoing his parents.

Larry's Tests
• Larry would sometimes talk about his successes to his father to see if his father still seemed hurt or vindictive.
• Larry would frequently talk about his successes to his friends to see if they seemed jealous or angry.
• In therapy Larry bragged about his sexual exploits and his weight lifting success to see if his therapist would be critical or jealous.

Larry's Insights
• Larry came to understand that many of his problems were based on his belief that his successes were achieved at the

expense of hurting other family members. This belief was based on a real experience — he *was* repeatedly punished, rejected, and attacked for his successes — by both his father and brothers. But even so, at this late date he would not be harming his father or his brothers by becoming successful.

• Larry gradually became aware of the connections between his lapses at work and his desire to avoid outdoing his father and his brothers.

• Larry saw that much of his self-defeating behavior — both at work and in a relationship — came as the result of acting in much the same way his father had acted. His efforts to avoid outdoing his father had led him to imitate his father's negative behavior patterns.

• Larry realized that as her favored son, he felt that he was responsible for making his mother happy. He felt that by achieving a close relationship with his girlfriend, he would be destroying the close relationship he had with his mother.

• Larry gradually came to understand that he felt that having a good relationship with his girlfriend meant outdoing his parents, who seemed so unhappy with each other.

Just the Beginning

The plan formulation exercise is not intended to produce instant results. You should not be concerned if you are not immediately able to identify every detail of your plan for psychological health. Becoming aware of previously unconscious material can be a complex, time-consuming process. Lasting insights do not come quickly or easily.

Indeed, this exercise should be considered a part of an extended process that will continue for many years. Even if your first plan formulation seems tentative or sketchy, it may prove extremely useful in giving a sense of direction and leading to further insights.

The Plan Formulation Exercise

On four blank pieces of paper, write the following headings: *Goals, Obstructions, Tests,* and *Insights.* As you read through the exercise that follows, write out a first draft of the elements of your own plan for psychological health.

GOALS

We all have similar basic life goals: A need for intimacy. A need for food. A need to care for our children. A need for financial security. A need to express ourselves in a fulfilling way.

Some life goals present us with no particular difficulty. Even though we know they will take a long time to achieve, we are quite satisfied with our ability to attain them. But most of us have certain life goals that remain elusive. Try as we might, we can't quite seem to get our act together in these areas.

For the purposes of this exercise, list *only your most troublesome or problematic life goals.* These are the goals that you sense you have some urge to sabotage.

Include both behavioral goals and feeling goals. Behavioral goals may include behaviors you might like to be able to perform (to concentrate and work hard on your law studies) and others you might like to be able to stop (overeating). There may be feelings you might like to start having (joy) and others you might like to stop (chronic anxiety).

Sample Behavioral Goals
- I want to be able to start dating appropriate partners.
- I want to be able to finish my work on time.
- I want to be able to stop screaming at my children.
- I want to be able to stop sabotaging my success at work.
- I want to be able to say no to my mother without feeling guilty.
- I want to feel free to choose and pursue a fulfilling, exciting career.
- I want to be able to be less involved with my parents.

Sample Feeling Goals
- I want to be able to feel close to my wife.
- I want to be able to withstand rejection without feeling devastated.
- I want to be able to feel confident and authoritative.
- I want to be able to feel less vulnerable and in need of help and support.
- I want to be able to enjoy sex with my partner.
- I want to be able to overcome my chronic depression.
- I want to be able to be less concerned with what my parents think.
- I want to be able to stop worrying constantly.

Divide your section on Goals into Behavioral Goals and Feeling Goals. Write down the behavioral and feeling goals that seem most important to you right now.

OBSTRUCTIONS

Your obstructions are the grim beliefs that keep you from achieving your goals.

Sample Grim Beliefs
• If I am angry, everyone will reject me.
• If things get too good, I will be punished.
• If I relax, something terrible will happen.
• If I get close to a man, he will ultimately reject me.
• If I trust a woman, I will always be betrayed.
• If I ask friends or family members for what I really want, I will be refused, punished, or will make them angry.
• If I have sex with a woman, she will end up hurt and bitter.
• If things appear to be going well, disaster probably lies just ahead.

Sample Grim Beliefs that Stem from Imaginary Crimes
• If I become a Democrat, I will be disloyal to my Republican father.
• If I don't eat dinner with my family three times a week, I will be abandoning my unhappy mother.
• If I try to get into a close relationship, I will only end up hurt and rejected because I am basically unlovable — I am guilty of basic badness.
• If I were to succeed in keeping my ideal weight, I would be guilty of outdoing and humiliating my overweight mother and sister.

Remember, you can feel guilty of a certain crime against one member of your family and a different crime against another. Consider each of the following imaginary crimes and ask yourself if it applies to you: outdoing, burdening, love theft, abandoning, disloyalty, and basic badness.

These are not all the possible imaginary crimes. Make your own categories if you find others that are important to you. Try to phrase your beliefs that stem from imaginary crimes in the same form as those we have outlined. For example:

"If I pursue or accomplish _____ [life goal], then _____ [negative outcome] will occur."

Take a few minutes now to list your most important grim beliefs in the section you have labeled Obstructions.

TESTS

As we saw in the last chapter, tests are experiments in which we challenge our grim beliefs — including our belief that we really *are* guilty of imaginary crimes.

Case Example: A Transference Test

Joyce, the office manager in the previous chapter, began a relationship with Orville, a kind and tolerant man. After they had been together for a few months she began to make a number of small, potentially irritating mistakes and also began to be somewhat moody. This behavior was an unconscious invitation for Orville to criticize her, as her father did when she was a child. By resisting these minor provocations, Orville greatly aided Joyce in overcoming her unconscious belief that she deserved bad treatment.

Joyce also tested her boss by neglecting small but important tasks at work. Whereas Orville had passed Joyce's test by refusing to be provoked, her boss's failure showed in his obvious dissatisfaction with Joyce's irresponsibility. Once she realized that she was testing her boss, Joyce was able to stop her self-sabotaging behavior.

Example of a Passive-into-Active Test

Felix was chronically late coming home from work. He'd promise to be home for dinner at 6:00, but wouldn't actually arrive until 6:45 or later. This was exactly the way his father had acted when he was a child, and it had made both Felix and his mother feel furious and helpless. Christa, his wife, angry and frustrated too, asked her own mother for advice. Together, they decided that Christa should set a time for dinner, then begin eating whether Felix was there or not. Christa stopped waiting for Felix to get home. Dinner went on the table at 6:00 sharp. And although Felix grumbled a bit, he soon began showing up on time.

By not allowing herself to be caught up in a sense of angry helplessness, Christa had passed Felix's test. She helped Felix overcome his unconscious belief that he was doomed to repeat his parents' conflict-filled relationship.

Ask yourself if you can identify a relationship — with your spouse, your friends, your children, your parents, your boss — in which you are testing the other person. Take a few minutes now to list these relationships and the nature of your tests.

Now go back to each person you have listed and ask yourself the following questions:

- Am I provoking this person to treat me like my mother or father did?
- Am I treating this person as my mother or father treated me?
- What grim, unconscious belief or imaginary crime am I attempting to overcome?
- Does this person usually pass or fail my tests?
- How does it feel when this person passes? How does it feel when this person is unable to pass?
- Which family members, friends, or business associates are testing *me?* Do I usually pass or fail their tests?

Write down your answers to these questions now.

INSIGHTS

In this section you will list any perceptions or insights that might help you overcome your psychological problems. Some of your insights may reflect an understanding of your grim beliefs or your imaginary crimes.

This portion of your plan may well be the longest. You may wish to add to it as you gain fresh insights over time. To help you organize your material, we have created subsections:

• The Origins of Your Grim Beliefs
• The Origins of Your Imaginary Crimes
• Your Identifications with a Parent
• Your Compliances with Parental Bad Messages
• Your Punishment Thoughts

The Origins of Your Grim Beliefs

List any important experiences of loss, abuse, or lack of love and attention you can remember: deaths, separations, illnesses, alcoholism, addictions, sexual abuse or other trauma, or neglect. Then try to understand how these incidents may have helped to shape your unconscious beliefs. Examples:

• Dad's binge drinking made his moods and behavior unpredictable. Whenever I started thinking things were OK, he'd go on a binge again. That's how I came to believe that if I relaxed, something bad was sure to happen.

• My older brother fondled me sexually beginning when I was nine years old. When I tried to tell my parents about it, they refused to believe me. The abuse continued until I was fourteen, when my brother left home. I felt guilty and invaded and angry. I ended up feeling that I had no right to stop people from abusing me because my parents acted as if I had no such right.

• Dad's plane crashed after I was angry and wouldn't kiss him good-bye. This was one of the experiences that taught me that anger was deadly.

• Since my parents always favored me, when my sister became a drug addict, I believed that I was responsible for the terrible way her life turned out.

• My relaxed, affable father frittered away the family fortune and made my mother extremely unhappy. That's why I unconsciously believe that whenever I feel relaxed and happy, I am courting disaster.

Write down any such experiences now.

The Origins of Your Imaginary Crimes

Review the hardships and unfulfilled life goals of each of your parents and each of your siblings. For each family member, ask yourself which imaginary crimes you may feel guilty of and what grim ideas you may have come to believe. For each imaginary crime, try to identify the experiences that led you to convict yourself of that crime. Examples:

• My dad seemed unsuccessful, so I keep myself from being successful in order to avoid outdoing him.

• My mom was unhappy except when she was telling me what to do. As a result, I've always felt afraid to make my own decisions and still check with her or somebody like her before I do anything. To become independent would constitute the imaginary crime of abandonment.

• My parents couldn't tolerate criticism. As a result, I find that if I consider a single critical thought about them, I feel guilty of disloyalty.

Write down your parents' or siblings' unfulfilled goals now.

Your Identifications with a Parent

Consider any thoughts, feelings, or behaviors that are currently a problem for you. Is your problem similar to a problem a parent or sibling had? If so, consider the possibility that your thoughts, feelings, or behaviors may be the result of identifying with that parent or sibling. Examples:

• I am excessively critical of my son just as my father was excessively critical of me.

• I am obsessed with my weight just as my mother and sister were.

• I can never seem to get my bills paid on time, just as my father never seemed able to.

Write down your identifications with a parent or sibling now.

Your Compliances with Parental Bad Messages

Look at your present problem behaviors and explore the possibility that you are complying with a parental bad message. Are you proving your parents right in their negative views of you or of life in general? List all the bad messages you got from your parents and older siblings. Remember to include both explicit and implicit bad messages. (You may find it useful to use the list of common bad messages at the end of Chapter 6.) Examples:

• My father said that no man would ever want me, and all my life I have arranged to get rejected by the men who interested me.

• My mother taught me not to trust anyone outside the family, and I am not really comfortable with anyone except family.

• My mother would never take a break or give herself a minute of rest. She would never go to bed and rest or go to the doctor no matter how ill she might get. That's how I learned that I shouldn't rest or take care of myself in any way.

• At my mother's funeral, my aunt told me that trying to satisfy my needs had killed my mother. That's why I cannot ask anyone to do anything for me even today, twenty years later.

Write down your compliances now.

Your Punishment Thoughts

Are you troubled by painful obsessive thoughts? If these thoughts arise when things are going well, when you have achieved an important goal (promotion, book publication), when you have planned to pursue your goal, or when you feel you have hurt or disappointed someone — they are likely to be punishment thoughts. Examples:

• After my recent promotion, I became obsessed by the fear that I wouldn't be able to do the job.

• After refusing to go out with a nice but somewhat depressed and boring man, I found myself thinking, I'm a bad person, I've hurt so many people in my life.

• After a brief period of feeling wonderfully happy and alive following my move to California, I became upset by the persistent thought that I might have AIDS or cancer, even though I felt fine and the medical tests were negative.

• After we signed a contract to write this book, I found myself worrying that my friends and colleagues would all end up repudiating me, that my coauthor would decide I was an illiterate dummy and would withdraw from our twenty-year friendship, and that no one would like the book anyway.

Take a few minutes now to list any painful, obsessive thoughts you can remember.

Your Plan May Be Quite Complex

You may well find that your own plan will be considerably more complex than the case examples we have used throughout this book. In retelling these case histories, we have frequently chosen to simplify matters to illustrate a particular point.

We are all complex individuals with strong bonds to a variety of family and friends. You may well find that you feel guilty of several different imaginary crimes. You may, for instance, feel guilty of burdening and abandonment toward your mother, outdoing toward your father, and love theft toward your brothers or sisters. You may find yourself involved in both identifications (repeating a parent's self-defeating behavior) *and* compliances (conforming to negative parental treatment or messages).

Once you have completed your own personal plan, you should have a more complete picture of the problems you are working on, the beliefs that underlie those problems, and the experiences that led you to those beliefs.

Your creation of this document will be valuable in its own right. But there is another way that the plan formulation may be helpful to you. When you are having a problem or some feelings that you don't understand, you may find it helpful to review what you have written. Just as a Control Mastery therapist may mentally review a client's plan formulation when she is confused about his lack of progress, you may go back to *your* own personal plan when your feelings or behavior seem confusing or self-defeating.

We suggest that you come back and repeat this exercise from time to time. You may find that you can develop an increasingly rich and helpful outline for progress.

The Continuing Process
of Psychological Self-Care

There are a variety of ways to continue the work you have begun by completing this exercise. You may wish to share your plan formulation with your spouse, a family member, or a friend. If you are in therapy, you may wish to share your plan with your therapist. If you are not, you may wish to consider entering therapy in order to make faster progress.

Therapy can be a particularly helpful way to free yourself from constricting unconscious beliefs. For those of us who suffered extreme trauma in childhood, individual or group therapy may be an indispensable part of the process of gaining insight.

But even for those of us with less serious problems, psychotherapy offers two special benefits: Your therapist's comments and interpretations can provide insights that are more specific to your particular situation than those in any book. And therapy can provide a safe arena for the testing process described in Chapter 11, "How Psychotherapy Works." Disproving your grim beliefs through such testing is probably the most potent way of weakening their tenacious grip.

If you suffer from debilitating or overwhelming psychological problems, you would be well advised to seek psychotherapy. But even if your problems are relatively minor, therapy may be extremely useful. While there are many paths to self-knowledge, help from a sensitive and well-trained psychotherapist is one of the best ways we know of freeing you from the unnecessary constraints that prevent you from living the fullest, most satisfying possible life.

Some clients enter psychotherapy not to overcome some particularly pressing problem, but in the spirit of wanting to enrich their life. Most psychotherapists are delighted to work with such clients. Psychotherapy at its best combines the process of solving problems with that of enrichment and discovery, for in the end they are ultimately the same.

Shopping for a Therapist

The best way to find a good therapist is to ask the people you know. If you have friends who are therapists, ask them for recommendations. If you have friends who are or were in therapy, ask about their experience. And ask them whether they would be comfortable with your seeing their therapist. If not, you may wish to ask their therapist to recommend a colleague.

Your minister or physician may know of a good therapist. University psychology departments, medical school psychiatry departments, and local associations of psychologists, psychiatrists, and marriage and family counselors can also provide referrals. Your telephone directory's yellow pages can give you a quick overview of resources.

Psychologists, marriage and family counselors, clinical social workers, psychiatrists, psychoanalysts, and other counselors all offer therapy in both private practice and clinic settings. Each of these traditions can produce excellent therapists, and there is no evidence that any one of them turns out better therapists than another. Choose the therapist that seems right for you — regardless of his background.

Trusting Your Own Reaction

No matter how you get your referral, it is important to make your own evaluation and decision. Once you have met with the therapist, ask yourself the following questions:

• Do you feel safe? Does the therapist seem like a person to whom you could tell your deepest thoughts, fantasies, and fears? Or does he or she seem somehow disrespectful, unreliable, sleazy, impatient, critical, or judgmental? People grow when it seems safe to do so, not when they are tense and frightened.

• Do you feel understood? Does the therapist really seem to be listening to the details of your predicament and seem really interested in understanding you? Or does she seem to have some theory (including Control Mastery Theory) to apply even before she understands you and your situation? Does the therapist seem to be getting a sense of what it is like to be in your shoes? A therapist who cannot understand your predicament is unlikely to be of much help.

• After meeting the therapist, do you feel at least a bit better? Do you feel a bit less anxious, less guilty, less depressed, more hopeful, or more clear? If you have been chronically depressed or hopeless, or if you have difficulty trusting people, you may need to give a therapist a long trial to see if he can help you. But before too long you should begin to feel some stirrings of hope, even if your grim beliefs cause you to distrust that hope.

It can sometimes be especially helpful if your therapist embodies some of the qualities that you wish to acquire. If you are depressed, you may benefit most from a therapist who is lively and cheerful. If you are anxious, you may prefer a therapist who is relaxed and confident.

And if you feel that the insights this book provides would be especially useful to you, discuss them with your prospective therapist. Although it is possible to get a great deal of help from a therapist who does not understand the key role of irrational guilt in his patient's problems, it is obviously a plus to have a therapist who does.

You may wish to see a therapist who is familiar with Control Mastery Theory. As this book goes to press, there are only a few hundred such therapists, most of them located in the San Francisco Bay Area. However, as time goes on, more and more therapists are being influenced by Control Mastery ideas. See p. 255 for information on ordering a current list of therapists familiar with Control Mastery Theory.

Choosing a Therapist

We suggest the following method for picking a therapist: Use the sources we discussed in the last few pages to find the name of a likely therapist. Call and make an appointment for three sessions. Spend those sessions getting a sense of whether you think that therapist could help you. If you feel comfortable, you may want to tell the therapist about your plan formulation and the insights you have obtained from this book.

Three sessions should be long enough to give you a sense of how the therapist works, how comfortable you feel, and whether she can help. If you *don't* feel good about the therapist by that time, don't go back. Simply call and cancel your future sessions. Don't worry about hurting the therapist's feelings; it's quite common for new patients to cancel. Try someone else. Continue this process until you find someone you trust.

Another good method for choosing a therapist is to make an introductory appointment with two, three, or four different therapists. Visit them all once or twice before making a decision. This method allows you to experience the approaches of a number of therapists before making a decision.

Therapy Groups

Another way to continue the process of psychological exploration is to join a support group or therapy group. Ironically, when it comes to finding a group, you have an advantage if you are the adult child of an alcoholic, the spouse of an alcoholic, an incest victim, or if you fall into some other easily identifiable group. As we mentioned in Chapter 10, people sharing these experiences have set up support groups in many communities. Many such groups are led by unpaid volunteers and do not charge a fee. In some communities you may also be able to find support groups that cater to the adult children of a variety of dysfunctional families. For information on finding such groups, see Appendix III, "Finding or Starting a Self-Help Group."

Those who live in cities and most larger towns will be able to find psychotherapy groups led by professional therapists. For help in finding these groups, contact your regional American Group Psychotherapy Association or write to American Group Therapy Association, 25 East Twenty-first Street, Sixth Floor, New York, New York 10010. Telephone: (212) 477-2677.

Keeping a Journal

Some people like to keep journals. If you are a journal keeper or would like to try to become one, you may have an excellent way to incorporate and build on the insights you acquired from reading this book. Keeping a journal is a highly personal matter, but here are some suggestions to get you started.

- Look for examples of self-defeating behavior in your daily life and see if you can discover the grim, unconscious beliefs or imaginary crimes that underlie this behavior.
- Keep an eye out for punishment thoughts in your daily life. When you notice such thoughts, record them in your notebook.
- Ask yourself, What are the most common ways that I punish myself for my imaginary crimes?
- Gather information from your siblings and parents in order to build up the most accurate picture of your childhood that

you can. Try to relate that childhood to the problems and strengths that you have today.

• Use the notes from your journal to update your plan formulation.

Keeping a journal is an excellent way to build on the insights you gained from the planning exercise and can also generate information to help you make your plan formulation more accurate and complete.

Using Novels and Movies

Reading novels or watching movies that illustrate the principles described in *Imaginary Crimes* is a fine way to continue the process of self-discovery. The principles that provide our deepest motivations have often been intuitively understood by novelists and playwrights. It is this very understanding that makes the characters' actions in these books ring true.

The plots of the following novels illustrate some important Control Mastery principles. The first three have been adapted into motion pictures, which are now available on videotape. All of them can be ordered from any good bookstore: *Prizzi's Honor* by Richard Condon, *Sophie's Choice* by William Styron, *Ordinary People* by Judith Guest, *The Prince of Tides* by Pat Conroy.

In addition, an extensive listing of professional and popular psychology books are listed in Appendix II, "Recommended Reading."

Where Do We Go from Here?

We have all been taught to think about our problems in ways that are primarily self-critical and self-accusatory. Psychological writers in particular have taught us that our problems were the result of our unconscious anger, repressed sexuality, and our unwillingness to give up the selfish pleasures of childhood. But while we all sometimes experience selfish, angry, and sexual impulses, these are not the source of most of our psychological problems. Most often our difficulties are caused by unconscious shame, unconscious fears, and unconscious guilt.

Although it is important to discover times when we are being unconsciously hostile, ungenerous, or seductive, this knowledge will generally not be enough to enable us to stop. Our natural aggression, self-interest, and sexuality do not usually create serious problems *except when these motives are distorted by our irrational, unconscious beliefs.* It is therefore crucial for us to understand the beliefs that underlie our inappropriate behavior. One of the most common grim, unconscious beliefs is that simply *having* a selfish, angry, or sexual feeling is in itself a crime.

It is our hope that this book has helped — and will continue to help — you to understand yourself and your psychological problems from a fresh, positive, and fruitful perspective:

• Instead of dwelling on the problems created by our selfish desires, we can begin to appreciate our guilt over wanting things for ourselves, our guilt over having things that others don't, our guilt over wanting to have lives of our own, and our irrational concerns about harming others.

• Instead of worrying about the effects of our anger, we can begin to look at the guilt we feel for *having* angry feelings, our fears that our angry feelings are dangerous to others, and our concerns that any expression of anger will cause us to be rejected.

• Instead of focusing on our unconscious sexual desires toward our parents, we can begin to look at our discomfort with the sexual quality of a parent's attentions, at our guilt over enjoying sex when a parent didn't, and at our irrational, unconscious fears that by expressing sexual feelings at all, we may endanger others.

You may be concerned that a reexamination of the dark side of your childhood may encourage you to "wallow in self-pity." Let us assure you, it will not. The idea that you would rather wallow in self-pity than get on with your life is the echo of a parental accusation: "You're just feeling sorry for yourself." Examining the pain you suffered as a child can actually be enormously liberating.

When we look into our childhood history, we will find two kinds of pain. There is the pain that we are accustomed to thinking of — pain caused by rejection, abuse, poverty, loss, neglect, or misunderstanding. For many of us, such suffering played a crucial role in our lives. But there is also another type of pain which we are *not* so accustomed to thinking of — the empathic pain we suffered from being a witness to the suffering of our parents or siblings — even though these sufferings may have been unconsciously self-imposed. It is this pain that most often gives rise to imaginary crimes.

And so we come to the end of our journey. In this book we have attempted to lay out a number of new and complex concepts from the cutting edge of contemporary psychotherapy research. We hope that the ideas presented here will give you, as they have given us, an increased appreciation of the depth, the complexity, and the wonder of the human spirit. For it must certainly stand as one of the great ironies of the human heart that so many of our most destructive patterns arise out of our most compassionate and altruistic impulses.

We hope these ideas will wear well, will become part of your habitual way of thinking about psychological problems, and will, in the end, become valuable psychological tools. We will be more than gratified if we help you a little further along the way of that long but vitally important journey we must each take if we wish to free ourselves from our grim beliefs and absolve ourselves of our imaginary crimes.

READER FEEDBACK

APPENDIXES

NOTES

INDEX

ABOUT THE AUTHORS

Reader Feedback

Although the ideas presented in this book are becoming well established in therapy and in research, their application to self-directed personal growth is still an exciting new area of study. We would appreciate your help in our continuing efforts to describe the ways individuals can use these ideas to deal with their own psychological problems and to attain their own psychological goals. We would be particularly interested in receiving feedback from readers who have attempted to apply these approaches in their own lives.

- What were the most important insights you got as a result of reading this book?
- Were there problems you hoped this book could help you with that you did *not* succeed in solving?
- How might we best improve the next edition of this book? What should be added? What should be cut?
- If we were to write a follow-up book, what should we cover? What kinds of exercises might we include?
- What successes and failures in your own psychological self-care efforts would you like to share with our readers?
- We are collecting case studies of people who have read this book, have done a plan formulation as described in Chapter 12, or have used it as the basis of a continuing plan for psychological self-care. We would love to receive a copy of your plan — along with comments on your progress. Please enclose your address and phone number so that we can contact you later for further information.

We will be any grateful for any feedback, anecdotes, or other comments you'd like to send. Please mail all responses to:
Lewis Engel, Ph.D.
Tom Ferguson, M.D.
P.O. Box 2997
San Rafael, California 94901

Appendix I

A Note to
Mental Health Professionals

My Search for a
Science of Psychotherapy

LEWIS ENGEL, PH.D.

I originally set out to be a physicist, not a psychologist. I wanted to be one of those dedicated scientists working to uncover the fundamental laws of the universe. Along the way I discovered that I found people a lot more interesting than subatomic particles. So I decided to become a scientist who worked directly with people, using the results of the latest research to help ease human suffering. I switched to the field of clinical psychology, hoping to apply the science of the mind to human problems. But once I made the change, I discovered that the science of clinical psychology was altogether different from the science of physics. It hardly seemed like a science at all.

There were well over a hundred different schools of psychotherapy in the U.S. alone. Each school had its own explanation of human behavior and had developed a jargon that was intelligible only to its followers. In many cases the followers of one school had no communication with those of another.

I learned that in most cases, these schools had been initiated by a gifted clinician who was also a brilliant and charismatic leader. The man or woman who founded a school (Sigmund Freud, Carl Jung, Eric Berne, Melanie Klein, Karen Horney) had developed important insights into human behavior. Each had made an important contribution to the field of psychotherapy. Unfortunately, their followers treated these psychological innovators like so many secular saints. Their writings were considered divine revelations, their teachings cited as a believer might cite the Bible, as the final arbiter to settle questions of theory or technique.

I studied many different systems of psychotherapy — Freudian, Jungian, Transactional Analysis, Gestalt Therapy, Neurolinguistic Programming, and others. At times I found each system very helpful for understanding a particular client. But in other cases they offered little or no help. Even more confusing, these different systems frequently suggested contradictory ways of dealing with a client. And I had no objective way of choosing between them.

I found myself feeling frustrated when followers of a given school would make dogmatic statements about a particular client or about psychotherapy in general. When I asked them how they knew these assertions were true, they would often act as if the truth was obvious. Or they would refer me to papers or books written by the founder or a member of their school. These writings usually consisted of no more than the elaboration of their own theories supported by anecdotal case material. Although these books and articles were sometimes quite thought-provoking, to my mind they proved nothing.

I was well aware from my first course in psychology that if everyone in a group expects things to be a certain way, they may well see them that way no matter what. Thus I could never be entirely sure that the loyal followers of the various masters weren't just fooling themselves. Especially when, at the next school down the block, everybody believed just the opposite.

In investigating the research literature, I became even more discouraged: virtually all of the studies I read seemed either anecdotal or trivial.[1] Certain psychoanalytic and psychotherapy journals seemed to rely largely on case studies, with an explanation of what the therapist believed she was doing. Such anecdotal evidence seemed insufficient to establish any general principles. In other journals I read research papers that were carefully controlled and statistically sound, but in most cases the phenomena they were studying seemed terribly remote from the day-to-day struggles I was experiencing with anxious, depressed, suffering clients.

This lack of rigorous scientific basis for my day-to-day work was very distressing to me. It often seemed that in becoming a psychotherapist, I had abandoned the realm of science altogether. I found that many of my colleagues felt the same way: they did not think of themselves as scientists, nor did they consider psychology a real science. They saw themselves as performing a social role in much the same way that witch doctors, shamans, and other unscientific healers had ministered to their fellows from the beginning of recorded history.

I gave up reading the research journals (as have a number of my colleagues[2]) soon after I finished my training. This was an error on my part because in the almost twenty years since I obtained my doctorate there have been a number of exciting developments in psychotherapy research. But I had become discouraged and convinced that psychology would always remain a loose confederation of splinter groups. I felt I would never find the kind of research tradition that exists in medicine, biology, physics, and chemistry, in which theoretical differences could be addressed and ultimately resolved by objective, fair-minded studies.

When confronted with a therapeutic problem, I would venture my best guess. If the client wasn't getting better, I would simply switch to another approach. In the end, I either found an approach that worked or the patient became discouraged and quit therapy. Although it seemed to me that I was an effective psychotherapist and was able to help most of my clients, I found it profoundly disturbing to think that I had no more to offer them than my experience, intuition, and a process of therapeutic trial and error.

From the beginning of my involvement with Control Mastery Theory, I found myself excited in a way I hadn't been since I first decided to become a psychologist. Control Mastery provided me with a very powerful way of understanding my own problems and those of my clients. Once I began to understand the principles of Control Mastery, I became much more effective as a psychotherapist, treating types of clients I had been unsuccessful in treating before. I also found that I was able to help those clients whom I had previously treated with some success even more successfully.

I soon discovered that the researchers who had developed Control Mastery Theory were much more than gifted therapists. They also had a deep commitment to the scientific examination of psychotherapeutic principles and techniques. I had finally found a group of professionals who shared my conviction that psychotherapy was a science as well as an art, and who had developed an effective approach for studying it. In fact, they had a large and rapidly growing research program, which included a variety of ongoing studies.

I began to sit in on the discussions and case conferences of the Mount Zion Psychotherapy Research Group, the group working to test and further develop Control Mastery Theory. I found an unaccustomed freedom from dogma and a striking intellectual openness. Unlike some other schools, Control Mastery not only allows but welcomes a variety of viewpoints. These discussions were never settled by statements such as "Freud said such and such in his 1927 paper on masochism — and that proves that I'm right and you're wrong." In fact, when presented with two conflicting points of view, the group would often design a formal research study that would attempt to settle the question objectively.

The Mount Zion Psychotherapy Research Group was established by Harold Sampson and Joseph Weiss in 1972. It has functioned as the research coordination arm of the Control Mastery movement and has achieved a number of important breakthroughs in solving some of the difficult problems that face psychotherapy researchers. The aim of the group is to "increase the effectiveness of psychotherapy by discovering the fundamental principles about how the psychotherapist helps the client to make progress."[3] Because of this, the group has never limited itself to examining Control Mastery therapy, but develops concepts and measures that can be used to study many different types of clients and many different varieties of therapy. In fact, the majority of the studies done by the group have involved therapists who had no knowledge of Control Mastery Theory.

But why hadn't other psychotherapy researchers established a coherent body of objective, shared knowledge in the field of psychotherapy years ago? It is not that psychotherapy researchers are unscientific or unintelligent. The problem has always been that those who study psychotherapy face enormous problems not faced by the physicist or medical researcher: *How do you start out with a matched group of study subjects?* Take three people who suffer from serious depression: one may have just lost his wife, one may feel guilty about succeeding and outdoing a parent, and one may have just been passed over for a major promotion. Are these subjects matched? Should they get the same treatment?

How do you make sure each patient in the study gets the same treatment? Therapists generally utilize a combination of theoretical considerations, life experience, personal characteristics (warmth, openness), and common sense in conducting psychotherapy. How can you standardize this process, without leaving yourself with something that doesn't resemble psychotherapy as it is practiced in the real world?

How do you keep your theoretical bias out of your research results? Most psychotherapy researchers have their own theories as to what makes psychotherapy work. It is, after all, essential to have some theory in order to plan one's research in a systematic way. But how do you avoid setting up your inquiry in such a way that it simply confirms what you already believe?

How do you evaluate progress in psychotherapy? Progress for one patient may not be progress for another. For example, anger from a patient who was previously unable to get angry might be an important sign of progress. But for a constantly angry patient, less anger might signal progress. Thus how then can you tell if a client is getting better, worse, or just not moving at all?

How do you evaluate the outcome of psychotherapy? If you study the effect of therapy on depression, you can give people tests at the end of treatment to measure how depressed they are. But the tests don't really tell you why they were depressed or why they cheered up. One patient may no longer be depressed because he has fallen in love with his therapist. Another may be depressed because his son was arrested with four kilos of cocaine in the trunk of his car. A third may be feeling better because a demotion has eased his success guilt. We don't really know from the degree of depression at the end of treatment whether the patient has received significant help with the problem that brought them into therapy or not.[4]

The Mount Zion Psychotherapy Research Group has developed approaches to address each of these questions. The result has been a fascinating body of research that sheds a great deal of light on the process of psychotherapy. One of the group's most crucial contributions has been the development of a technique that allows researchers to devise an individualized plan formulation for each client. (This technique is based on Joseph Weiss's unconscious plan concept, discussed in Chapters 11 and 12.) Being able to create a reliable plan formulation turned out to be a tremendous breakthrough because it overcame a problem that had hindered most researchers — developing an objective picture of each individual.

Once a plan formulation has been developed, the therapist's behavior can be compared to the plan and rated by neutral judges. If the therapist behaves in accord with the plan (that is, makes interpretations that are according to the plan and passes the client's tests), her behavior gets high marks. If her behavior is neither for nor against the plan, the therapist gets neutral marks. And if her behavior opposes the plan (that is, makes interpretations that are contrary to the plan and consistently fails the client's tests), she gets low marks. Repeated studies have shown that at those times in the treatment when therapists get high marks, the client usually shows immediate progress. If the therapist gets high marks all through the course of therapy, the patient will show a positive outcome. If the therapist gets intermediate scores, passing some tests and failing others, making some pro-plan and some anti-plan interpretations, the client will make small to moderate progress. If the therapist gets consistently low marks across the board, the client will either make no progress or will actually end up worse off than when he entered therapy.

The group has also tested some of the assertions made by the various schools of psychology. One such study looked at the level of anxiety that accompanied the emergence of old memories or other new material in the course of psychoanalysis.[5] Classical psychoanalysts would predict that the emergence of new materials would be accompanied by high anxiety — because in their view such memories and insights must be forced to the surface. Control Mastery therapists (and others who adhere to the ideas Freud expressed in his later work) would expect that new material would emerge when the client was experiencing low levels of anxiety. These theorists believe that new material comes up when the client feels safe enough to lift her repressive defenses.

The study indeed showed that new material typically comes into awareness when the client is experiencing low levels of anxiety. This and other studies have provided support for the idea that it is the client's level of perceived safety that allows him to progress in psychotherapy.

With repeated studies of this type, evidence could be gathered that would support certain psychotherapeutic ideas and would cast doubt on others. This is the way that progress is made in the other sciences. And this is the way that progress can now be made in the realm of psychotherapy. Mount Zion Psychotherapy Research Group members are now training researchers at other psychotherapy research programs to replicate their studies.[6] Even though Control Mastery Theory research is aimed at uncovering basic principles underlying the process of psychotherapy, because we use the transcripts of real psychotherapy sessions as our data, the results often have immediate and practical relevance to psychotherapists.[7] For example:

• The discovery that the client comes to therapy with a plan for getting better can help the therapist to focus on discerning that plan and assisting the client in carrying it out.
• The notion of testing on the part of the client can help the therapist behave in a way that will help the client accomplish his plan and make troublesome testing behavior more understandable and endurable.
• The notion that the client will improve when it seems safe to do so can help the therapist to avoid pushing the client in ways that are unproductive.
• The notion that a client will get better if the therapist is acting in accord with the client's plan can help a therapist notice when he is acting or interpreting in ways that are not helpful.

A few brief notes on the research techniques of the Mount Zion Psychotherapy Research Group are provided in the Notes.[8] Interested readers can find an annotated bibliography of key journal articles on Control Mastery

Theory in Appendix II, "Recommended Reading." We would especially recommend *The Psychoanalytic Process,* by Joseph Weiss, Harold Sampson, and members of the Mount Zion Psychotherapy Research Group.[9] This definitive work, written for professionals, includes a detailed description of Control Mastery Theory and the basic research techniques and findings of the Mount Zion Psychotherapy Research Group.

Interested readers are invited to write to me to request the "Updated Control Mastery Resource List for Professionals," describing current journal articles, monographs, tapes, and training opportunities in Control Mastery Theory. This listing will be updated from time to time as new material becomes available. Mental health professionals are encouraged to copy the list to share with friends and colleagues.

In addition, I am compiling a "Nationwide Listing of Therapists with an Interest in Control Mastery Theory." Mental health professionals with an interest in Control Mastery Theory are invited to add their names to the list by writing me. Please indicate if you would like to be included and provide your full name with appropriate degrees and licenses and your full professional address and phone number. Copies of the list are available on request — either to professionals or to interested laypeople. If there are a number of interested professionals in your area, you might wish to join with others to set up your own local Control Mastery Theory Study Group.

Please send your name and address to Lewis Engel, Ph.D., P.O. Box 2997, San Rafael, California 94901. A donation of $5.00 to help cover printing, postage, and handling would be appreciated but is not required.

Appendix II

Recommended Reading

NONFICTION BOOKS ON RELATED TOPICS

Overcoming the Fear of Success
Martha Friedman
Warner Books, New York, 1980
    This useful book is written by a psychologist who specializes in treating clients who suffer from fear of success, and is especially appropriate for anyone who suffers from this common syndrome. It is fascinating to note the great similarities between her thinking and Control Mastery Theory, even though each line of thought was developed completely independently.

The Drama of the Gifted Child
Alice Miller
Basic Books, New York, 1981
    In this powerful book, Miller makes the point that from an early age, children adapt themselves to their parents' needs. When parents are insensitive or self-preoccupied, the child may end up almost completely disconnected from his own deep feelings.

For Your Own Good: Hidden Cruelty in Child-rearing and the Roots of Violence
Alice Miller
Farrar, Straus and Giroux, New York, 1983
    Miller points out the inhumanity of many widely accepted child-rearing practices and traces their historical roots. She argues that particularly authoritarian and brutal childhoods can contribute to brutal adulthoods, by presenting short biographies of a prostitute, a serial killer of young boys, and Adolf Hitler.

Thou Shalt Not Be Aware
Alice Miller
Farrar, Straus and Giroux, New York, 1984

In this volume, Miller continues her explorations into the effects of the abuse of children in their adult lives. As the title suggests she focuses on the damage done when children are not even allowed to be aware that they have been hurt or abused. She emphasizes, as does Control Mastery Theory, that psychological problems in adulthood are not due to the aggressive or sexual feelings that an adult experienced as a child but to his parents' sexual or aggressive feelings directed toward him.

Bradshaw on the Family
John Bradshaw
Health Communications, Deerfield Beach, Florida, 1988

Bradshaw has been popularizing many of the same ideas that underlie Control Mastery Theory. He assumes, as do we, that the child learns guilt and shame in his family of origin and that these emotions and the beliefs that underlie them cause trouble later in life. In addition, he incorporates some of the best thinking from family therapy and from the adult children of dysfunctional parents movement. Although he emphasizes what he calls toxic shame, it is, in many cases, quite similar to what we call unconscious guilt and unconscious shame.

A thought-provoking videotaped lecture series by the same name airs from time to time on public television and is well worth watching.

Healing the Shame That Binds You
John Bradshaw
Health Communications, Deerfield Beach, Florida, 1988

In this volume Bradshaw explores his concept of toxic shame in more depth.

BOOKS ON RELATIONSHIPS AND SEXUALITY

The Intimate Enemy
George R. Bach and Peter Wyden
William Morrow, New York, 1969

This book has been around for a long time. For handling problems with anger, whether the problem is overcontrol of anger or destructive expression of anger, George Bach's writings can be extremely helpful. There is also an excellent section on negotiation skills.

After the Honeymoon: How Conflict Can Improve Your Relationship
Daniel B. Wile
John Wiley and Sons, New York, 1988

This is one of the most helpful and original recent books about dealing with marital conflict. Like Bach, Wile understands that conflict is an inevitable part of intimacy, and in this humorous but profound book, he suggests a variety of fascinating strategies for using existing conflicts to help promote intimacy. Highly recommended.

For Each Other, Sharing Sexual Intimacy
Lonnie Barbach
New American Library, New York, 1982, 1984
   This and Dr. Barbach's other books are among the best things written on sexual problems and sexual enrichment.

Male Sexuality: A Guide to Sexual Fulfillment
Bernie Zilbergeld
Little, Brown, Boston, 1978
   An excellent self-help guide to resolving male sexual problems.

ADULT CHILDREN OF DYSFUNCTIONAL PARENTS

Toxic Parents: Overcoming Their Hurtful Legacy and Reclaiming Your Life
Susan Forward with Craig Buck
Bantam, New York, 1989
   A useful book on the problems of adult children of disturbed or impaired parents. Many of my clients have found it extremely helpful, and many of its ideas are very similar to those in *Imaginary Crimes*.

Changes: A Magazine for and About Adult Children of Alcoholics
Published six times a year by the U.S. Journal of Drug and Alcohol
   Dependence, Inc., 1721 Blount Road, Suite 1, Pompano Beach, Florida
   33069
   This magazine has a variety of articles written from many viewpoints as well as listings of conferences and workshops all over the country. It's a valuable resource for people interested in becoming involved with the Adult Children of Alcoholics movement.

It Will Never Happen to Me!
Claudia Black
Ballantine Books, New York, 1981, 1987
   One of the first and the best books for and about adult children of alcoholics.

A Time to Heal: The Road to Recovery for Adult Children of Alcoholics
Tim Cermak
Avon Books, New York, 1988

Cermak, a psychiatrist and pioneer in this field, has written a powerful book that includes a lot of case material, including his own story — he himself is the child of an alcoholic father.

Treating Adult Children of Alcoholics: A Developmental Perspective
Stephanie Brown
John Wiley and Sons, New York, 1988
In this excellent book written for a professional audience, Dr. Brown, a pioneer in the group treatment of children of alcoholics, develops an in-depth theoretical link between the childhood experience of living with an alcoholic parent and the resulting disturbances in adult functioning.

The Courage to Heal: A Guide for Women Survivors of Sexual Abuse
Ellen Bass and Laura Davis
Harper and Row, New York, 1988
A moving and powerfully written book for women who were sexually abused as children.

Children of Alcoholism: A Survivors Manual
Judith S. Seixas and Geraldine Youcha
Harper and Row, New York, 1986
A highly readable book for adult children of alcoholics which dovetails particularly well with Control Mastery Theory.

Outgrowing the Pain: A Book for and about Adults Abused as Children
Eliana Gil
Dell, New York, 1983
A concise and direct book, particularly useful for adults who were physically abused or neglected as children.

RESEARCH METHODOLOGY

The Psychoanalytic Process: Theory, Clinical Observation, and Empirical Research
Joseph Weiss, Harold Sampson, and the Mount Zion Psychotherapy Research Group
Guilford Press, New York, 1986
This book, written for the professional, is the best and most detailed description of the development and details of Control Mastery Theory and research.

"Developing Reliable Psychodynamic Case Formulations: An Illustration of the Plan Diagnosis Method"
John T. Curtis
Psychotherapy, vol. 25, 1988

A description of how the plan diagnosis method is applied with a detailed case example.

"Research on the Process of Change in Psychotherapy: The Approach of the Mount Zion Psychotherapy Research Group"
George Silberschatz et al. In L. Beutler and M. Crago (eds.)
International Psychotherapy Research Programs, American Psychological Association Press, Washington, D.C. In press.
A comprehensive overview of the work of the Mount Zion Psychotherapy Research Group to date.

"How Do Interpretations Influence the Process of Psychotherapy?"
George Silberschatz, P. B. Fretter, and J. T. Curtis
Journal of Consulting and Clinical Psychology, vol. 54, no. 5, 1986
This study compared two predictors of patient progress. It found that plan compatibility of therapist interpretations was a better predictor of patient progress than was the type of interpretation (i.e., transference interpretations versus nontransference interpretations). Plan compatibility was highly correlated with patient progress whereas type of interpretation did not correlate with patient progress.

"Using the Patient's Plan to Assess Progress in Psychotherapy"
George Silberschatz, J. T. Curtis, and S. Nathans
Psychotherapy, vol. 98, 1989
This paper describes the development of a case-specific outcome measure (plan attainment) that overcomes many of the problems of traditional standardized outcome measures.

"The Effects of Shame, Guilt, and the Negative Reaction in Brief Dynamic Psychotherapy"
M. O. Nergaard and G. Silberschatz
Psychotherapy, vol. 26, 1989
This study found that high levels of guilt predicted poor therapy outcome. Guilt was a better predictor than shame and a broadly defined "negative indicators" scale.

THEORETICAL PAPERS

"Toward a Reconceptualization of Guilt"
Michael Friedman
Contemporary Psychoanalysis, vol. 21, no. 4, 1985
Our ideas regarding the importance of human altruism were largely shaped by this fascinating monograph. We would heartily recommend this

groundbreaking work to anyone interested in a detailed discussion of the vital roles of altruism and guilt within the human psyche.

"The Role of Unconscious Guilt in Psychopathology and Psychotherapy"
Marshall Bush
Bulletin of the Menninger Clinic, vol. 53, no. 2, 1989
This excellent paper makes a case for the power of unconscious guilt in shaping our psychological problems. The March 1989 issue of the *Bulletin of the Menninger Clinic* contains *nine* articles relating to Control Mastery Theory, including two critiques, and is well worth reading.

"Is Altruism Part of Human Nature?"
M. L. Hoffman
Journal of Personality and Social Psychology, vol. 40, no. 1, 1981
This excellent paper provides a wide-ranging review of the overwhelming evidence for human altruism.

CLINICAL PAPERS

"Unconscious Guilt as a Cause of Sexualized Relationships"
Suzanne Weatherford
Bulletin of the Menninger Clinic, vol. 53, no. 2, 1989
In this paper Dr. Weatherford summarizes four years of intensive psychotherapy with a patient who engaged in various forms of self-destructive behavior including the sexual fondling of his fourteen-year-old stepdaughter.

"Crisis Intervention Through Early Interpretation of Unconscious Guilt"
Nicholas H. Nichols
Bulletin of the Menninger Clinic, vol. 53, no. 2, 1989
Dr. Nichols describes the use of Control Mastery Theory in a hospital crisis clinic.

"Survivor Guilt in the Pathogenesis of Anorexia Nervosa"
Michael Friedman
Psychiatry, vol. 48, 1985
Excellent discussion of anorexia nervosa with a wealth of clinical examples, focusing on the role of survivor guilt in causing anorexic behavior.

"Clinical Implications of Research on Brief Dynamic Psychotherapy I. Formulating the Patient's Problems and Goals"
John Curtis and George Silberschatz
Psychoanalytic Psychology, vol. 3, no. 1, 1986

"Clinical Implications of Research on Brief Dynamic Psychotherapy II.
How the Therapist Helps or Hinders the Patient's Therapeutic Progress"
George Silberschatz and John Curtis
Psychoanalytic Psychology, vol. 3, no. 1, 1986
These two articles provide case examples of the application of Control
Mastery Theory to brief therapy.

Appendix III

Finding or Starting
a Self-Help Group

For many of us who *are* adult children of dysfunctional families, discussing our problems openly in groups composed of people with similar experiences can be a key factor in our own healing. Just sitting and listening to other group members tell of experiences that could have happened to us can be enormously moving and helpful. It makes us feel that at last someone else can really understand what it was like. It can provide a sense that our suffering is not unique, that we are not alone.

Most important of all, these groups can help us see that we were not to blame, that we were not responsible for what happened to us as children. Participation in such a support group can really bring home the idea that our guilt is irrational and our crimes imaginary.

The best way to find a group is through your network of friends and family members. Ask them if they know of such groups, or if they know others who do. Some of the larger groups maintain national offices that supply printed information on their organization and referrals to local chapters. We have listed the national offices of some of the largest and best-known groups.

There may well be other excellent groups in your community. You can get a good local overview of all the groups in your area by calling one or more regional self-help clearinghouses. We have also listed two national self-help clearinghouses, which will provide local referrals.

Mental health workers, other health professionals, or a local mental health association may also be able to help you find a group. If you can't find a local group that is specific for the dysfunctional patterns in your own family, you may wish to consider starting your own.

SUPPORT GROUPS FOR CHILDREN OF DYSFUNCTIONAL FAMILIES

National Association for Children of Alcoholics
31706 Coast Highway
South Laguna, California 92677-3044
(714) 499-3889
    An association of persons interested in the problems of children of alcoholic parents.

Adult Children of Alcoholics
P.O. Box 3216
Torrance, California 90505
(213) 534-1815
    A clearinghouse for twelve-step self-help meetings for adult children of alcoholics. Information is available about meetings both in the United States and in other countries.

Al-Anon/Alateen Family Group Headquarters
Madison Square Station
New York, New York 10010
(212) 302-7240
    Headquarters of groups for family members of alcoholics.

Alcoholics Anonymous
P.O. Box 459
Grand Central Station
New York, New York 10163
(212) 686-1100
    For those seeking to recover from alcoholism.

Al-Anon Family Group
P.O. Box 862
Midtown Station
New York, New York 10018-6106
(212) 302-7240
    For family members and friends of problem drinkers.

Alateen/Ala-Preteen/Alatot
P.O. Box 862
Midtown Station
New York, New York 10018-6106
(212) 302-7240
    For children of any age who live with an alcoholic.

Parents Anonymous
6733 Sepulvida Boulevard, No. 270
Los Angeles, California 90045
(800) 421-0353
    For parents who fear that they may be physically or emotionally abusing their children.

Parents United
P.O. Box 952
San Jose, California 95108
(408) 280-5055
    For adults who were sexually molested as children and for parents of molested children. Groups nationwide.

Nar-Anon Family Groups
P.O. Box 2562
Palos Verdes, California 90274-0119
(213) 547-5800
    For relatives and friends of individuals with drug problems.

Families Anonymous
P.O. Box 528
Van Nuys, California 91408
(818) 989-7841
    For relatives and friends of individuals with drug problems.

National Alliance for the Mentally Ill
1901 North Fort Meyer Drive
Arlington, Virginia 22209
(703)524-7600
    For relatives of the seriously mentally ill.

REGIONAL SELF-HELP CLEARINGHOUSES

California*	(800) 222-LINK (California only)
Connecticut	(203) 789-7645
Illinois	(800) 322-MASH (Illinois only)
Iowa	(800) 383-4777 (Iowa only)
Kansas	(316) 689-3170
Massachusetts	(413) 545-2313
Michigan*	(800) 752-5858 (Michigan only)
Minnesota	(612) 642-4060

* Maintains listing of additional local clearinghouses operating within that state

Missouri — Kansas City	(816) 561-HELP
Nebraska	(402) 476-9668
New Jersey	(800) 367-MASH (New Jersey only)
New York State*	(518) 473-3655
New York City	(718) 596-6000
Long Island	(516) 348-3030
Westchester	(914) 347-3620
Oregon — Portland	(503) 222-5555
Pennsylvania — Pittsburgh	(412) 247-5400
Pennsylvania — Scranton	(717) 961-1234
Rhode Island	(401) 277-2231
South Carolina	(803) 791-2426
Tennessee — Knoxville	(615) 584-6736
Texas*	(512) 454-3706
Vermont	(800) 442-5356
Washington, D.C.	(703) 536-4100

* Maintains listing of additional local clearinghouses operating within that state

NATIONAL SELF-HELP CLEARINGHOUSES

National Self-Help Clearinghouse
25 West Forty-third Street, Suite 620
New York, New York 10036
Director Frank Riessman and his staff can provide information on other self-help groups for specific concerns. They request that you write rather than call. The center also publishes a useful manual, *How to Organize a Self-Help Group,* by Andy Humm. $6.00 postpaid.

The Self-Help Clearinghouse
St. Clares–Riverside Hospital
Denville, New Jersey 07834
(201) 625-9565; TDD (201) 625-9053
Director Edward J. Madara and his staff provide consulting services to individuals interested in starting a self-help group. The center also publishes a national directory of self-help groups. Their brochure, *Ideas and Considerations for Starting a Self-Help Group,* is free. Please send a stamped, self-addressed legal-sized envelope along with your request.

Notes

1. Control Mastery Theory is named for two of its key concepts: *control* and *mastery*.

   Part of the way that psychotherapy heals us is by helping us recall long-forgotten memories and feelings. Once these feelings and memories are available, we can use them to help overcome the unconscious irrational beliefs that cause our psychological problems. Control Mastery Theory holds that we unconsciously *control* whether to bring these repressed memories and feelings to the surface on the basis of whether we perceive it as safe to do so.

   While some therapists believe that psychological problems develop when we hold on to primitive, immature impulses, Control Mastery Theory holds that we do *not* really want to hold on to our problems (even though it may sometimes look as if we do). We want to *master* our problems. In fact, Control Mastery Theory assumes that we have a powerful unconscious drive to master our psychological problems. If we fail to master our problems, it is not because they provide us with childish satisfactions, but rather because we unconsciously fear that we ourselves or those we love will be terribly hurt if we do. And because we believe ourselves guilty of imaginary crimes, we don't feel we *deserve* to have the things we really want.

2. The term *imaginary crime* is not used by Weiss in his writings. We have used it in order to make Weiss's ideas more accessible to a general audience.

3. The notion that unconscious beliefs cause psychological problems is shared by a number of other important psychological theories. Freud argued from time to time in his voluminous writings that unconscious beliefs caused some psychological problems, although he never embraced the idea that unconscious beliefs caused virtually all psychological problems. More recently Aaron Beck, Albert Ellis, and other

Notes • 267

members of the Cognitive Therapy movement have also asserted that it is beliefs that cause psychological problems. However, cognitive therapists do not explore the origin of unconscious beliefs as thoroughly as does Control Mastery Theory, and this makes their work less helpful than it otherwise could be.

4. Freud was a prolific thinker and writer who struggled throughout his life to present the truth of the human psyche. His ideas changed and evolved over his lifetime, and it is possible to find in his work a variety of points of view, some of them contradictory. One very consistent theme, however, is the idea that *human beings are motivated solely by selfish interests*. Freud felt that human tendencies toward altruism merely represented "an underlying contrary attitude of brutal egoism." Sigmund Freud, *The Complete Works of Sigmund Freud, Standard Edition*, vol. 13 (London: Hogarth, 1953), 72. For additional examples of Freud's conviction that human beings are fundamentally self-serving, see Michael Friedman, "Toward a Reconceptualization of Guilt," *Contemporary Psychoanalysis*, vol. 21, no. 4 (1985): 501–47.

5. M. L. Hoffman, "Is Altruism Part of Human Nature?" *Journal of Personality and Social Psychology*, vol. 40, no. 1 (1981): 121–37. This excellent paper provides a wide-ranging review of the overwhelming evidence for human altruism.

6. One of the reasons most of us believe that it is sentimental and unrealistic to think that human beings have instinctive altruistic tendencies is our impression that the "lower animals" are driven only by selfish instincts. If lower animals don't have a drive to care for or protect one another, why should human beings? Again, however, new data and a reevaluation of older data has led biologists to the conclusion that although some species of animals exhibit almost no altruistic behavior, other species exhibit a great deal.

The most universal example of this is the way that mothers and sometimes fathers in certain species will give food and care to their offspring while neglecting themselves. Moreover, parents of a number of species will even risk their lives to protect their offspring. They will fight dangerous intruders or try to attract their attention to lure them away from the helpless young. In the process, these animals unselfishly disregard their own needs to aid their young.

But it is not only in protecting their young that they ignore their own welfare. Particularly in some of the species that live in groups, individuals instinctively sacrifice themselves for the good of other group members. For example, worker bees will sacrifice their lives to protect the hive, even though they are sterile and have no offspring.

Wolves, crows, and chimpanzees, and other social animals are instinctively programmed to look out for one another. Individual chimpanzees will sometimes share food and lead each other to food, thereby having less for themselves but increasing the fitness of the whole group.

But the idea that animals can be altruistic seems to contradict Darwin's theory of evolution. Doesn't that theory tell us that each animal competes with every other member of his species and that only the fittest survive? Not quite. What Darwin actually says is that animal species that are successful in reproducing themselves under changing environmental conditions will thrive, and those that can't will become extinct. Competition is certainly an important element in Darwin's thinking. However, if a species has powerful altruistic and cooperative instincts that help it survive and reproduce, that altruism and cooperation are much in accord with Darwin's theory, also.

Thus, social animals that live in groups gain considerable evolutionary advantage by having some strong altruistic tendencies. Archaeological and paleontological evidence clearly shows that humans have always lived in groups. This information combined with research demonstrating the empathic and helping behavior of young children and infants can now provide us with a new view of human motivation. This more sophisticated conception of human motivation is that it is not completely selfish nor is it completely unselfish. Like many other animals, along with our selfish and competitive instincts, there exists an instinct to protect and care for others.

7. A. Sagi and S. Hoffman, "Empathic Distress in Newborns," *Developmental Psychology*, vol. 12, no. 4 (1976): 175–76.

8. C. Zahn-Wexler and M. Radke-Yarrow, "The Development of Altruism," *The Development of Pro-social Behavior*, ed. M. Eisenberg (New York: Academic Press, 1982), 115. These researchers used mothers (after a rigorous training program) as observers of their children's behavior in the face of the distress of others. In a surprising percentage of situations when the children observed the distress of others (between 30 and 39 percent for the one-year-olds), the children exhibited altruistic behavior. That is, they attempted to comfort the distressed parent or sibling, they tried to get help from an adult, or they tried to cheer up the distressed individual. This excerpt is a typical mother's report of an altruistic event from that study, but has been edited for brevity and clarity.

9. Ibid., 111. "Whereas some investigators find interpretable prosocial behaviors occurring in preschool-aged children . . . most existing developmental theories propose a much later age of occurrence of real,

mature prosocial behaviors. The age of reason and the beginning of operational thought (about seven years) and the age of resolution of Oedipal conflicts (about six years) are thought to mark the approximate time of emergence of altruism in cognitive and psychoanalytic theories."

10. Although the existence of altruistic behavior among animals and human beings is widely accepted by evolutionary biologists, there is controversy as to the evolutionary mechanism of that behavior. A school of thought that is currently gaining ascendence is the "selfish gene" theory of Richard Dawkins. This theory holds that genes use organisms to propagate themselves and any behavior (including altruistic behavior) that tends to increase the survival of closely related genes is therefore evolutionarily advantageous — even if it is to the detriment of the individual organism. For more details, see Richard Dawkins, *The Selfish Gene* (New York: Oxford University Press, 1976) and R. Trivers, "The Evolution of Reciprocal Altruism," *Quarterly Review of Biology*, vol. 46, no. 4 (1971): 35–57.

11. The Control Mastery Theory view of omnipotence is different from the classical Freudian idea that the child has an innate tendency to see himself as all-powerful. Whereas other theorists see omnipotence as innate, gratifying, and renounced as part of the maturation process, in our view it is learned, burdensome, and difficult to free oneself from.

12. People become chemically dependent for a variety of reasons other than unconscious guilt, and we are not here asserting that unconscious guilt is the only, or even the most common, cause of chemical dependence. However, my colleagues and I have treated a substantial number of clients for whom unconscious guilt was a key factor in their addiction.

CHAPTER 2

1. There has been a recent upsurge of interest in what has come to be called "cognitive science," i.e., man as a theory-making animal. Workers in this new field — which combines psychology, anthropology, linguistics, and neuroscience — emphasize the importance of goals and mental representations in shaping behavior. They stress that from very early in life, children are working hard to develop their own theory of how the world works. For a good introduction to the field, see Howard Gardner, *The Mind's New Science: A History of the Cognitive Revolution* (New York: Basic Books, 1985).

2. The notion of the grim, unconscious belief is the cornerstone of Joseph Weiss's reformulation of psychoanalytic theory. In his early works,

Freud attributed most psychological problems to the continuing conflict between our lustful and murderous impulses on the one hand, and our repressive ego on the other. In Weiss's view, which is closer to the view expressed in Freud's later work, most psychological problems come about because of our grim, unconscious beliefs that pursuing our normal, healthy impulses will bring injury to ourselves and our family. So a therapist following Freud's earlier work might see a symptom as a compromise between the lustful desires of the id and the repressive forces of the ego, but Weiss would see it as an attempt to avoid the horrible consequences predicted by our unconscious beliefs.

3. Weiss often refers to these beliefs as grim, unconscious, pathogenic beliefs. By including the word *pathogenic,* he emphasizes that these beliefs are the cause of our psychological problems. We have not used this term in our text because it is a specialized medical term that could be confusing to a lay readership, but in this chapter and in other places, we have tried to make clear that we share Weiss's conviction that grim, unconscious beliefs are the source of most psychological problems.

4. Martha Friedman's *Overcoming the Fear of Success* (New York: Warner Books, 1980) provides a useful discussion of the reasons people sabotage their own success. Friedman is a psychologist who specializes in treating patients who fear success. This is a useful resource for anyone who suffers from this common syndrome.

5. The term "thousand-repetition grim belief" is not used by Weiss or Sampson. Weiss uses the term "strain trauma" to refer to those many small, repetitive incidents that cause a grim, unconscious belief to be inferred.

6. Paul's case is a condensed and adapted version of the case of Mr. S., from Joseph Weiss, et al., *The Psychoanalytic Process: Theory, Clinical Observation, and Empirical Research* (New York: Guilford Press, 1986), 79.

CHAPTER 3

1. Mike had to face a combination of circumstances that is all too typical of a family with an alcoholic father: although his father was unreliable and often intoxicated, his alcoholism was never spoken of (if his problem became public knowledge, Mike's father might lose his hospital privileges and his patients). This placed a tremendous burden on Mike's mother. The children felt responsible and all took on "family roles" — with Mike as the perfect little man who tried to make up for the pain his mother suffered at his father's hands.

2. "The experience of guilt, or just the threat of it, produces anxiety because anxiety is a reaction to danger, and guilt is one of the most dangerous human emotions. The danger it poses lies in the fact that guilt feelings can become almost intolerably painful. They produce a need to incur punishment and make restitutions, they destroy feelings of self-worth and self-esteem, they undermine one's belief in one's good intentions, and they make one less able to defend oneself in the face of false accusations and unmerited mistreatment." From an unpublished paper entitled "The Role of Unconscious Guilt in Masochism" by Marshall Bush (1985).

3. These crime categories are not part of Control Mastery Theory as originally formulated by Weiss. In terms of Weiss's formulations, burdening, outdoing, and love theft are closely related to survivor guilt, while abandonment and disloyalty are related to separation guilt. Basic badness would be considered a compliance to negative parental messages and treatment.

4. In their excellent guidebook, *Know Your Child*, Stella Chess and Alexander Thomas (New York: Basic Books, 1987), present the importance of "goodness of fit" between parental styles and the child's innate temperament, along with practical suggestions about how to achieve that goal. Chess and Alexander base much of their thinking on their thirty-year longitudinal study of 133 people from infancy through adulthood. It is refreshing to find a child-rearing book based on solid and widely respected research.

   Some completely healthy, normal children are hard for most parents to deal with. These kids can exhibit a number or all of the following hard-to-deal-with traits from birth: restlessness and vigorousness; difficulty in adapting to changes in routine; tendency to avoid new people, food, situations, etc.; high intensity; irregular feeding and sleeping habits; easily bothered by noises, lights, the texture of clothes; and general negativity and fussiness. If you suspect you or someone close to you has such a child, we strongly recommend *The Difficult Child* by Stanley Turecki and Leslie Tonner (New York: Bantam, 1987).

5. An excellent book on the subject of divorce is Judith Wallerstein and Joan Kelley's *Surviving the Breakup: How Children and Parents Cope with Divorce* (New York: Basic Books, 1980). This book is based on a large study in which divorced parents and children were followed for many years. The authors state that approximately one-third of the children accepted significant blame for the divorce and that younger children were more likely to feel guilty about the divorce than were the older children. In addition, over half the children were intensely worried about their mothers.

6. H. Leowald, "The Waning of the Oedipus Complex," *Journal of the*

American Psychoanalytic Association, vol. 27 (1979): 751–75. For the children of many depressed, dependent parents, the assumption of responsibility for one's own life may seem psychologically tantamount to killing one's parents. In this fascinating paper, however, Leowald argues that guilt at becoming independent is an important part of *everyone's* development.

7. My concept of basic badness is very close to John Bradshaw's concept of "toxic shame." See *Healing the Shame That Binds You* (Deerfield Beach, Fla.: Health Communications, Inc., 1988), vii. "To have shame as an identity is to believe that one's being is flawed, that one is a defective human being."

8. Stella Chess and Alexander Thomas, *Know Your Child* (New York: Bantam, 1987), 67. The authors report that the "high activity" children in their study who lived in circumstances that allowed them space and activities to discharge that energy developed no behavior disorders, whereas a number of the "high activity" children who lived in small apartments on unsafe streets did.

CHAPTER 4

1. Judith Guest, *Ordinary People* (New York: Penguin Books, 1976), 223.

2. A frequently made psychoanalytic explanation for the guilt we feel toward a deceased sibling involves sibling rivalry. A therapist who understands guilt in this way may explain that since our wish to get rid of our competitor for our parents' attention has come true, we will conclude that our wish has magically caused his death. Control Mastery holds that such competitive or angry feelings may intensify survivor guilt, but just the simple fact of being alive when a sibling is dead is sufficient to produce these intense guilt feelings.

3. William G. Niederland, "The Survivor Syndrome: Further Observations and Dimensions," *Journal of the American Psychoanalytic Association,* vol. 29 (1981): 413–23. A case that Niederland mentions briefly demonstrates the survivor guilt of those whom the Nazis spared. "[A] guilt-ridden survivor blames herself for having 'deserted' her mother, when the latter at their arrival in the concentration camp was placed on the left side, *die schelchte Siete,* while she — a strong and tall young woman — was put on the right, that is, forced to labor in the *Schneiderie,* and later do kitchen work." Like Sophie this unfortunate woman blamed herself even though the decision as to who would live and who would die was beyond her control.

4. Although concentration camp survivors are all afflicted with survivor

guilt to a considerable degree, some are able to deal with that guilt much better than others. An inspiring example is Victor Frankl, the psychiatrist who, while in a concentration camp, wrote extensively on the role of meaning in maintaining psychological health. It is beyond the scope of this book to investigate the complex topic of why some survivors were crushed by guilt and others were not. However, I suspect that Frankl was able partially to assuage his guilt by devoting his life to helping others.

5. Niederland, 421. "On the basis of my long-standing research, I have reason to believe that the survival is unconsciously felt as a betrayal of the dead parents and siblings, and being alive constitutes an ongoing conflict as well as a source of constant feelings of guilt and anxiety."

6. Ibid., 413–23. Niederland's paper primarily describes survivors of the Nazi concentration camps. Psychological problems are probably more extreme in this group of survivors than survivors of floods, fires, and natural disasters for two reasons: 1) The loved ones who died at the hands of the Nazis died brutally, with much pain and suffering. This undoubtedly has the effect of intensifying the guilt and sorrow the survivor feels for them. 2) Those survivors who had been in the camps themselves suffered extreme deprivation, horror, and brutality. Therefore they were troubled not only by survivor guilt but by memories of their own terror, anxiety, and humiliation.

7. Weiss's thinking on the subject of survivor guilt was strongly influenced by the psychoanalyst Arnold Modell. It was Modell who originally extended the idea of survivor guilt from the guilt of those whose parents or siblings had died, particularly under horrible circumstances, to those who have simply fared better than their parents or siblings. In an excellent paper, Modell states: "I am referring to a sense of guilt that is the response to the awareness that one has something more than someone else. This sense of guilt is invariably accompanied by a thought which may remain unconscious, that what is obtained has been obtained at the expense of taking something away from somebody else." For further details, see "The Origin of Certain Forms of Pre-Oedipal Guilt and the Implications for a Psychoanalytic Theory of Affects," *International Journal of Psychoanalysis*, vol. 52 (1971): 339.

CHAPTER 5

1. For a fascinating discussion of the universality of and centrality of separation guilt, see H. Leowald, "The Waning of the Oedipus Com-

plex," *Journal of the American Psychoanalytic Association*, vol. 27 (1979): 751–75

2. Jay R. Greenberg and S. A. Mitchell, *Object Relations in Psychoanalytic Theory* (Cambridge, Mass: Harvard University Press, 1983), 274–81. Object relations theorists focus to a much greater extent than classical psychoanalysts on the real effects of parental behavior on the child's development. Greenberg and Mitchell's excellent book contains synopses and comparisons of many object relations theorists. Prominent among these theorists is the child psychoanalyst Margaret Mahler, who first coined the term *separation-individuation* and who also reported and analyzed the way that young children return periodically to their mothers for "emotional refueling." Control Mastery Theory actually places more stress on the child's relations with his parents than any of the theorists discussed by Greenberg and Mitchell.

3. Freud felt that children always viewed their parents as powerful, and his conception had a strong influence on the mental health profession and the public at large. "Throughout his writings Freud assumed that children perceive their parents as powerful. Parents may be frustrating or gratifying, cruel or kind, loving or unloving, but they are always strong authorities." Michael Friedman, M.D., "Toward a Reconceptualization of Guilt," *Contemporary Psychoanalysis*, vol. 21, no. 4 (1985): 505. Freud felt children were motivated exclusively by self-interest and fear. Friedman points out that even a child's affection for a parent, something most people would consider an exception to Freud's theory, is considered by Freud to be no exception at all. He quotes from Freud: "Children love themselves first, and it is only later that they learn to love others and to sacrifice something of their own ego to others. Even those people whom a child seems to love from the beginning are loved by him at first because he needs them and cannot do without them — once again from egoistic motives."

4. C. Zahn-Wexler and M. Radke-Yarrow, "The Development of Altruism," *The Development of Pro-social Behavior*, ed. M. Eisenberg (New York: Academic Press, 1982), 116.

5. I believe that Control Mastery Theory and family therapy have a lot to contribute to one another. Control Mastery Theory can provide family therapy with a deep and highly compatible understanding of the intrapsychic effects of family dynamics. Family therapists can enrich our understanding of how family systems actually operate and how we can intervene to change them.

6. Many key concepts of Control Mastery Theory are immediately recognizable to family therapists. The idea that a child may become delinquent or troubled in a misguided attempt to help other family

members is only one example. Another concept that the two approaches have in common is the importance of childhood omnipotence in causing psychopathology. One of the common techniques in family therapy is to help an overly responsible child feel less responsible for everything that goes on in the family.

7. Ann's irrational worries are an example of punishment thoughts. (See Chapter 7.)

8. Dan Greenburg, *How to Be a Jewish Mother* (Los Angeles: Price Stern Sloan, 1964). This best-selling book is a tongue-in-cheek compendium of techniques parents use to instill guilt in their children. Some may find the book offensive because they may feel it fosters an unfair stereotype, that Jewish mothers are the only parents who use guilt as a means of controlling their children. In my own experience as a psychotherapist, Jewish mothers are no more likely to use guilt as a means of controlling their children than fathers or parents of other races, creeds, or ethnic backgrounds. Indeed, the reason the book was such an enormous best seller was that people of all backgrounds recognized their own experiences in the guilt-inducing techniques Greenburg describes.

9. Like any across-the-board advice, the notion that it is important to put energy into one's own activities and interests in order to be happy does not apply equally to all parents. There are parents who put all their energy into their career, their social life, etc., and do not spend enough time and emotional energy on their children. This is more common with fathers than mothers, who are much more likely to err on the side of being overinvolved with their children. These parents are missing out on the happiness and joy that comes from a truly close and loving relationship with their children.

10. In standard psychological terminology, the feeling that a young child has when separated from his mother or mother figure is called separation anxiety. Separation anxiety is a readily observable phenomenon in young children and young animals for that matter. It consists of distress and efforts to get close to the mother that occur when the mother is too far away or when some potential danger or threat appears.

This phenomenon has been most extensively investigated by the British psychologist Dr. John Bowlby, who got interested in the subject when he was studying what happened to English schoolchildren who were taken out of London, away from their mothers, to avoid the danger of German bombings during World War II. These children got very depressed and developed a variety of other symptoms, which impressed upon Dr. Bowlby the fact that separation from the primary parent during childhood causes serious and long-lasting psychological damage. Bowlby theorized that separation anxiety and the resultant effort to get close to the parents is an adaptive, instinctual pattern of behavior. See John Bowlby, *Separation: Anger and Anxiety* (New York: Basic Books, 1973).

11. It is interesting to compare Lydia's response to her abandonment by her parents with the very different reaction to abandonment we saw in the case of Paul, who was sent away at age two and a half to protect him from his brother's illness. As an adult, Paul became timid, tense, dependent, and unable to have intimate relations. Lydia was successful while Paul could barely hold a job. Lydia was intimidating and fierce while Paul was timid and retiring. But they had one thing in common: both felt distrustful of others and avoided close relationships.

When the caretaker of a young child has been away for too long the child becomes anxious and upset. When the caretaker returns the child will be clingy for a period of time, fearful that the caretaker may again disappear. Psychotherapists and researchers call this phenomenon separation anxiety. Paradoxically, however, when adults behave in a clingy, insecure way, it is rarely due to separation anxiety. Like Ann, whose parents were doting and overprotective, their clinginess is usually due to separation guilt: unconscious concern that a loved one will feel abandoned if they grow up, become independent, and leave. People like Lydia and Paul, who as children suffered more from separation *anxiety* than from separation *guilt,* are usually not clingy. In fact, they may tend to avoid close relationships altogether.

CHAPTER 6

1. The notion of basic badness has much in common with John Bradshaw's concept of toxic shame: "toxic shame is about being flawed as a human being. Repair seems foreclosed since no change is really possible. In its ultimate essence, toxic shame has the sense of hopelessness." *Healing the Shame That Binds You* (Deerfield Beach, Fla.: Health Communications, Inc., 1988), 9.

2. For a wealth of examples of cruel and destructive child-rearing practices all too common in our society, see Alice Miller's *For Your Own Good: Hidden Cruelty in Child-rearing and the Roots of Violence* (New York: Farrar, Straus and Giroux, 1983). This book shows how mistreated children grow up to be apologists for their parents' brutality and often repeat the same behavior with their own children. Miller also makes the case that the brutality of Hitler's father eventually

contributed to the dictator's need to be brutal to those who were helpless to oppose him. She also argues that the enormous emphasis on obedience in German child-rearing practices of the time allowed many Germans to take part in the Nazi madness.

CHAPTER 7

1. Joan Harvey with Cynthia Katz, *If I'm So Successful, Why Do I Feel Like a Fake?* (New York: St. Martin's Press, 1985).

2. Harvey with Katz, 160–62. "They can feel guilty about their success as well, thinking that it is somehow wrong for them to be doing better than a parent or a sibling. A woman may feel guilty about having a college education or professional career because her mother never had the opportunities for these things. Or a man may feel guilty about making more money than his father because this implies that he has somehow eclipsed his father's position in the family.

"The fear of success can penetrate our personal lives as well. A woman may feel guilty about having a happy love relationship if her own mother was unhappy in marriage. The man whose brother is shy and withdrawn might restrain himself from becoming too popular.

"Anyone can avoid his fear of success if he believes he is getting ahead through fraud, rather than through his own abilities. He's not aware of this mental process, but it is as if he's telling himself, 'I'm not really a successful person, I'm just a phoney who's been fooling other people. So it's okay for me to be doing well at this.' "

3. Stephanie Brown, *Treating the Alcoholic* (New York: John Wiley and Sons, 1985), 286–87. The effective treatment of alcoholism provides a nice example of the distinction between remorse as self-punishment and constructive remorse. Alcoholics usually do hurt and wrong many people while they are actively alcoholic. Spouses, children, and colleagues may be lied to, let down, and abused in various ways. Many alcoholics alternate between dramatic remorse for and complete denial of the harm they have done. The tremendous guilt they feel contributes to their depression and tendency to return to drinking.

As part of the Alcoholics Anonymous program of recovery, alcoholics are encouraged to make a list of all persons they have harmed. Then they are urged to make direct amends to those people wherever possible. This is the essence of steps 8 and 9 of the Twelve Steps of AA.

There are many excellent books and articles that delineate the AA approach to alcoholism. They are available from AA chapters. There are chapters in almost every community in the United States and in major cities around the world. Dr. Brown's book will particularly interest mental health professionals and focuses on a developmental model of recovery.

CHAPTER 8

1. W. H. Grier and P. M. Cobbs, *Black Rage* (New York: Basic Books, 1968), 114–20.
2. Very often the fear of being hurt and the fear of hurting others are intertwined. For example, the parent you fear hurting will also hurt you in return by attacking, rejecting, or humiliating you.

CHAPTER 9

1. The marriage categories of vital, devitalized, conflict-habituated, and passive-congenial are taken from a fascinating book by two sociologists, John F. Cuber and Peggy B. Harroff, *Sex and the Significant Americans* (New York: Penguin Books, 1968). Cuber and Harroff interviewed 437 "distinguished Americans" about their marriages. The interviewees were generals, judges, heads of large businesses, and other highly successful persons and their spouses. Although the sample was not random, the study showed that vital marriages were very much in the minority. Since the subjects were exclusively upper- or upper-middle class we can't know for sure how the results would apply to middle- and lower-class couples, but our guess is that the situation is not very different.
2. We agree that the infatuation that is common in the early phase of a relationship rarely lasts. Instead a sense of mutual acceptance and openness can be achieved that not only lasts but builds as the years go by. It requires a deep commitment of each partner to 1) be there for the other and to listen and 2) share his deepest feelings. Both of these commitments are very hard to carry out. To really listen to your spouse, to put aside your own viewpoint for the time that you are listening, can sometimes be terribly hard, particularly if your spouse's words are critical or threatening in some other way. And to bare your own deep feelings, including those that may threaten your spouse, can also be extremely difficult. But this is, in large part, what it takes to maintain a lifelong intimate relationship. There is a good discussion of this question in M. Scott Peck's *The Road Less Traveled* (New York: Simon and Schuster, 1978). See particularly pages 85–130.
3. We recommend the following books for those who would like to enhance their relationship skills:

George R. Bach and Peter Wyden, *The Intimate Enemy* (New York: William Morrow, 1969). An excellent place to start. Includes an extremely helpful discussion of the fight-phobic partner who avoids conflict at all costs and of the partner who easily explodes in angry outbursts. The authors recommend that couples learn to fight fairly and constructively while avoiding destructive conflicts and pointless bickering. There is also a good section on negotiation skills.

Daniel B. Wile, *After the Honeymoon: How Conflict Can Improve Your Relationship* (New York: Wiley, 1988). In one of the most helpful and original recent books about dealing with marital conflict, Wile explains an ingenious strategy that involves cultivating, rather than trying to ignore or get rid of, the differences between partners.

4. TA (Transactional Analysis), a popular school of psychotherapy begun by Eric Berne with the popular and influential *Games People Play* (New York: Grove Press, 1964), has a lot to say on the subject of bad messages. In TA theory, what I call bad messages are divided into injunctions and attributions. Injunctions are implicit or explicit messages such as: don't be happy, don't be successful, don't be sexual. Attributions are characterizations by parents such as: you've always been angry from the day you were born; your brother is the brilliant one, but you are the hard worker; you're a troublemaker. Attributions, too, often become self-fulfilling prophecies. For another good discussion of these distinctions, see Claude Steiner, *Scripts People Live* (New York: Grove Press, 1972), 71–75.

5. One of the best treatments of this subject is Lonnie Barbach's *For Each Other, Sharing Sexual Intimacy* (New York: New American Library, 1982, 1984). This and Dr. Barbach's other books are among the best things written on sexual problems and sexual enrichment.

6. Portions of this case were freely adapted from the case of Mr. R. in Joseph Weiss et al., *Psychoanalytic Process: Theory, Clinical Observation, and Empirical Research* (New York: Guilford Press, 1986), 81–82.

CHAPTER 10

1. Estimates of the number of children of alcoholics in the general population run from 20 to 40 million. Whether we accept the lower or higher figure, there is still a huge portion of our population that has suffered effects of being raised in an alcoholic family and is at greatly increased risk for having difficulties in relationships, chronic anxiety, low self-esteem, an increased susceptibility to alcoholism and other addictions, and an inability to relax and have fun. Any movement that can make a significant change in the lives of so many people in

our society will make an important difference in society itself. We think that the ACA movement will do that.

2. Although there have been occasional studies of children of alcoholics since the late 1940s, the concept of them as a group with a common set of serious problems became widely disseminated only in the late 1970s. In 1979, *Newsweek* interviewed Dr. Stephanie Brown and Claudia Black. That article introduced the public to the idea that there were particular problems that resulted from being raised in alcoholic families. It was also about this time that Dr. Brown and others at Stanford University began long-term group treatment of children of alcoholics.

Ten years later, the ACA movement is skyrocketing. In a local bookstore in the small California town where I live, there are over a dozen titles directly relating to the problems of children of alcoholics. A national magazine devoted exclusively to the ACA movement has been launched — all this in a field where a few short years ago there was no information available in your bookstore. (The magazine is called *Changes*, "a magazine for and about adult children of alcoholics," and is published six times a year by the U.S. Journal of Drug and Alcohol Dependence, Inc., 1721 Blount Road, Suite 1, Pompano Beach, Fla. 33069.) Groups are proliferating at an enormous clip, under the auspices of Al-Anon and other private and public agencies. Many workshops for both children of alcoholics and the professionals who work with them are being offered *and* are getting overflow responses.

3. In April 1989 there was a conference of people from the ACA and the CM movements. Transcripts are available from Larry Edmonds, Mount Zion Psychotherapy Research Group, 2420 Sutter Street, San Francisco, California 94115. There is a fee to cover duplication costs.

4. "It is of vital importance that we acknowledge, from the beginning, that the symptoms and behaviors of adult children of alcoholics (ACoAs) are directly related to the experience of being raised in an unsafe, dysfunctional, alcoholic family system." Wayne Kritsberg, *The Adult Children of Alcoholics Syndrome* (Pompano Beach, Fla.: Health Communications, 1985), 1.

5. This list of characteristics was adapted from Judith S. Seixas and Geraldine Youcha, *Children of Alcoholism: A Survivors Manual* (New York: Harper and Row, 1986), 47–48.

6. It is striking how often adult children of alcoholics, who are not alcoholics themselves, marry alcoholics. This is particularly true of daughters of alcoholic fathers. It seems likely to me that these un-

happy choices are at least partly an unconscious unwillingness to outdo the unhappy and burdened nonalcoholic parent.

7. As the idea of codependency was developed in clinical studies of alcoholics, the codependents were originally called co-alcoholics. As the field was broadened to include other drugs and, later, addictive behaviors not related to drugs (compulsive gambling, compulsive eating, etc.), the term *codependency* began to be used. For a good overview of codependency, see Melody Beattie, *Codependent No More* (New York: Harper and Row, 1987), 27–28.

8. Claudia Black in Rachel V., *Family Secrets: Life Stories of Adult Children of Alcoholics* (New York: Harper and Row, 1987), xxiv.

9. Ibid., xxiii. But although many incidents of sexual and physical abuse occur when the abusing parent has been drinking, this behavior is not simply a product of alcoholism. Many alcoholics stop being violent or inappropriately sexual after they quit drinking, but others do not. Physical or sexual abuse must be considered a serious problem in its own right, often requiring treatment over and above the treatment a parent may receive for alcoholism.

10. Dr. Claudia Black makes this point in her excellent and best-selling book *It Will Never Happen to Me!* (Denver: M.A.C., 1981), 15. "While working with adult children of alcoholics, I discovered an interesting phenomenon: in their childhood, these particular adults did not fit the stereotype of what I had been led to believe was representative of children of alcoholics. These adults were not necessarily the children who developed into runaways, who filled our juvenile justice systems, who were asthmatic or hyperactive, who performed poorly in school, or had low self-images. . . . The majority of these people indicated, instead, that they had strong tendencies to appear 'normal' and to be from 'typical' American families. They did not exhibit problematic behavior, and they rarely, or never, talked about the alcoholism in their primary family."

11. As far as we know, the varying descriptions of alcoholic family roles were developed through clinical observation rather than any kind of formal research. Because of this, the categories of family roles are somewhat different from expert to expert. The family hero is the most striking and perhaps most common child's role in the alcoholic family, and all the books I have consulted refer to this category. Other categories seem to command less agreement.

12. The family therapy movement has recognized for years that the roles that each member plays serve a purpose for the whole family. In 1964, Virginia Satir introduced the term *identified patient* to indicate that the child who got into trouble was probably not the source of diffi-

culty in the family. Family therapists noticed if they "cured" the "sick" member of the family, another family member often started showing symptoms. *Conjoint Family Therapy*, rev. ed. (Palo Alto, Calif.: Science and Behavior Books, 1967).

13. Claudia Black in Rachel V., op. cit., xxvii.
14. This list of sexual abuses was adapted from Ellen Bass and Laura Davis, *The Courage to Heal: A Guide for Women Survivors of Sexual Abuse* (New York: Harper and Row, 1988), 21.
15. Ibid., 22.
16. The Adult Children of Alcoholics movement is taking steps to bring the issue of parental alcoholism out into the open in the schools. The National Association for Children of Alcoholics has instituted the National Elementary School Education Project, which provides materials for school counselors to *all grammar schools in this country*. These resources include posters featuring comic book heroes who express such messages as: "If your mom and dad drink too much, you're not alone. There are millions of kids with alcoholic parents." "All your feelings are okay. If your mom or dad is an alcoholic, then being sad or scared is normal." "Hulk says you can still love your mom and dad and get help for yourself." At the top of each poster is the line SOME MOMS AND DADS DRINK TOO MUCH . . . AND IT HURTS. Not surprisingly, the organization that is spearheading this effort is primarily composed of people who are or who work with children of alcoholics. Gerry Myers, "National Elementary School Education Project," *The NACoA Network*, vol. 4, no. 2 (Summer/ Fall 1987). Published by the National Association for the Children of Alcoholics, 31706 Coast Highway, Suite 201, South Laguna, Calif.

CHAPTER 11

1. Psychotherapy has been practiced in many ways: body therapies, scream therapies, psychodramatic therapies, art therapy, music therapy, etc. Nevertheless the vast bulk of psychotherapy and counseling in the United States today consists of regular meetings between one therapist and one client, during which the client talks and the therapist comments on what he has said.
2. For more on how these researchers were able to formulate each client's plan — and for guidelines for formulating *your* own plan — see Chapter 12.
3. K. Howard et al., "The Dose-Effect Relationship in Psychotherapy," *American Psychologist*, vol. 41, no. 2 (1986): 159. "There is a grow-

ing consensus in the literature that psychotherapeutic treatment is generally beneficial to patients."

4. Traditional psychoanalysis is usually conducted on a three-to-five-day-per-week basis over a period of three to six years. Typically the client lies on a couch with the analyst sitting behind him. Psychoanalysis is obviously both time-consuming and expensive and only a tiny fraction of psychotherapy clients today are in analysis. However, the psychoanalytic understanding of psychological problems remains the most widely held point of view among American psychotherapists.

5. There have been a number of studies by Control Mastery researchers that have provided support for the idea that a client makes progress when she feels safe to do so. See George Silberschatz, "Testing Pathogenic Beliefs," in Joseph Weiss et al., *The Psychoanalytic Process: Theory, Clinical Observation, and Empirical Research* (New York: Guilford Press, 1986), 256–66. See also George Silberschatz et al., "Testing Pathogenic Beliefs Versus Seeking Transference Gratifications," 267–76. The first of these studies provides evidence that when the therapist made it safer for the client by passing her test, the client immediately improved on a number of progress rating scales. The second study provides evidence that it is not the frustration of infantile wishes but rather evidence that the client's grim beliefs are false that causes patients to progress.

6. Of course, there are times in therapy when the therapist can make things safer by confronting a client. For example, if a client tells the therapist he proposes to do something dangerous, self-destructive, or illegal, the client is often reassured if the therapist takes a strong stand against that plan of action. This is particularly true if the client's parents didn't take a stand against self-destructive behavior.

7. Unfortunately, however, not every client can be cured by the proper therapy. Sometimes a client may have been so traumatized in childhood that even with the help of a skilled and sensitive therapist, he is unable to overcome his grim, unconscious beliefs.

8. Most clients have received a combination of good and bad treatment from their parents. The good treatment does not create psychological problems because it does not induce the client to form grim, unconscious beliefs. Since the client's primary purpose in therapy is to free herself from these beliefs, she invites the therapist to replicate the bad treatment she received, not the good.

9. Alice Miller, *Thou Shalt Not Be Aware: Society's Betrayal of the Child* (New York: Farrar, Straus and Giroux, 1984), 12.

10. Sometimes when a therapist passes a test, it will make the client feel comfortable enough to attempt more strenuous tests. A client who

makes a few mild complaints about his therapist may begin to complain even more vigorously if the therapist is able to pass his initial test.

11. Some therapists reading this book may realize that they have made some of the harmful recommendations we describe, without any obvious harm resulting. In fact, at times a client can extract value from an interpretation that will tend to be harmful to most people most of the time. It depends largely on how the interpretation fits into the client's unconscious plan. Sometimes, for example, the *process* of interpretation may be more important than the content. If a client's parents were never definite about anything and the client is working on his difficulties in being definite — just the fact that the therapist makes an interpretation in a forceful way and sticks to it may be helpful, even if the interpretation is incorrect. The effect of any given interpretation on a client's progress is determined by a complex web of factors which is beyond the scope of this book. For a fuller discussion, see Joseph Weiss et al., *The Psychoanalytic Process: Theory, Clinical Observation, and Empirical Research* (New York: Guilford Press, 1986), 84–116.

CHAPTER 12

1. The plan formulation technique was originally developed by Joe Caston, M.D., and is described in his article "Reliability of Diagnosis of Patient's Unconscious Plan" in Joseph Weiss et al., *The Psychoanalytic Process: Theory, Clinical Observation, and Empirical Research* (New York: Guilford Press, 1986), 241. The development of the plan formulation has been a tremendous breakthrough in psychotherapy research. It allows researchers to evaluate a psychotherapist's interventions and to determine whether they support or interfere with the patient's real goals.

APPENDIX I

1. C. Morrow-Bradley and R. Elliot, "Utilization of Psychotherapy Research by Practicing Psychotherapists," *American Psychologist*, vol. 41, no. 2 (1986): 188. "With virtual unanimity, psychotherapy researchers have argued that (a) psychotherapy research should yield information useful to practicing therapists, (b) such research to date has not done so, and (c) this problem should be remedied."

2. L. H. Cohen et al., "Use of Psychotherapy Research by Professional

Psychologists," *American Psychologist*, vol. 41, no. 2 (1986): 198. "Clinical psychologists are not frequent readers of the research literature."

3. George Silberschatz et al., "Research on the Process of Change in Psychotherapy: The Approach of the Mount Zion Psychotherapy Research Group," International Psychotherapy Programs, eds. L. Beutler and M. Crago (Washington, D.C.: American Psychological Association Press). In press.

4. George Silberschatz et al., "Using the Patient's Plan to Assess Progress in Psychotherapy," *Psychotherapy*, vol. 98 (1989). This paper reviews and details the successful application of the plan concept to measuring patient progress. In addition, it describes research under way to use the plan to measure patient progress, thereby producing a case-specific measure of outcome that overcomes the problems we have pointed out.

5. A number of studies have been done which compare the predictions that are made by classical psychoanalytic theorists with those made by Control Mastery theorists. Each of these studies has supported the Control Mastery Theory point of view. Most of the studies in Joseph Weiss et al., *The Psychoanalytic Process: Theory, Clinical Observation, and Empirical Research* (New York: Guilford Press, 1986) contain an explicit comparison with some aspect of classical psychoanalytic theory. New studies are under way which will be comparing Control Mastery Theory with other theories such as Cognitive Therapy.

   To reiterate, however, this is not to say that Control Mastery Theory contradicts all of Freud's thinking. Control Mastery Theory is partially based on ideas that Freud emphasizes in his later work.

6. Other centers that are replicating Control Mastery research are the University of Cincinnati Medical Center and Rutgers University.

7. For a brief but excellent description of the relation of Control Mastery Theory research findings to clinical practice, see John Curtis and George Silberschatz, "Clinical Implications of Research on Brief Dynamic Psychotherapy I. Formulating the Patient's Problems and Goals," *Psychoanalytic Psychology*, vol. 3, no. 1 (1986): 13–25, and its companion article, "Clinical Implications of Research on Brief Dynamic Psychotherapy II. How the Therapist Helps or Hinders the Patient's Therapeutic Progress," 27–37.

8. With few exceptions, the Mount Zion Psychotherapy Research Group has used verbatim transcripts of completed psychotherapies for its data. These include short-term psychotherapies consisting of sixteen sessions, and also full-length psychoanalyses, consisting of many

hundreds of sessions. The clients studied knew from the outset of psychotherapy that their treatments would be used for research purposes and that their anonymity would be safeguarded. Tape recordings were made of each session, which were then transcribed. Plan formulations were devised by having a group of trained judges develop a consensus on a written description of the clients. This process was handled in a rather complex way, designed to ensure scientific objectivity and reliability, and described in John Curtis et al., "Developing Reliable Psychodynamic Case Formulations: An Illustration of the Plan Diagnosis Method," *Psychotherapy*, vol. 25, no. 2 (1988): 256–65.

9. Joseph Weiss et al., *The Psychoanalytic Process: Theory, Clinical Observation, and Empirical Research* (New York: Guilford Press, 1986). Available from the publisher at 72 Spring Street, New York, NY 10012 (800-221-3966) or it can be ordered from your bookstore. This book is the best source for an overall understanding of Control Mastery Theory and research.

Index

About the Authors

Lewis Engel, Ph.D., is a San Francisco clinical psychologist. He attended Reed College (where he and his coauthor, Tom Ferguson, were freshman roommates), earned bachelor's and master's degrees in psychology at San Francisco State University, and received his doctorate in psychology from the California Institute of Professional Psychology. In 1981, Engel requested a professional consultation on an especially difficult client with psychologist Harold Sampson. It was through Sampson that he first learned about Control Mastery Theory. Engel is currently a working member of the Mount Zion Psychotherapy Research Group, the group that coordinates ongoing research on Control Mastery Theory. He also teaches the principles of Control Mastery Theory to psychologists and graduate students. He lives in San Rafael, California, with his wife, psychologist Brandy Engel, and their son, Nicholas.

Tom Ferguson, M.D., is the author of *Trusting Ourselves: A Crash Course in the Psychology of Women* (with Karen Johnson, M.D.) and many other self-help books. He attended Reed College, earned bachelor's and master's degrees in English at San Francisco State University, and received his M.D. from the Yale University School of Medicine. He was the founding editor of the journal *Medical Self-Care* and is founder and editor-at-large of the *SelfCare Catalog*. He served for many years as medical editor of the *Whole Earth Catalog*. He has received the National Educational Press Association's Distinguished Achievement Award for his writings on raising health-responsible children and the Lifetime Extension Award for his writings on the rapidly expanding area of self-help and self-care. He is a popular speaker and workshop leader for professional and lay audiences. He lives in Austin, Texas, with his wife, Meredith Dreiss, and their daughter, Adrienne.